AF784680

SUBCOMMITTEE ON CAPITAL MARKETS, INSURANCE AND GOVERNMENT SPONSORED ENTERPRISES

RICHARD H. BAKER, Louisiana, *Chairman*

DOUG OSE, California, *Vice Chairman*
CHRISTOPHER SHAYS, Connecticut
PAUL E. GILLMOR, Ohio
SPENCER BACHUS, Alabama
MICHAEL N. CASTLE, Delaware
PETER T. KING, New York
FRANK D. LUCAS, Oklahoma
EDWARD R. ROYCE, California
DONALD A. MANZULLO, Illinois
SUE W. KELLY, New York
ROBERT W. NEY, Ohio
JOHN B. SHADEGG, Arizona
JIM RYUN, Kansas
VITO FOSSELLA, New York,
JUDY BIGGERT, Illinois
MARK GREEN, Wisconsin
GARY G. MILLER, California
PATRICK J. TOOMEY, Pennsylvania
SHELLEY MOORE CAPITO, West Virginia
MELISSA A. HART, Pennsylvania
MARK R. KENNEDY, Minnesota
PATRICK J. TIBERI, Ohio
GINNY BROWN-WAITE, Florida
KATHERINE HARRIS, Florida
RICK RENZI, Arizona

PAUL E. KANJORSKI, Pennsylvania
GARY L. ACKERMAN, New York
DARLENE HOOLEY, Oregon
BRAD SHERMAN, California
GREGORY W. MEEKS, New York
JAY INSLEE, Washington
DENNIS MOORE, Kansas
MICHAEL E. CAPUANO, Massachusetts
HAROLD E. FORD, JR., Tennessee
RUBÉN HINOJOSA, Texas
KEN LUCAS, Kentucky
JOSEPH CROWLEY, New York
STEVE ISRAEL, New York
MIKE ROSS, Arkansas
WM. LACY CLAY, Missouri
CAROLYN McCARTHY, New York
JOE BACA, California
JIM MATHESON, Utah
STEPHEN F. LYNCH, Massachusetts
BRAD MILLER, North Carolina
RAHM EMANUEL, Illinois
DAVID SCOTT, Georgia
NYDIA M. VELÁZQUEZ, New York

THE FASB STOCK OPTIONS PROPOSAL: ITS EFFECT ON THE U.S. ECONOMY AND JOBS

HEARINGS

BEFORE THE

SUBCOMMITTEE ON

CAPITAL MARKETS, INSURANCE AND

GOVERNMENT SPONSORED ENTEREPRISES

OF THE

COMMITTEE ON FINANCIAL SERVICES

U.S. HOUSE OF REPRESENTATIVES

ONE HUNDRED EIGHTH CONGRESS

SECOND SESSION

APRIL 21, MAY 4, 2004

Printed for the use of the Committee on Financial Services

Serial No. 108–80

U.S. GOVERNMENT PRINTING OFFICE

95–438 PDF WASHINGTON : 2004

For sale by the Superintendent of Documents, U.S. Government Printing Office
Internet: bookstore.gpo.gov Phone: toll free (866) 512–1800; DC area (202) 512–1800
Fax: (202) 512–2250 Mail: Stop SSOP, Washington, DC 20402–0001

HOUSE COMMITTEE ON FINANCIAL SERVICES

MICHAEL G. OXLEY, Ohio, *Chairman*

JAMES A. LEACH, Iowa
DOUG BEREUTER, Nebraska
RICHARD H. BAKER, Louisiana
SPENCER BACHUS, Alabama
MICHAEL N. CASTLE, Delaware
PETER T. KING, New York
EDWARD R. ROYCE, California
FRANK D. LUCAS, Oklahoma
ROBERT W. NEY, Ohio
SUE W. KELLY, New York, *Vice Chair*
RON PAUL, Texas
PAUL E. GILLMOR, Ohio
JIM RYUN, Kansas
STEVEN C. LATOURETTE, Ohio
DONALD A. MANZULLO, Illinois
WALTER B. JONES, JR., North Carolina
DOUG OSE, California
JUDY BIGGERT, Illinois
MARK GREEN, Wisconsin
PATRICK J. TOOMEY, Pennsylvania
CHRISTOPHER SHAYS, Connecticut
JOHN B. SHADEGG, Arizona
VITO FOSSELLA, New York
GARY G. MILLER, California
MELISSA A. HART, Pennsylvania
SHELLEY MOORE CAPITO, West Virginia
PATRICK J. TIBERI, Ohio
MARK R. KENNEDY, Minnesota
TOM FEENEY, Florida
JEB HENSARLING, Texas
SCOTT GARRETT, New Jersey
TIM MURPHY, Pennsylvania
GINNY BROWN-WAITE, Florida
J. GRESHAM BARRETT, South Carolina
KATHERINE HARRIS, Florida
RICK RENZI, Arizona

BARNEY FRANK, Massachusetts
PAUL E. KANJORSKI, Pennsylvania
MAXINE WATERS, California
CAROLYN B. MALONEY, New York
LUIS V. GUTIERREZ, Illinois
NYDIA M. VELÁZQUEZ, New York
MELVIN L. WATT, North Carolina
GARY L. ACKERMAN, New York
DARLENE HOOLEY, Oregon
JULIA CARSON, Indiana
BRAD SHERMAN, California
GREGORY W. MEEKS, New York
BARBARA LEE, California
JAY INSLEE, Washington
DENNIS MOORE, Kansas
MICHAEL E. CAPUANO, Massachusetts
HAROLD E. FORD, JR., Tennessee
RUBÉN HINOJOSA, Texas
KEN LUCAS, Kentucky
JOSEPH CROWLEY, New York
WM. LACY CLAY, Missouri
STEVE ISRAEL, New York
MIKE ROSS, Arkansas
CAROLYN MCCARTHY, New York
JOE BACA, California
JIM MATHESON, Utah
STEPHEN F. LYNCH, Massachusetts
BRAD MILLER, North Carolina
RAHM EMANUEL, Illinois
DAVID SCOTT, Georgia
ARTUR DAVIS, Alabama
CHRIS BELL, Texas

BERNARD SANDERS, Vermont

Robert U. Foster, III, *Staff Director*

CONTENTS

ADDITIONAL MATERIAL SUBMITTED FOR THE RECORD

THE FASB STOCK OPTIONS PROPOSAL: ITS EFFECT ON THE U.S. ECONOMY AND JOBS

Wednesday, April 21, 2004

U.S. House of Representatives,
Subcommittee on Capital Markets, Insurance,
And Government Sponsored Enterprises
Committee on Financial Services,
Washington, D.C.

The subcommittee met, pursuant to call, at 10:05 a.m., in Room 2128, Rayburn House Office Building, Hon. Richard Baker [chairman of the subcommittee] presiding.

Present: Representatives Baker, Ose, Gillmor, Lucas of Oklahoma, Royce, Manzullo, Oxley (ex officio), Kelly, Ney, Shadegg, Biggert, Capito, Hart, Kennedy, Tiberi, Kanjorski, Hooley, Sherman, Inslee, Moore, Capuano, Frank (ex officio), Hinojosa, Lucas of Kentucky, Crowley, Clay, McCarthy, Matheson, Lynch, Miller of North Carolina, Emanuel, Scott and Velazquez.

Chairman Baker. [Presiding.] I would like to call this meeting of the Capital Markets Subcommittee to order.

This morning we are convened for the purpose of reviewing the pending Financial Accounting Standards Board stock option expensing proposal and the potential effect its adoption may have on job creation and our economic recovery, which I believe to be fully engaged. I have given some thought to my opening statement this morning and the past few days, but I had the occasion to read press reports of yesterday that changed my intentions to open the hearing.

The congressional process is a very open and public process. No one ever has accused the Congress of moving too fast, to my knowledge, on anything. It is a process subject to hearings and review which we will benefit this morning from our panel of witnesses in getting additional comment, and then subject to our ability, a markup subsequent to recorded vote, publicly recorded, then a full committee review, then if leadership so chooses for consideration, then of course a bicameral process and subject to the presidential veto. Although many criticize the political process, it is the one forum in which every person's perspective can be vented, can be put on the public record, and elected officials held accountable for the decisions they make.

In the matter before the committee today, it is the presumption that the Financial Accounting Standards Board is an entity which will conduct and review appropriate financial standards absent such political necessities, and that professionals for the public good shall make determinations in the best interests of our economic stability. Given that history of the Financial Accounting Standards Board, I am the first to acknowledge that I have on prior occasions disputed the decisions of the Standards Board on various other matters of accountancy practice. I felt, as a public official, the right to express those opinions and to disagree on occasion where I thought it in the public interest to do so.

However, it has always been past practice of the Board to refrain from engaging in the seamier side of the public policy business and was surprised to learn that FASB now has engaged its own lobbying firm. But what really got me more engaged in this matter were the comments of the Chairman of the Board, and again let me quickly add, if this press report is true, I have also been on that side of the coin where my representations have not always been accurately reflected, and quick to respond that should this press account be accurate, from the Wall Street Journal, it raises concerns which I think appropriate to bring to the committee's attention.

When Chairman Herz yesterday criticized a well-organized lobbying effort within the Congress, but then went on to say, "One thing I cannot control is Congress." I would say, that is a good thing. No one person should control the Congress, nor enterprise. It acknowledged in the comment that the proposed rule is now open to public comment until the end of June. Apparently, members of Congress are the only group that can have no comment on the matter until the close of the consideration at the end of June, but calling on all in the investor class and those within the business community to make your views known to people in Washington; a call for investors, again, to make your views known.

We cannot have it both ways. If you expect the Congress to have a hands-off approach and allow a regulatory entity to act without comment from anyone, I question the need for a public comment period because in the midst of the public comment period, this hearing has been called for the sole purpose of having those make comment on the effect of this proposed rule on the broader economy. To engage the resources of a lobbyist and for the chairman of the board to then make a political request of constituencies to affect and influence the Congress has now opened the door. If you want to have a public discussion where all interested parties express their opinion, there is no more open venue, no more free of influence, no more publicly recorded venue than the United States Congress.

Now, I do not always agree with the outcomes of the congressional process, but I have great regard for the process and respect the wisdom of 435 members of the House and 100 members of the Senate in coming to what is the best-balanced conclusion for the public interest. I make no apologies today about having introduced a bill and brought this matter to public discussion. I happen to personally believe it is the right thing to do. I will acknowledge there are other people with different opinions and I may be wrong, but today we have had a group historically known for its nonpolitical determinations open the door to political judgments. I hope we can do it going forward in a professional manner and all have respect for each other at the conclusion of the process, that professionals with differing opinions can come to some resolution that ultimately is in the best interest of the public.

I apologize to the committee for going on at length, but I felt the necessity to express those views.

Mr. Kanjorski?

Mr. KANJORSKI. Mr. Chairman, I am not aware of the press comments, but it strikes me that it poses the question of whether you will respect me in the morning.

Chairman BAKER. No.

[Laughter.]

Mr. KANJORSKI. Actually, Mr. Chairman, I think this is an important issue, and we meet for the third time in the 108th Congress to study the accounting treatment of stock options. I have a prepared statement that I will submit for the record. I guess the interests are that this is a recognized problem, one for the accounting industry and the need for certainty in how things are done.

I am not an accountant by profession, but I also feel that it perhaps is a dangerous ground for us to tread on that the Congress will interpose its position on a board that is dedicated and structured to make these determinations. That is not to say that that board's determinations come with the weight of the Constitution or perhaps the actions of God to Moses on the mount.

It is, however, a struggle that could be off-course in terms of I think there are two major issues here. One is whether or not this Congress supports the fact that we have a structured entity in the private sector to make final determinations of accounting rules. I think that is vitally important for our system domestically and internationally. Two, my interest in this is that I truly believe that accounting is for the purposes of transparency of investors and people, that they have a right and a want to know what is the structure and the commitment of the organizations they potentially want to invest in.

I have had the occasion over the last several weeks to visit with people that are on both sides of this issue. I have listened to them as hard as I can. I remember having a discussion with the president and CEO of one of the major California new-tech companies just 2 weeks ago. He struck me with the importance of this for his industry. I have great sympathy that in that particular industry, this could create a problem, the rule as it is structured. But as we discussed it together, he tended to agree with me with the need for transparency; that we cannot have every company doing with their stock options as they will and anticipate that analysts will discern every one of the 27,000 public companies in the United States. That is not going to happen, and particularly with the loss of respect for the analysts over the last several years. They probably will not be performing that function sufficiently to give transparency.

So I do not understand why we get to the point of one way and not another. I think potentially, and it is too bad we do not have both the SEC and FASB here today, but I understand most of those groups are on travel internationally and are not available for us today. So in that regard, before we conclude and go to markup on this subject, I think it is only right that we bring representation of FASB and SEC before the committee so that they can spell out their arguments, because quite frankly I have a question that I would like to pose to them that I think is very fundamental and important.

Are there other ways, in accordance with accounting principles, that we can get to transparency without necessarily going the full gamut of a single rule applying across the board that could disadvantage some of our major technology companies? I do not know what the answer to that is, but being rather Burkean in my philosophy that unless you show me the benefits of change, I am more apt to hold with tradition. My natural proclivities lead me to support the institutions, whether they are courts of law or organizations such as FASB, that they have the ultimate insight and interest and intention of doing the right thing and propounding the proper rules, always subject to review.

But before we get to the final decision and whether or not the Congress should take up singular activity of reviewing, sometimes under pressure, the implementation of a rule across the board, I think it could be fundamentally destructive to our system if we encourage people to believe that FASB is okay to some extent, but where there are interest groups that can rise above that and put significant pressure on the Congress of the United States to interpose their will and its will on an organization like FASB, that could be very destructive to the entire process of the system.

Those that favor that position today on a particular accounting rule may find out that when they become less significant or less important or less apt to be able to affect the actions of Congress, they can have suppressive activity brought on them by other special interest groups or pressure groups within our system. That tends to go to the destruction of the system as we have it.

With that in mind, Mr. Chairman, I do ask that we have an additional hearing before we go to markup on this situation, having in FASB and the SEC. I look forward to today's hearing. I think the weight of the witnesses, as I discern them, are significantly disadvantaged one side of this proposition right now, although I look forward to the testimony particularly given by some of our industrial leaders that are here today to give us an insight on how the impact will be in the capital markets and on these particular corporations that exist, and that had some advantage by using stock options as a methodology of not tapping into their capital assets when they were at the beginning stage or formative stage of their endeavors.

With that in mind, I offer my full statement in the record, Mr. Chairman, and look forward to it. I guess I will read The Wall Street Journal the day before such hearings so that I am fully equipped to respond to the Chairman's views.

[The prepared statement of Hon. Paul E. Kanjorski can be found on page 82 in the appendix.]

Chairman BAKER. I thank the gentleman for his statement. It certainly will be made part of the record, as will all members's opening statements.

Mr. Ose, did you have an opening comment?

Mr. OSE. Thank you, Mr. Chairman.

I am appreciative of the fact that you are having another of these hearings. I remain somewhat bemused by our ongoing debate here. We have yet to define a system whereby we can accurately value these options, whether it be Black-Scholes or binomial equation or something of that sort. And yet we are hurtling down a path, at least from a regulatory standpoint, to impose a requirement of a blanket nature on America's corporations without defining yet exactly how we are going to value it.

I would submit to the body that the various opinions that are being put forth by people who have moved to expense options on their financial statements, as opposed to those who have yet not made that move, largely track the enterprise models that they speak from. For instance, let us take Mr. Buffett. Mr. Buffett has argued in favor of expensing options, but I think if you look at Mr. Buffett's investments, you will find very few of them in the technology business, where options are used for significant compensation to employees.

I would submit to the body that the difference of opinion in corporate America as to how to treat options, whether to expense them or make them transparent within the notes to financial statements, reflects the needs of different enterprises to either compensate their employees or reduce their tax liability. Those who are advocating for leaving options in the current situation whereby they are disclosed within the notes, are using options as a compensation tool, by and large. Those who are advocating for the expensing of options look at the net impact on their tax liability by expensing those options. The net income for that enterprise would be less.

It is perfectly logical, but we still come back to this same point, and that is however you value these options, whether you are a strong advocate for leaving it the way it is or a strong advocate for changing the system, however you value these options your valuations are based on assumptions. If it is the assumptions that are driving FASB's concern, that is if the assumptions may or may not be valid, we ought to talk about that, rather than whether or not to put them into the financial statements.

I thank the Chairman for having this hearing. I am still waiting for somebody to definitively quantify for me how you value these options. Thank you, Mr. Chairman.

Chairman BAKER. I thank the gentleman for his interest in the subject and his statement.

Ranking Member Frank?

Mr. FRANK. Thank you, Mr. Chairman. I appreciate the attention you are giving to this.

This is a very difficult issue for me. Intellectually, it is one of the harder ones that we deal with. When I was in law school, accounting overlapped with my duties as a state legislator. I was absent a lot of times that day when we came up with the issue. I am continually impressed both with the complexity of accounting issues and even more difficult for us with their fluidity.

We have an issue here, though, where I am conflicted. I have been convinced by people, particularly in the high technology industry, that this change could do them some damage. I will get in a minute to what I think of that, but facts have to be taken into account. On the other hand, setting a very strong precedent of this Congress setting rules on a specific and technical accounting issue is difficult. So we often in this body use procedural arguments to reinforce our substantive preferences. The tough time comes when you have both a genuine procedural preference, as the Ranking Member talked about, and a substantive view which will not be well served by following that procedural preference. If it is up to me, I would not be demanding that these be expensed, but I do not want to go into a situation where we become the appellate Financial Accounting Standards Board.

I must say, while I accept what the high technology people tell me, they are a lot of very smart, very decent people who have done a lot of good for this economy, and they are overwhelming in their view. I must say that what they tell me is somewhat distressing because I have to say in substantive terms, this issue to me is frankly like some other issues where the reality seems to me to have been swamped by perceptions that have taken over. That is, whether or not the accounting is changed, whether options are expensed or not, does not change the reality.

Currently, I am told, they are available in the footnotes. I am not a regular reader of the footnotes of financial company statements. If we changed the rule, they will not be in footnotes; they will be treated differently. The reality will not change. So what we are being told, and this is a disturbing fact for me, is that the investment community of America will react very differently to an identical reality depending on how it is presented in financial statements. That is disappointing to me.

Perhaps one of my illusions was that these cold-headed, hard-hearted financial people would be less influenced by whether it was in the footnote or not in the footnote. But being told that without a change in the reality, the method of presentation of the reality will have an enormous impact, but both sides seem to agree that it would have this impact, whether or not there is a nominal profit or not. I am hoping that people in the high tech industry if this does go through will turn out to have underestimated the financial community, and that they will be able to tell the difference between reality and perception, but I understand this is troubling.

I have an alternative that I am going to be introducing later. I will be filing the bill later in the week. As I have looked at this, I find it hard to see what damage has been done by the current accounting treatment of options. I have not had anybody write to me and say I was terribly misled because they did not expense the options and I invested in them, and look what happened to me. But there have been problems with options.

It seems to me, from what I have learned in my role here on this committee, is that the problem with the stock options in our economy is the perverse incentive they have given in some cases to the top decision makers in some corporations to spike the stock price and then cash in and walk away. There have been large corporate entities that have done things that made no sense from the standpoint of the corporation over time, but did make sense because there were some corporate executives who benefited short-term.

I am going to file legislation that would direct the SEC to promulgate rules that will deal with a situation in which the top decision makers in corporations cash in stock options and there is subsequently a drop in the value, because I think that is the public policy issue. I am not at this point ready to tell FASB what to do or what not to do on a subject which is such a difficult one intellectually. But I would hope that the existence of this option, the ability of the regulators to deal with the abuse of the perverse incentives given by stock options to chief executives, would be a relevant factor in the field, because we do have a genuine comment period. I think it is possible for some of us to say to the FASB that we are skeptical of the rectitude of their action, without being committed to overturning them congressionally because I am in that bind.

So I am going to be filing this legislation later that would direct the SEC to deal with what seems to me the serious problem here, which is the perverse incentive that the current stock option rules give to a handful of irresponsible and unethical chief executives and their top aides, and hope that that might be a factor in the debate.

Thank you, Mr. Chairman.

Chairman BAKER. I thank the gentleman for his statement.

Chairman Oxley?

Mr. OXLEY. Thank you, Mr. Chairman.

Let me congratulate my friend from Massachusetts, the Ranking Member, for his thoughtful statement. I think his statement does point out some of the difficulties that we as policymakers have in dealing with this complicated issue.

This is the third time in this Congress that we will discuss stock option accounting. The number of hearings this subcommittee has held demonstrates how important this issue is. I applaud Chairman Baker for his good work on this subject. In light of the Financial Accounting Standards Board's recent proposal, it is particularly important now.

The question of whether stock options should be expensed has been debated for many years. Some, like the former Chief Accountant of the Securities and Exchange Commission, Walter Schuetze and numerous experts in accounting, believe that the FASB's position that the issuance of employee stock options creates an expense is simply improper accounting. Mr. Schuetze observes that the issuance of a stock option to an employee does not change the market capitalization of the corporation, as measured by the market value of the outstanding shares and the value of the outstanding option. Thus, there is no expense. If there had been a true expense, which he defines as the "using up" of an owned asset or the decline in the value of an owned asset, then the market value of the outstanding shares and option should have declined, but that is not the case. It also makes me particularly glad that I did not take accounting in college.

Others, like FASB, as evidenced by its recently released proposal, take the contrary view, arguing that employee stock options do constitute a corporate expense. FASB's position is that all employee stock options have value, which employees purchase with the services they provide. Because they have value, FASB asserts, when stock options are given to employees they give rise to compensation costs that are properly included in measuring an enterprise's net income.

Some point out that the grant of an employee stock option is an opportunity cost to the issuer. They argue that if a company were to grant stock, rather than options, to employees, the company's cost for this transaction would be the cash it otherwise would have received if it had sold the shares at the current market price to investors. But this situation is not analogous to that of the issuance of employee stock options. Not only are employee stock options issued exclusively to employees of the issuer, but each employee stock option is written for a specific individual. Thus, there is, by definition, no market into which these options can be sold.

Another significant problem is the accurate valuation of stock options, and we have been through this many times. While there is a diversity of opinion on the merits of requiring the expensing of employee stock options, there is uniform agreement on at least one aspect of this debate. It is extremely difficult to value these options. This gives rise to concerns that strike at the heart of financial statements. What use are they if not for purposes of comparing one company's statement against another's?

The FASB itself recognizes that there is no options-pricing model that gives an accurate assessment of the value of options across all enterprises. The Black-Scholes model has been shown to have significant deficiencies for purposes of valuing employee stock options. The Binomial method has similar problems. FASB's solution is to provide no guidance as to what method a company must use to calculate value.

The lack of a uniform, reliable valuation method creates problems of comparability among companies, accuracy of the financial statements themselves, and, as one of our witnesses today suggests, even opens up the possibility of manipulation of earnings by management. These are concerns that merit further consideration. But as Craig Barrett, the CEO of Intel, has observed, whether or not stock options should be expensed is not just an accounting issue. It is also an economic issue. And that is the focus of today's hearing.

Preserving the independence of the Financial Accounting Standards Board is a consideration. That is an issue of process and jurisdiction and certainly the members of this panel have a great respect for FASB's expertise. However, some issues go beyond that of accounting and enter the mainstream of economic policy. If it is true that the adoption of FASB's employee stock option expensing rule would cause significant and serious damage to job creation, then it becomes an economic policy issue and one that Congress should certainly review.

Dozens of chief executives have publicly stated that their firms will reduce or eliminate options if the FASB proposal is enacted in order to avoid the negative impact that expensing will have on earnings per share, and in turn, the company's share price. If this is the case, then shareholders and our economy as a whole will sacrifice some measure of economic growth.

The venture capital community has been quite outspoken on this issue. One of our witnesses today discusses the great extent to which venture-backed companies rely on stock options to attract and retain talent. He also points out that in over 70 percent of venture-backed companies, stock options were awarded to all employees, not just top executives. These companies are a significant component of our economy. He cites statistics illustrating that venture-backed companies directly or indirectly accounted for 27 million jobs in 2000 and had sales constituting about 11 percent of our GDP. These are compelling figures. If the FASB proposal will undermine job creation and economic growth, then it calls for closer scrutiny by the Congress.

The Congressional Budget Office study concluded that expensing employee stock options will not have a significant effect on the economy. The study argues that the information has already been disclosed in footnoted financial statements and thus is reflected in the stock price. We will examine today whether this analysis is correct.

While there are many informed experts on both sides of this issue, there are some aspects of this debate on which there is agreement. First, expensing employee stock options is not a silver bullet for achieving better corporate governance. Second, the importance of transparent, accurate financial statements cannot be overstated.

Mr. Chairman, I look forward to hearing from our esteemed panel of experts today as we consider once again the far-reaching implications of the FASB proposal.

I yield back.

[The prepared statement of Hon. Michael G. Oxley can be found on page 74 in the appendix.]

Chairman BAKER. I thank the Chairman for his statement and for his attendance here today.

Ms. Velazquez?

Ms. VELAZQUEZ. Thank you, Mr. Chairman.

First, I want to thank Chairman Baker and Ranking Member Kanjorski for holding this important hearing. Stock options have contributed significantly to the economic growth of the U.S. economy, allowing smaller firms to grow and expand in a time when the labor markets may have chosen otherwise. During periods of strong economic growth and low unemployment, such as the late 1990s, the demand for specialized labor outstripped supply. As a result, wages and benefits were bid up to levels unseen in previous periods.

During such previous periods, companies that were rich were often able to attract and retain employees, effectively beating out smaller firms that lacked the cash flow of the larger competitors. During the 1990s, however, stock options leveled the playing field and permitted startups to compete with Fortune 500 companies for talented employees. Instead of economic oligopoly, new firms sprouted up across the country, providing the critical mass for new industries and markets.

The accounting treatment of stock options is a complex issue. If it were not, this issue would not be before us today. First and foremost, I am concerned about any regulatory change that will threaten entrepreneurial activity. I believe that the churning of ideas is necessary for the U.S. economy to move forward and create the jobs that we so desperately need. Such creative destructionism can provide the U.S. with a model for long-term economic stability.

FASB has proposed a rule that will alter the accounting treatment of stock options. While the proposed rule does not prohibit firms from issuing stock options, it will require firms to expense these options in their financial statements, a distinct departure from FASB's current approach. I do have serious concerns with this proposed rule as it appears that it will disproportionately impact smaller companies relying on stock options to finance their early development and growth.

While it is not clear to me that the proposed rule will result in more accurate or comparable financial information for public companies, it is apparent that the rule will impose substantial compliance costs on startups. In addition, I am suspicious of any proposal that restricts smaller firms's access to the equity markets. By impeding smaller firms's ability to be competitive, as I believe this proposed rule does, our national economy and more importantly our local communities will be less likely to realize the benefits that innovation and risk-taking bring: new jobs, an expanded tax base, and opportunity for future generations.

Mr. Chairman, I too echo Mr. Kanjorski's request for an additional hearing with the FASB Chairman and the appropriate SEC officials before we move to mark up the legislation. With this in mind, I thank you for your leadership on this issue and I look forward to hearing the testimony of the witnesses on this complex issue.

Thank you, Mr. .Chairman.

Chairman BAKER. I thank the gentlelady for her statement.

Mr. Royce?

Mr. ROYCE. Thank you, Mr. Chairman. Once again, I want to thank you for the hearing, and I want to thank you for introducing H.R. 3574, the Stock Option Accounting Reform Act.

Also, on behalf of my colleague from California, Representative Eshoo, and Representative Eshoo is your lead co-sponsor of H.R. 3574, I would like to submit for the record a letter from our California Treasurer, Philip Angelides in which he endorses this bill.

[The following information can be found on page 161 in the appendix.]

Let me say, Mr. Chairman, that I am extremely troubled by FASB's proposal which would require firms to expense employee stock options. Expensing options will have very negative consequences. In fact, just the threat of expensing has already changed the behavior in many firms. Mandatory expensing of employee options will effectively end the practice of granting employee stock options as we know it.

Stock options enable firms, often new economy-oriented firms, to attract talent that otherwise would go to companies able to pay higher salaries through cash compensation arrangements. Newer growth companies tend not to have large stable cash flows. However, through stock options, they can compete by offering employees an up-side in the event that the firm succeeds.

Incentive is perhaps the most important driver of economic growth. People advocating expensing are taking incentive for success away from the very companies that could be producing the next generation's goods and services. No economic model can dispute this argument.

California rests on the banks of the Pacific Rim. All of our country's new economy firms, but particularly those in California face greater and greater competition from businesses in Central and

East Asia. I ask my colleagues to reflect on the fact that companies in China are striving to take away our global edge in technology. China graduates now 195,000 engineers and computer programmers annually. Many have made the point that the Chinese government has embraced stock options in its 5-year plan. Here is my point. I am worried that while communist China is learning capitalism, we are forgetting it.

Again, Mr. Chairman, thank you for the leadership on this issue. I look forward to the testimony of our distinguished witnesses. I yield back.

Chairman BAKER. I thank the gentleman.

Mr. Crowley?

Mr. CROWLEY. Thank you, Mr. Chairman. Thank you for holding this hearing today. I want to thank the ranking member as well, Mr. Kanjorski, for his input and his presence here today, as well as the Chairman and the Ranking Member of the full committee for their interest in this issue.

I want to begin by expressing my gratitude for FASB and the role that it plays in our economy, that of ensuring independence and credibility of our nation's accounting systems. At the same time, I also have to state that I disagree with FASB's recently proposed rule change, the mandatory expensing of all stock options as I believe this rule does not deal solely with accounting principles, but rather also deals with economic policy as well.

While accounting standards should be left to FASB, economic policy should and must remain with Congress and the executive branch. I believe this differentiation between accounting policy and economic policy must be made when discussing this proposed rule change. This proposed regulation will not address concerns about excessive executive compensation or reliability of a company's financial statements. Rather, I believe this rule will adversely affect employees who receive stock options, especially employees whose companies provide broad-based stock option plans, thereby hurting wealth creation and weakening or eliminating the basic economic instrument that created the economic boom of the 1990s and is still used frequently today by venture capital startups.

Besides delving into economic policy, which is not I believe the role of FASB, I have additional concerns about this rule, such as that this expensing mandate will provide less, not more, integrity in accounting. Supporters of this rule will argue that it makes accounting more honest. I have to differ. In fact, this rule will allow two different methods for companies to expense their options, either binomial or Black-Scholes, both of which are not considered accurate evaluation models. In essence, this rule will allow companies to pick and choose their accounting methods, providing more confusion, I believe, and more dishonesty in financial statements. This rule will allow corporate accountants to decide which expensing system works best for their company's goals.

Whereas today, to keep accounting honest, those same firms with stock options must, under FASB's guidelines, disclose the value of their options in the company's financial footnotes, as mentioned earlier, or charge it directly against income, leaving no economic surprise for any investor.

Additionally, supporters of this rule will argue that there is nothing in this rule that prevents the issuance of stock options and that the CBO report states that expensing of options will not have any adverse consequences. They go on to argue that some companies such as Coca-Cola expense their options now and have not seen a drastic adverse affect in their stock price. But when referencing Coke as an example or using the CBO report to justify this expensing mandate, supporters of expensing do not take into account the issue of broad-based stock option plans that benefit all company employees, not the regular stock option plan that benefits the few at the top of the corporate pyramid. Companies like Coke provide and expense their options, but they are not broad-based plans. They are options for top corporate executives.

The mandatory expensing of stock options would effectively destroy broad-based stock option plans which enhance financial opportunities for workers at all levels, stimulate economic growth, and help create the new economy of the 1990s, a new economy, as I mentioned before, that we are still feeling the effects of today. In fact, it is these broad-based plans that have spread wealth throughout all sectors and to all employees of our new economy, from CEO to secretary. Ninety-eight of the nation's top 100 largest high-tech firms that focus on the Internet provide options to most or all of their employees, and most of these options go to the rank-and-file workers, helping stimulate wealth creation for employees while allowing employers to attract the best talent.

Contrary to popular belief, these people receiving broad-based stock options are not all located in Boston and San Francisco. Statistics show that 41 percent of those receiving broad-based stock options live in the South and 24 percent live in the Midwest. Unfortunately, we already are starting to see, as was mentioned before, the negative effects of this FASB rule. It has not even been finalized as of yet. Some companies are already beginning to scale back their broad-based option plans in anticipation of the FASB rule, and I believe this hurts employees and not the executives.

I am supportive of an independent FASB for the purpose of making accounting rules, but again this rule is not about accounting. It is about economic policy, and I believe that belongs with Congress and the executive.

I yield back the balance of my time.

Chairman BAKER. I thank the gentleman for his statement.

I have no further members on our side seeking recognition for an opening statement, so the next person to go to is Mr. Scott.

Mr. SCOTT. Thank you very much, Mr. Chairman. Certainly, this is an extraordinarily important and yet complex issue.

I think that as we move forward on this, and I have enjoyed working with the Chairman on this issue, but it is clear that the legislative process is really working here and raising some questions and putting some issues on the table that certainly need to be dealt with as we move forward.

My understanding of H.R. 3574 is that it does indeed immediately dispense with the stock options requirement for the top five executives in a corporation. It provides for a study before moving forward, and certainly exempts small businesses from the first three years. The question is, though, is that enough.

I think there are three issues here that we certainly have to exhaust before we move forward. First of all, what impact does this have by immediately stopping the stock options for the top five executives in a corporation, for the rank-and-file members who for years have benefited from stock options. I think we have to move gingerly to make sure that is continued.

The other issue, of course, is small startup businesses. Is the exemption enough for the first 3 years, especially our technology companies. It is very important that we respond to that concern. The third area of concern for me, of course, is to hear from the SEC, to hear from FASB, to make sure as we move forward we are doing the right thing in dealing with the abuses and to stop that and regain the confidence of the American people in our most treasured possessions, and that is in our corporations that are the bulwark of our economic system, without doing tremendous damage otherwise.

So Mr. Chairman, I really look forward to this, going forward, and I hope that we can address those three concerns as we move forward as we deal with this very complex issue.

Thank you.

Chairman BAKER. I thank the gentleman.

Mr. Sherman?

Mr. SHERMAN. Thank you, Mr. Chairman. As the only member who will begin his statement by saying I am glad the FASB is looking at this issue, I do have a lot to say.

Let me begin by looking at this whole idea of broad-based options. I have drafted the option plans. I have consulted with the companies on their option process. Yes, there are a few companies that have broad-based plans, but in general you are talking about 80 percent of this benefit going to the top 8 percent of the employees across the board in this economy. When we look at the bill that is being proposed to deal with this, it supposedly is there just to protect broad-based.

Look at two important details in the bill. First, even when options are granted to the top five people in the company, you have to assume zero volatility. So it is not just a bill to protect broad options. It is a bill to massively undervalue options given to the top five executives. Second, if you are number six at GM, you are probably doing pretty good. We should instead, if we want to focus on broad-based options, look at options which when valued at time of grant are less valuable than $100,000 per employee per year. That would allow us to make sure that we are giving a special benefit only to those options that are not being used for the purpose that options have been used for, and that is to make our corporate executives the richest corporate executives in the world by far.

Now, we should be matching expenses and revenue. That is basic accounting. So we are told that somehow a stock option is not really an expense. It is not anything of value. Well, if it was not anything of value that was being given up, why does everybody want it? More importantly, what is an option? It is a piece of the future growth of the company, transferred from the current shareholders to the option grantees, the executives. That is very much a transfer of something of value.

That is why if the company were to grant options which could be very similar in their form to employee stock options, would it grant those to private investors? That would be a recognized transaction. The proof of what I am saying is this. Let's say we really cared not about whether the executives got compensated, but there was health care for the bottom half of the employees, particularly in big companies that may not even use stock options now.

We told corporate America, you can grant stock options to insurance companies if those insurance companies are giving health care to the bottom half of your employees. That is an expense. It has always been an expense. That is why companies do not use that as a device to pay their insurance companies. Instead, they have to pay them in cash, and increasingly they decide not to pay the cost of today's health care.

If the transfer of an option to acquire something use for the company, like the work of the employees, is not an expense, why just employee stock options? Why can't you buy your building for stock options and not list that as a cost? Why can't you pay your telephone bill with stock options and not list that as a cost? The reason is because stock options is another way of paying an expense.

Now, if we do things right and expense stock options, then we will I think show the world that perhaps unlike China, unlike some others, we have the best, clearest, most transparent, fairest, most logical accounting system being imposed, even when powerful interests disagree. The effect will be to reduce executive compensation in this country. The effect will also be, and it will not be a major effect, but it will be an effect. There will be a slight reduction in the amount of capital flowing to those companies that use stock options and that capital will instead flow to some older companies that tend not to use stock options. Is it better that a stock that somebody invest in Intel than invest in Proctor and Gamble? Gee, I do not know, but picking winners and losers has never been a proper role for this Congress.

So I would like to argue that FASB is doing its job and we should leave them alone. There is one problem. FASB is not doing its job, two huge problems up there in Connecticut. First, this exposure draft just kind of leaves drifting do you use binomial? Do you use Black-Scholes? When do you use one? When do you use the other? Any guidance? Or do you just hire the accounting firm, there are not many left, but do you just hire the accounting firm that will give you the lowest stock option value? If they are going to do their job, they ought to do it.

But there is a much greater problem with FASB and it is a related issue. We cannot talk about stock options without talking about research expense, because the biggest argument against what FASB is doing is that it will hurt high tech. Well, let's talk about something that really hurts high tech, not just something that may disadvantage a few executives in high tech, but rather that disadvantages high tech in general. FASB will admit it is completely wrong as a matter of accounting theory, but they have left it in place for over 30 years, and that is the expensing of all research. The effect is for us as an economy to under-invest in research, for stockholders to under-invest in companies that do research.

Why is this related? Because if we are going to hit tech with bad accounting for research, should we also hit them with good accounting for stock options? Is it fair to take a sector of our economy and require them to expense stock options, which is good accounting, while at the same time requiring them to expense the nearly $2 billion they do every year of research, which is bad accounting.

So when this bill comes up, I will propose an amendment that it remains in effect only so long as FASB fails to allow for the capitalization of successful research and development expenditures. When FASB solves that problem, it will have a far greater affect on encouraging investment in high tech than anyone ever argued that this stock option thing has a negative affect. If I am able to get that amendment passed, and I realize it will be a matter of first impression to most of my colleagues, I will support the bill, in which case, and I think right now I am the only one speaking against it.

So we need to have a fair accounting system for tech companies, one that recognizes that when you give a stock option, you have given something, but when you have done research and it is successful research, you have bought an asset.

I yield back and I thank the Chairman for his indulgence.

Chairman BAKER. I thank the gentleman.

Mr. Lucas?

Mr. LUCAS. I am ready to hear from the witnesses.

Chairman BAKER. Thank you, Mr. Lucas.

Mr. Miller?

Mr. MILLER OF NORTH CAROLINA. I agree with Mr. Lucas.

Chairman BAKER. And Mr. Hinojosa?

Mr. HINOJOSA. Thank you, Mr. Chairman.

Chairman Baker and Ranking Member Kanjorski, I want to thank you for holding this very important and timely meeting. Chairman Baker, I want to note first and foremost that I am a co-sponsor of your legislation, H.R. 3574, the Stock Option Accounting Reform Act. I remain an ardent supporter of this legislation despite FASB's March 31 proposed rulemaking that would require companies to report as an expense the value of stock options they give to executives and rank-and-file employees.

In fact, FASB's recent proposed rulemaking demonstrates how important it is that Congress pass your legislation, particularly section three of your bill. Section three would prohibit the SEC from recognizing as generally accepted any accounting principle established by a standard-setting body relating to the expensing of stock options pending the completion of an economic impact study by the Secretary of Commerce and the Secretary of Labor.

What everyone here needs to recognize is that stock options are an important tool to attract talent to new ventures, and that mandatory expensing of stock options will stifle their issuance, reduce company profits, and deter innovation and economic growth. FASB's proposed rulemaking likely would result in the disappearance of stock options. The disappearance of stock options will inhibit a company's ability to attract and retain skilled employees.

If the FASB rule takes effect, many of the companies will stop issuing options to their rank-and-file employees. There is no reliable nor accurate formula to properly value them, contrary to what FASB contends.

In closing, I want to include in my comments concerns that I see in global competition with large importing nations like China. Mr. Chairman, the Chinese government has incorporated stock options into its 5-year economic plan to boost its technology industry. As a member of the House Manufacturing Caucus, I know all too well that many of America's manufacturing jobs have already been outsourced to China, thus negatively impacting our U.S. economy. FASB's proposed rulemaking poses a similar risk in that venture capital companies and high-tech companies might relocate to China or other stock option-friendly nations if registered companies are required to expense their stock options in the United States.

Mr. Chairman, I want to work with you and other co-sponsors of your legislation to at least delay the implementation of FASB's proposed rulemaking, either by passing your legislation as a standalone measure, or working together to incorporate it into other legislation to ensure its passage. Hopefully, we will succeed in this endeavor.

I yield back the balance of my time.

[The prepared statement of Hon. Rubén Hinojosa can be found on page 81 in the appendix.]

Chairman BAKER. I thank the gentleman.

If there are no other members desiring to make an opening statement, I want to welcome our witnesses to our hearing. I hope you have enjoyed it today. We would like to remind each of you that despite the length of members's comments, we do request that each of you try to limit your remarks to 5 minutes. Your formal statement will be made part of our hearing record. I welcome each of you. We look forward to your comments.

I would turn first to Mr. Jeff Thomas, field applications engineer, Altera Corporation. Welcome.

STATEMENT OF JEFF THOMAS, FIELD APPLICATIONS ENGINEER, ALTERA CORPORATION

Mr. THOMAS. Chairman Baker, members of the subcommittee, I want to thank you for hearing my testimony today.

My name is Jeff Thomas. I am a field applications engineer for the Altera Corporation in San Jose, California. Altera Corporation manufactures and sells programmable logic devices, which are semiconductor chips used in a broad range of applications. In my role as an FAE, it is my responsibility to provide on-site technical support to one of our largest customers, which is a major telecommunications company.

In my daily work, I train engineers on how to use our chips. I present our new technology to our customers and I ensure that their systems are successful. I am here today because I volunteered to participate in this hearing because stock options have played a large role in my decision to pursue a career in the high-tech field. I wanted to communicate to you the impact that they have on employees as well as companies that offer broad-based stock option plans.

I graduated from Carnegie Mellon University in 2000 with a bachelor's degree in electrical and computer engineering. I had job offers from a broad range of companies at the time of my graduation. During my time at CMU, I had a couple of summer internships at Fortune 500 companies, and both companies offered me a job upon graduation. However neither offered a broad-based stock option plan.

I also interviewed with a number of high-tech firms, and every job offer that I got from a high-stock firm did include stock options. So I decided that I wanted to work where I had a stake in the success of the company. I decided I liked the idea of being able to profit not only from my salary, but also from the growth of the company.

In retrospect, I can definitely say I have seen a difference in both the behavior and performance of employees in high-tech firms that have a vested stake in their company, compared to the people that I worked with at companies where they did not have that ownership stake.

My first day at Altera, I was granted stock options that would vest over the next four years. So after one year if I stayed with the company, 25 percent of those options would vest. If the stock price had gone up, I could buy and sell those options and realize a profit. I could not transfer those options or sell them on an open market of any kind. I could only use them for my own personal gain.

Also each year at my annual review, I was granted a new batch of stock options based on my performance that would follow a similar vesting schedule. This ensures that I was constantly motivated to stay with the company and continue to work for its long-term growth .

Stock options are a great incentive for employees. People work hard not only to advance their personal companies, but to grow the company as a whole. They allow all employees to grow into the success of the company. As the sales and profits of a company increase, the employees benefit through the appreciation of the stock price. This fosters an environment where employees will go out of their way and beyond their job descriptions to grow the company as a whole.

Stock options are also a strong motivation to stay with a company. Because of their vesting schedule, employees are incentivized to stay with a good company. Since I believe in Altera's long-term vision, I want to stay with the company and continue to build my ownership share in that company through the stock option program. Because everybody at Altera has a stake in the company, we are all committed to making the company successful in the long term.

This behavior is not unique to Altera. I see this type of dedication and work ethic at companies all around Silicon Valley. All my friends, whether they work at big telecom companies or small startups, share the same desire to see their company become successful because they share a stake in that company. Engineers in the valley often work long hours and weekends to make sure their company succeeds because each person has a personal stake in the enterprise beyond just their salary.

Already in my career I can say I have seen the effect of broad-base stock option plans in action. I have been able to compare the atmosphere at a high-tech company in Silicon Valley to some of the

Fortune 500 companies I worked at as a summer intern. I can definitely say that people in Silicon Valley work harder, longer and care more about the long-term performance of the company than employees that are just there to get a paycheck.

Throughout my career, I want to continue to work at companies like Altera that offer stock options to a broad base of employees so that I can continue to work towards the shared goal of increasing the company's value. I believe this promotes an extremely valuable working environment.

I also believe that anything that would make it more difficult for a company to grant stock options would hurt the company's performance overall. The success of Silicon Valley is based on the work ethic and dedication of its employees. This work ethic is a direct result of the fact that employees know that they will share in the success of their company. If anything happens that would not allow the companies to offer their employees a share in that success, I believe the overall performance of that company would be hurt.

I sincerely hope you will consider these positive impacts of stock options on both employees and their companies while you are determining the fate of this bill.

Thank you again, Mr. Chairman and members of the subcommittee. I am happy to answer any questions you have at this time.

[The prepared statement of Jeff Thomas can be found on page 157 in the appendix.]

Chairman BAKER. Thank you very much, sir.

I follow a script, Mr. Kruse, and I should have recognized you first, but your name did not appear first on my list. So I recognize you at this time, Mr. Douglas Kruse, professor, School of Management and Labor Relations, Rutgers University. Welcome, sir.

STATEMENT OF DOUGLAS KRUSE, PROFESSOR, SCHOOL OF MANAGEMENT AND LABOR RELATIONS, RUTGERS UNIVERSITY

Mr. KRUSE. Thank you. I am pleased to be here.

I am a professor at the Rutgers University School of Management and Labor Relations. I am also Research Associate at the National Bureau of Economic Research in Cambridge, Massachusetts. At the NBER, I am working with Professor Richard Freeman of Harvard University and my Rutgers colleague Joseph Blasi. We are co-directing a project looking at shared capitalist programs in U.S. companies.

I am also co-author of a book that came out last year, In the Company of Owners, that looks at broad-based stock options in U.S. companies, co-authored with Joseph Blasi and Aaron Bernstein. I regret that I did not bring a copy of the book to wave around. As Doug was pointing out, my publisher will never forgive me for forgetting that today.

As part of the NBER project, we added some questions to the 2002 General Social Survey, a representative survey of working Americans. I want to summarize a few results from that and some other evidence for you very quickly. What we found was that 13 percent of private sector employees say they hold stock options. That translates into 14 million stock option holders. We also found that 23 million workers say they own company stock, 15 million of them through employee stock purchase plans.

Contrary to popular impression, most stock option holders are not rich executives. In fact, a very striking finding, the one that I would really point to, is in appendix one of my testimony. It turns out that 79 percent of stock option holders earn less than $75,000 a year, and well more than half earn less than $50,000 a year. We provide a variety of breakdowns in appendix two showing that the majority of the stock option holders are non-managers. More than 90 percent say that they are in the middle-or working-class, and they are spread across regions and across the social and political spectrum. We do the same thing in appendix three for holders of company stock, and find very similar results. They are very representative.

I have strong reservations about expensing, since many companies say that they are going to first cut broad-base stock options if expensing takes place. There were four studies last year in 2003 that analyzed hundreds of corporations. They found that one-half to one-third were already making large cuts in stock option plans. One-half to two-thirds planned cuts in employee stock purchase plans.

One might say, well, maybe the companies are just crying wolf. In the last few days, Joseph Blasi and I looked at the first 10 companies to file SEC proxies for 2003 out of the largest 20 companies, the Fortune 20 companies. Of these 10, six had already announced that they will expense stock options. Five of those six have already increased the share of stock options going to the top five executives from 2002 to 2003, and all six of them increased the share going to the CEO. If this trend continues, we think it will be deeply troubling. It could be bad not just for regular employees who will be cut out of stock options, but it could be bad for company value as well.

We did a recent study on executive compensation over the past 11 years in the 2,000 largest companies. We found that increases in executive compensation, including different measures of stock options, do not predict future shareholder returns. In contrast, we surveyed over 20 years of evidence on broad-based employee ownership, profit sharing and stock options in chapter seven of our book, that I should be waving around now. The evidence clearly shows that broad-based plans are linked to higher productivity and shareholder return on average; not in every company, of course, but on average.

It would be a shame if expensing discourages companies from using and extending these plans that can improve performance. Public policy should be encouraging policies that improve performance.

So our conclusion is if there is expensing, it makes sense to somehow preserve broad-based plans. One good approach could be to expense just for the top five executives, as the current bill proposes. If expensing does go through for all employees, another possibility is to create a tax credit that would offset the option expense only for companies with truly broad-based plans. This could be an alternative to the existing deduction when options are exercised, so it could end up actually being revenue-neutral, a tax credit that would end up being revenue-neutral.

Finally just as a last note, I call attention to another House bill that would create a presidential commission on employee ownership. Given the importance of all these issues, given the debate around this, we think a presidential commission on employee ownership could be a good way to explore those issues.

Thank you very much.

[The prepared statement of Douglas Kruse can be found on page 125 in the appendix.]

Chairman BAKER. We thank you very much. You may wave the book at any time you choose. Thank you.

[Laughter.]

We welcome next Mr. Douglas Holtz-Eakin, Director of the Congressional Budget Office. Welcome, sir.

STATEMENT OF DOUGLAS HOLTZ-EAKIN, DIRECTOR, CONGRESSIONAL BUDGET OFFICE

Mr. HOLTZ-EAKIN. Mr. Chairman, Congressman Kanjorski, members of the committee, the CBO recently delivered to Congress a study entitled Accounting for Employee Stock Options, which details the fact that employee stock options are an economic cost to firms. They represent an exchange of value in return for labor services, and displaying that value—measured by the fair value or cash equivalent of the option and recognized over a period that the labor services are used, the vesting period—leads to a more accurate portrayal of net income in economic terms.

Correspondingly, the failure to display this on financial statements leads to an overstatement of economic net income. Valuing employee stock options is a difficult task and is complicated by features such as vesting periods, forfeiture provisions and non-transferability of these options. However, advances in financial analysis permit reasonable valuation of such options, as they do comparable instruments such as warrants which are currently held in many entities portfolios. And such valuations are similar in their accuracy to those of such complicated issues involving uncertainty as retiree health benefits, the impairment of goodwill, or the cost of environmental cleanup, which may occur in the future.

These are all currently displayed in the firm's financial statements. One would anticipate that the increased use of these techniques under the prospect of the proposed FASB standard might lead to further advances in the ability to value these options more accurately. Recognizing the expense of employee stock options would not alter the economic fundamentals of any business. It would not alter the markets in which they compete for customers, their international or domestic competitors, or the prices that they charge.

It would not have any impact on the labor markets in which they hire their workers or the need for compensation and appropriate incentives for those workers. It would not alter the technologies that they currently deploy nor the incentives to acquire and deploy new technologies. And fundamentally, it would not alter the cash flows used to conduct their operations.

Any potential economic impact of expensing employee stock options will come through changes in investors's evaluations of these firms. For savvy investors and for most firms, no new information will be provided by moving the disclosure from the current notes onto the face of the statement. Expensing would simply make it easier and more broadly possible to do the same valuations that are available today.

It is the case that some valuations may decline. If so, those firms and their workers would suffer the costs and experience disruption from the reduced availability of equity capital to those firms in the near term. However some may also rise, and on balance one would expect that there would be no great overall impact on the U.S. economy and that any targeted impacts on particular firms would be outweighed by the improved allocation of capital on the economy, resulting in increased employee productivity, and improved economic performance.

One cannot know for sure the overall economic impact in advance of the adoption of the FASB standard. However, the experience as displayed thus far for those firms which have voluntarily undertaken expensing or from the experience from countries such as Canada which has not only proposed, but implemented an expensing standard, or the area of the European Union which has announced a standard, but not yet implemented it, all suggest that there would be no broad-based economic impact.

Mr. Chairman, we thank you for the chance to discuss our report today and look forward to your questions.

[The prepared statement of Douglas Holtz-Eakin can be found on page 107 in the appendix.]

Chairman BAKER. I thank you very much for your participation in our hearing today and your statement.

Next, I wish to welcome Mr. Kevin Hassett. Please proceed at your leisure.

STATEMENT OF KEVIN HASSETT, DIRECTOR OF ECONOMIC POLICY STUDIES, AMERICAN ENTERPRISE INSTITUTE

Mr. HASSETT. Thank you very much, Mr. Chairman.

I agree with Mr. Oxley and Mr. Ose, Mr. Chairman, that the best reading of the literature is that right now the literature is not exactly sure how to value these options. The literature is not sure how to value these options because of issues mentioned by Mr. Holtz-Eakin, but also because the options have a much longer life than the type of options that are marketed these days. To my mind, having been immersed in the technical details since my dissertation, I think that is the most relevant issue here.

Indeed, Warren Buffett himself said in the Financial Times that the minute you get into longer-term options, it is crazy to use Black-Scholes. The fact is that is true. In fact, this issue has even made it into the leading text books, as is mentioned in my testimony, and developed in more detail in a recent paper prepared by Glenn Hubbard and Charles Calomiris for the American Enterprise Institute.

So I think this explains why it is that FASB has been going so slowly on this issue, given their clear designs on expensing. The fact is, as you get close to expensing and think about how to do it, contrary to Mr. Holtz-Eakin's statement, you find that it is not the case that there is an accepted way to do it, which is why FASB has refused to specify, it appears to me in reading their documents, precisely how firms are supposed to do it.

So in my testimony, what I do is really go after the question that Mr. Frank raised in his opening statement. How is it that you could actually change the world if the market is efficient, if it is looking at the details on options already, then if you move an expense calculation maybe that is incorrect up to the top line, what effect does that really have on anything? Just like if we subtracted 10 from earnings, then what a rational investor would do is they would just add 10 back in. So if we do something wrong, the rational market ought to see through it.

What I found after studying this issue with my colleague Peter Wallison at the American Enterprise Institute, who as you know is a very distinguished attorney who has worked for President Reagan and has had other positions in town, is that it is very likely that if we do not tell firms how to expense options and know that we are basically giving them a problem to solve that has not been solved by the literature, then we are going to open up a real legal mess that will potentially tie firms up in class action lawsuits for years and cause you to have to consider new legislation.

In my testimony, I provide a simple example of the state that I think we might end up in if FASB has its way. That is, suppose that for example a publisher that finishes a book in 2003 and plans to send it to the book stores in 2004, is required to forecast the sales in 2004 for that book by FASB and include that in their 2003 statement. And FASB does not tell them how to forecast it. They just say, you have to say, since you paid for the expenses of the book in 2003 what the sales are going to be in 2004.

Well, the firm would presumably try its best to develop a model to forecast sales, but of course on average there would be a whole lot of firms that would make errors. As soon as they make those errors, the earnings will be misstated, and that will open the firm up to class action lawsuits. It is my belief and Mr. Wallison's belief, and we have spelled this out in great detail in a paper that is just coming out in Regulation magazine, that the real reason why the expensing of options is going to cause firms to not use them as much as they do now, and to shy away from them, is because if you do not specify a model, then everybody is going to get the expense wrong. Probably about half the firms at least are going to have over-stated their earnings because their model led them to do that. With that over-statement, they are going to find themselves enmeshed in really difficult lawsuits.

So I think it would be a big mistake for FASB to require the expensing of options without expressly stating how to do it. If they expressly state how to do it, then the firm will at least have the defense that we are just following FASB's directions and that defense might well be a reasonable one and a successful one. Absent that, I think that FASB is creating a real mess for our corporations and one that will lead them to shy away from the use of options.

Thank you.

[The prepared statement of Kevin A. Hassett can be found on page 90 in the appendix.]

Chairman BAKER. Thank you very much. I appreciate your participation.

Our next witness is Mr. Phil Smith, chairman of the board, Taser International. Welcome, sir.

STATEMENT OF PHIL SMITH, CHAIRMAN OF THE BOARD, TASER INTERNATIONAL, INC.

Mr. SMITH. Thank you, Mr. Chairman and subcommittee members. It is a pleasure to be here. Let me give you a quick background and then launch into what I have to say.

I have an undergraduate degree from West Point, MBA and I have a PhD in business and a specialty in finance, so I clearly understand all the theoretical arguments. I have been a corporate officer in three Fortune 500 companies and I have done five high-tech startups. I spent the last 35 years in this business, so I have lived it from almost the inception.

I guess I am one of the few guys here who can talk from practical reality and not some theory. I really get a kick out of most of the people testifying yesterday in the Senate and have never seen an option, used an option, have ever benefited from an option or ever used them to try and attract employees to a company. That is what is most disappointing to me. The people that are really involved have had very little voice in what is going on. I hope that this committee takes this to heart.

I can give you one example, of these five startups. I did one in the Silicon Valley in 1983 that we sold in 1985 very successfully. The employees out of that company started 12 new companies. They took the money they earned from the options and literally like a thing exploding with seeds, 12 new companies started in the Silicon Valley in 1985 from the people from that company.

I can go through example after example. I do not have the time. Options are used not only for employees. As I pointed out in my testimony, when we went public 3 years ago at my current company, Taser International, we were in need of some interesting board members to comply with the corporate governance that Chairman Oxley has been kind enough to levy on all corporations in America. When you go out and talk to significant board members and people with a strong background, there is a real risk in coming on a public company's board today. The trial lawyers love to have them. People are very concerned about joining public boards, especially young public companies. One of the ways we got the people we did, the caliber we got, was the ability to use options.

Now, it turned out they have been very successful. They all have made quite a bit of money as a result of that. But at the time they took those options, they accepted the risk. You take this option away from us and force to expense and I do not know how we are going to attract these board members. We could not have afforded to pay them the money it would have taken to get them on our board and provide the governance that the Congress is looking for.

The second thing is, it is a double whammy for small companies. A current thing, our stock is extremely volatile. It fell 32 percent yesterday, which happens to be just one data point. The stock is up 6000 percent over the last 12 months. We have what is called a very high volatility. We get penalized because, one, we are a small company and secondly, we are highly volatile. You take the measurement of our company. We will get two penalties, not just one. One, we are small; second, we are highly volatile.

Those will really impact the bottom line of our company, and obviously a lot of our investors are retail investors. I agree, the sophisticated investor can read the footnotes in our balance sheet. They are cops. They are police officers around the country that own 100 or 200 shares. They do not understand the sophistication of footnotes, and they are not going to understand when all of a sudden the earnings drop on the company compared to other companies in the industry.

Third, I would like to talk about the issue of tax. Our corporation has not paid tax for the last couple of years because of employee options. When they exercise their option and make the profit, they pay a personal tax. The corporation gets the benefit. We have been able to retain that tax and use it to grow, and we have grown our employee base to 199 employees from 70 a year ago by using that cash flow. It would normally have been paid as corporate income tax. Nobody has talked about the tax issue here, about the corporations that are allowed to retain that tax, the cash on their balance sheets and use it to grow.

Let me give you one last thing. We have stopped issuing options. We have given all our employees their final options this year. They vest by the end of the year, merely because of this legislation. We do listen to what goes on in Washington. We do watch what is going on and we are not about to penalize our shareholders and ourselves by issuing a bunch of options that we have to expense in future years. We have told our employees there will be no more options if this passes, and the only people that are going to get it are the top five.

My last comment, as Mr. Sherman mentioned, he tried to contain executive compensation with the $1 million salary cap, and we all see how effective that was. They just reported the highest executive compensation in the country this past year, I think it was in USA Today. So it had very little effect on the top five. Your proposal will address the top five and let the average employee have a chance to benefit in the success of their company. At Taser, we have 20 millionaires, from secretaries to production employees, right up the line. They are the ones who are going to lose out. Those are the ones who will not get the options. It will still go to the top five. I certainly hope you are successful, Mr. Chairman.

Thank you.

[The prepared statement of Phil Smith can be found on page 152 in the appendix.]

Chairman BAKER. Thank you very much for your contribution here.

Our next witness is Mr. Robert Grady, managing partner, Carlyle Venture Partners. Welcome.

STATEMENT OF ROBERT E. GRADY, MANAGING PARTNER, CARLYLE VENTURE PARTNERS

Mr. GRADY. Thank you, Mr. Chairman and members of the subcommittee. I appreciate the opportunity to present this morning, not only on behalf of the Carlyle Group, which is one of the world's largest private equity firms, but also I serve as a member of the board of directors of the National Venture Capital Association. By coincidence, I also have taught for the last decade on the faculty of the Stanford Business School, which we will come back to in a minute.

The FASB has asked for comment on this exposure draft, and our comment is simple. The proposal is inappropriate. It is incorrect as a matter of financial and accounting theory. I think it is poorly thought-out and it is very definitely unworkable.

Before I comment directly on the exposure draft, let me just offer a little context that makes clear the typical use of stock options today in the economy.

The two venture capital funds that I spend every day managing, which were started in 1997 and 2002 respectively, have investments in about 38 different companies, all started from the ground up. Those 38 companies employ over 4,000 people. In the five private companies on whose boards I sit, Blackboard here in Washington, DC; Panasas in Fremont, California; USBX in Los Angeles; Secure Elements out in the Virginia suburbs; and Ingenio, also in California; incentive stock options are granted to every single employee, from the receptionist to the CEO. That is typical in the venture capital world. In fact, according to a recent survey by the NVCA, over 70 percent of venture-backed companies award stock options to every single employee. You heard Professor Kruse state that half of all option holders in the country earn less than $50,000 a year.

The standard type of grant in a venture-backed company is a grant that is vested to encourage an employee to stay at the company. A typical structure, in fact the most commonly used in venture-backed companies, calls for the grant to vest over 4 years, just like the grants that Mr. Thomas received when he joined his company, with so-called "cliff vesting" on the first anniversary of employment of one-quarter of the options and then monthly vesting of the remaining three-quarters each month over the next 3 years.

That is an important point to understand about how options work, because under the FASB's exposure draft, with its provisions for graded vesting, the normal grant of stock options, the one that virtually every venture-backed company in America uses, will have to be valued 37 different times per grant. Somehow, the FASB believes this will make financial statements more understandable.

Let me turn to the FASB's exposure draft and how its policies will work or not work if implemented. First, I do feel compelled to start with a fundamental conceptual point, and that is that options are units of ownership. They are shares. They are not expenses. They are not claims of cash against the company's resources. They are not the use of a company asset. Basically, they should be treated and disclosed, in my view, in the denominator, if you will, of the earnings-per-share calculation. If you account for them in both the numerator and the denominator, you are double-counting them.

So if in fact FASB were proposing in this exposure draft that when companies report earnings per share, they had to disclose in every case the fully-diluted share count, that is, including all options outstanding in the denominator, I think that would be a fair and very workable proposal. I think this point is essential, because at its heart, what this debate is all about is that many Americans, and in fact people all over the world, are willing to trade off cash compensation for units of ownership. They are willing to earn less cash today and thereby create less in terms of ongoing expenses by the company, so that over the long term the company will be worth more. In other words, they are thinking like owners. It is good for other shareholders who might choose to join them along the way that they are thinking like owners, because their interests are aligned as mutual owners of the securities of the company.

Ironically, the proponents of expensing say that requiring it will not have the dire effect that many predict, that some of us predict, because they say investors will just in effect ignore it. Investors will basically strip out the effect of expensing and look straight to cash EPS. So in other words, they will ignore GAAP. The reason they will do it is precisely because it will not be representative of the company's true expenses. That is exactly what I believe Representative Frank was saying, if reality does not change. So the irony of the FASB proposal, in other words, is that it is likely to undermine confidence in and the use of GAAP accounting, which one presumes to be the exact opposite of the objective of the proposal.

In the gymnastics that FASB has had to go through to get over this fundamental point, in trying to define units of ownership as expenses instead of shares, they have created a number of problems that I would just like to touch on and enumerate briefly.

The first obstacle, of course, is trying to define the appropriate measurement date at which to value an option. There are two different possibilities. The FASB has suggested that the grant date is appropriate. The problem with this, of course, is that the value of the option at grant date is highly uncertain. It may never vest. The employee might leave. It may never be exercised because the stock may never be "in the money" during the appropriate time frame.

An alternative is to move the measurement date to the exercise date, and that would even be worse because it would simply penalize the most successful companies, those with the brightest prospects, for the mere fact that their stock has appreciated. You have heard the example of Taser. Their profits would be wiped out by the mere fact that their stock had appreciated, regardless of the performance of the company.

A second problem which the committee has discussed today is how to value what an option would be worth. FASB suggests using observable arms-length transactions, but of course for private company options they have never traded, so the value of the option has to be modeled somehow. There is a choice of modeling and methodologies to use, and whatever choice you make leads to a radically different assessment of value.

That, of course, leads to the third problem, which is that any of the models that one could choose, including Black-Scholes, named for the late Fisher Black and my former colleague at the Stanford Business School, Myron Scholes, and a binomial model for that matter, rely on one key variable and that is the estimate of the volatility of the underlying stock. Of course, since private company shares have not traded, any estimate of volatility is basically a guess. Actually, FASB makes it worse because they say we are not to look at historical volatility; you are to estimate future volatility. So any estimate of volatility will be subject to both potential manipulation and inaccuracy.

That, of course, leads to a fourth problem, which is to try to get around this problem of estimating in advance the volatility, FASB has given private companies in the proposal the option to use intrinsic value as a way of valuing options. Under this methodology, the value of the option is adjusted for every reporting period, every quarter, or in some cases of private companies, every month, and is changed to reflect an estimate of value or stock price if it is a public company. That is basically a form of variable accounting which brings stock price directly into the income statement of the company, and of course introduces the potential for wild swings from quarter to quarter of the value of any given option, so it will be massively confusing for investors.

The fifth problem is that FASB ignored that most private company employee options are highly restricted. That is, they are not only subject to vesting, but they cannot be transferred; they cannot be hedged; they cannot be pledged; they cannot be sold. So it is very hard to value these restrictions. Interestingly, FASB argues that no restrictions that exist during the vesting period should even be considered in valuing the options. Clearly, an option that is subject to restrictions is worth less than an option that is subject to no restrictions, yet FASB would have them be recorded at exactly the same price. So much for the concept of fair value.

Finally, in seeking to identify the proper time period over which to attribute the expense that the exposure draft would require, the FASB creates a whole new set of problems. For example, the exposure draft suggests that companies should try to model or predict the groups of their employees for purposes of predicting their exercise behavior. That is because the proposal calls for them to adjust the contractual term for expected early exercise or post-vesting behavior. Obviously, that would be a completely speculative exercise that would be almost preposterous in its unreliability.

All of these obstacles, by introducing theory, uncertainty and subjectivity in place of the actual experience, which is what financial statements are supposed to reflect, will make the income statements of companies less reliable, not more reliable.

In the end, Mr. Chairman, I think what is clear from FASB's proposal is, as you suggested in your opening statement, that it is responsive not to the volume of comments it has received from the venture capital community or companies that use options, but rather to the political process. I do believe this is fundamentally a political proposal and, as you said, Mr. Herz is quoted as inviting people to contact their representatives. I do believe it is in response to something that has nothing to do with employee options, which is the reported abuses at places like Tyco, WorldCom, Adelphia, et cetera, where people stole company resources, allegedly, or reported incorrectly the financial performance of the company.

In this regard, the National Venture Capital Association does support the legislation you have proposed. We believe it is responsible. We believe it is appropriate to exempt private companies where it is impossible to value the options from the expensing requirement. Having taken 175 or so companies public in my career,

I believe it is appropriate to exempt companies during their first three years of being a public company so that you can get some trading experience and understand how to assess the volatility of the stock. With that, we do hope that the Congress will act on your proposal.

Thank you, Mr. Chairman.

[The prepared statement of Robert E. Grady can be found on page 84 in the appendix.]

Chairman BAKER. Thank you very much.

Our final participant this morning is Mr. George Scalise, president of the Semiconductor Industry Association. Welcome.

STATEMENT OF GEORGE M. SCALISE, PRESIDENT, SEMICONDUCTOR INDUSTRY ASSOCIATION

Mr. SCALISE. Thank you, Mr. Chairman and members of the committee. I am George Scalise. It turns out I have been in the semiconductor industry for about 45 years, so I have seen it from the very earliest days and I have seen what stock options have done to help build this industry from a startup to what is now a $200 billion a year industry. I also have been the beneficiary of that process of stock options.

First of all, the SIA strongly supports H.R. 3574 and we commend the leadership of the Chairman as well as the 30 members of the committee that are co-sponsors of the legislation. Going back to the industry for just a moment, the U.S. semiconductor industry, the U.S.-based companies, are the most competitive in the world today and have been since the onset of this industry. We currently have about 50 percent of that $200 billion a year market. It turns out that only 20 percent of that market is here in the U.S. However, about 70 percent of our manufacturing is located here in the U.S. The average employee earns about $97,000 and we have about 255,000 employees here.

So this program that we are talking about is very vital to this industry and has been since the onset. Semiconductors, as you probably know, are the building blocks for the whole information technology market, which is now a $1 trillion export market for the U.S. So whether you are talking about equipment or software, it does not really matter; whether it is games or automobiles, they all embody semiconductors.

The other thing that is important about this is that semiconductors and the IT industry now represent about 8 percent of the economy, but it turns out they are more than 30 percent of the growth; they reduce inflation by about 1 percent a year; they increase productivity by about 1 percent a year. As a consequence, they make a major contribution to the overall economy.

Keep in mind, our prices go down every year by at least 30 percent. Every year the prices go down by at least 30 percent. So if you bought a bit of memory in 1995 for $1, you would be paying about 2 cents for that today. In a few more years, you will be paying 1/100th of a cent or less than that as we go along. So this kind of contribution is something that we need to find ways to encourage and support and make continue to happen going forward.

Going on to the competition, as I said, this is a worldwide market. It is also worldwide competition. As someone said earlier, our competitors overseas have now seen the wisdom of using stock options as a method of dealing with their employees, compensating their employees. In a recent forum that we had at Stanford University, about a month ago, we had representatives from Taiwan, China, Korea and the U.S. talking about the industry and what was going on, and what the competition was all about. One of the folks from Taiwan pointed out that they do not really have a cost associated with stock options because there is no tax benefit, therefore they can grant these very lavishly, if you will, and the employee gets a great benefit from it.

As a consequence, they have now attracted about 5,000 of some of the very best engineers we have in this industry, to go to Taiwan to be a part of the industry there today. Now, granted, a number of our employees are foreign-born. They come to our universities, are trained, and they come to work with us here. But up until very recently, they have been employees that stayed with us. We are now beginning to see that migration reversing and going the other direction. In large part, it is because of the kind of compensation and the kind of tax structure that is associated with stock options.

Let me just turn for a moment to the accounting side of this, because I know that is one of the important arguments that is being put out here. I think that our greatest concern, I think you have seen editorials on the part of some of our CEOs in the industry, who are making it very clear that if there is going to be a change, the investing public is going to have to see something that is very transparent, that is very accurate, and is very comparable from company to company. I think the evidence that we have heard about here today, and I do not want to go into it again because I think you have heard it, is that that is not possible with the proposal that is in front of us today.

Therefore, I think the legislation that is being proposed to take a hard look at this and make sure we understand just what the consequences are, is very, very critical, so that we do not make that mistake of adopting something that is not going to be transparent, that is not going to be accurate, and will not be comparable from company to company. That would create more confusion, and in particular it will disadvantage the small investor versus the professional investor by a wide margin. That is the last thing that we should have happen.

The other point that I would like to make is on the stock purchase plan, which is a very important part of all of our companies. Again, the companies that have stock purchase plans is for 100 percent of the employees, just like our stock options are for anywhere from 80 to 95 percent of our employees; in some cases 100 percent. That will absolutely destroy the employee stock purchase plan if this proposal goes forward.

Again, I think this is one of the great opportunities for young people to get their first real shot at building equity for themselves and their families is through these stock purchase plans. They are very, very quick to unfold, and again if the company does well, these people can do very well and they can begin to buy their homes and do the other things that young families do. So I think it is very important that we make certain that we maintain the vigor and the opportunity associated with employee stock purchase plans.

Finally, as far as international convergence is concerned, I do not really see why we have to rush to try and come together with IASB and whatever their proposal happens to be, because first of all I do not think there is a timetable associated with that that is going to necessarily come to pass. There is a lot of controversy with the European companies on the IASB proposal, and therefore I think we ought to set that aside as having no real validity as far as consideration as we take a look at this FASB proposal that is in front of us.

Thank you. I am ready to answer any questions.

[The prepared statement of George Scalise can be found on page 148 in the appendix.]

Chairman BAKER. Thank you, sir. Before I proceed with questions of my own, I just want to yield time to Mr. Shadegg for purposes of an introduction. Mr. Shadegg?

Mr. SHADEGG. Thank you, Mr. Chairman.

I simply want to welcome Mr. Phil Smith of Taser International, chairman of the board. I apologize. I was across the hall in a hearing of the Commerce Committee which happens to be dealing with some issues that affect Arizona, Luke Air Force Base, the Goldwater Range right now, so I had to be there and could not be here during opening statements.

I welcome Mr. Smith. Taser is located in the metropolitan Phoenix area where my congressional district is. I appreciate his testimony here today. Mr. Chairman, as you know as a member of the Congress who is deeply concerned about the FASB proposal and believes the better alternative is in fact the legislation you have introduced, I appreciate Mr. Smith's comments on that point, and I simply wanted to be able to welcome him to the committee as a fellow Arizonan.

Thank you, Mr. Chairman. I yield back.

Chairman BAKER. Thank you, Mr. Shadegg.

Professor Kruse, I am interested based on your study of industry practice that is evident in the book. In identifying the problem that started the current academic discussion, was there evidence in your view of broad-based plans being manipulated adverse to either the corporate or public interest?

Mr. KRUSE. With respect to broad-based plans, no. We came to this interest in broad-based plans out of a couple of decades of research we have done on broad-based employee ownership, profit sharing, programs that involved employees in company performance. That is where we came at it from.

When we looked into broad-based plans, doing very extensive research on this, both quantitative and qualitative research, we did not find the broad-based plans being manipulated in the way that a lot of the executive plans obviously have been.

Chairman BAKER. Is it not true that with regard to SEC rule treatment of the top five proxy requirements for disclosure and disclosure of compensation, that there is now precedent for the top five being treated differently today from others within a corporate reporting structure?

Mr. KRUSE. Yes, that is true.

Chairman BAKER. So I can make the legitimate claim that the selection of the top five is consistent with other body of law and regulation by way of special disclosure for those set of individuals?

Mr. KRUSE. I believe so.

Chairman BAKER. Thank you.

Mr. Grady, you made comment with regard to the difficulty of predicting accurately volatility in a startup company. Is it not the case that FASB now and has historically allowed privately held corporations to set volatility at zero?

Mr. GRADY. Yes. The current rule allows minimum value to be the methodology used in calculating the value of an option, but the proposed rule disallows the use of that going forward. It actually complicates matters by allowing three different ways for options to be valued. It says for the old options, you can use minimum value, but going forward you have to switch to using one of the models I suggested, one of the lattice or binomial models.

Chairman BAKER. Let me help make that point. Where you have a historic record and could possibly predict volatility, you do not have to; and going forward on startups that you can't, you are going to be required to.

Mr. GRADY. Right. Well, for all options going forward under the proposal. Yes.

Chairman BAKER. Mr. Smith, you discussed the fact that in your corporation you have now given notice to employees going forward that this year's grant of options is it. It has also been stated by others on the panel and from other reports that foreign competitors now put banners up at job fairs, "options granted." What is the potential impact from your perspective on future startups on innovation if we, within the United States, preclude granting of options without expensing, and our competitive industries in international markets are allowed to proceed as they have historically, given the allegations of job economic recovery and all the concerns about outsourcing.

Mr. SMITH. In our company today it is not as important as it was. We are now a pretty visible company and we have a lot of cash. But when we started the company, over the 11 years it took to get there, it was extremely important. We were hiring people at below-market wages, no question about it. Our average people make $40,000 a year, by the way, that have the stock options that I referenced in my written statement. So it is not the high-paid people.

We have a lot of people who come into the company and take those jobs. Think about it. A person is sitting in a large corporation with a 401(k), a pension plan, great health benefits, and you are going to give him a chance to come into a less-than-ideal working environment, nothing is fancy in a small startup company. It is pretty rough-going. You ask him to work 12 or 14 hours a day, and they don't generally have very good health benefits and certainly do not have 401(k) or pension plans. What is the incentive for a person to do that? And you are going to pay him less money?

I remember when I left Boston, I was working for Computervision. It was a Fortune 500 company at the time. We were standing in a 9,000 square-foot house, and my wife says: let me understand this; you are taking a cut in pay to 40 percent of what you are making now; you have options in a company which is out of money, it was a venture startup; and I am going to have a house that is about as big as the garage on this house. Why am I not excited about moving to the Silicon Valley?

That is the issue. You have to have some compensation for these people to take that risk and make those moves. I have done it multiple times in my life. I have been broke more times than I have made money by doing that, but that is the whole part of an entrepreneur. Getting these people to take that risk, you have to offer them something.

One thing I would like to point out. I do not know why we are in such a rush to be like everybody else. The last thing I want to be is like everybody else. Everybody else in the world did not create the growth engine and jobs that we did in the Silicon Valley, right out to the beltway here with AOL and MCI and many great companies got started. These options were an instrumental part of it.

I do not know why we are in such a heck of a hurry to go out there and dismantle the machine that has worked and served us so well in the past, especially now when we need to develop the next new thing to put people back to work in this country. I would not be tampering with anything in this area for the next couple of years until we find what the next new thing is and get these people back to work.

A long-winded answer.

Chairman BAKER. I thank you for the answer. It is sort of like the fire department showing up when the house is on fire and simply burning the rest of the neighborhood. It just does not seem to be a responsive solution to the problem at hand.

Mr. Frank?

Mr. FRANK. Thank you, Mr. Chairman.

I would just say to the previous witness that I do not know when you sold that house, but given what has been happening to house prices in Massachusetts, a 9,000-square-foot house, you would have to have some pretty good options to beat what you could have made on that if you had held it.

I want to just expand on what I said before. Let me talk to the people who are in the industry, who have told me, and I take this with great seriousness, that if the expensing requirement goes through they will stop giving options. I guess we ought to be very specific why. Obviously, the reality will not have changed. Why will you have to stop giving options? Is it the reaction of the investor community, the lender community? What will require you to stop granting these if the reality has not changed, but the way in which you are to account for them does?

Mr. SMITH. Is that question for me, sir?

Mr. FRANK. Any of you.

Mr. SMITH. I will take a shot at it. We stopped it because we do not want to impact our operating performance next year for our shareholders because of these options being expensed.

Mr. FRANK. Excuse me. The question is this, it is not the reality. So the shareholders, what will cause the share price to drop? Is it the reaction of an investor community that says, hey, they moved this from the footnote to the bottom line. That is my frustration.

Mr. SMITH. Let me explain it to you. I think you were out of the room. A lot of our shareholders are policemen. They are cops. They own 100 to 200 shares of our stock. When they look at the income statement, they have no idea what footnotes are or anything else. All of a sudden they are going to see this dramatic change next year. I would say a good 40 percent——

Mr. FRANK. There are two problems with that. I would hope we could try to just educate the community. Cops have to be fairly sophisticated about something. The other thing is, unfortunately your arguments cuts a little bit both ways because one of the arguments people have now is, well, that information about the options is already there. It is in the footnote. When you argue that while it is in the footnote, they will not read it, you are unfortunately frankly giving support to some who say people do not know it is there. It cannot be both. It can't be available and impervious.

Mr. SMITH. I am going to make one comment and pass it off to some of my colleagues. If it ain't broke, don't fix it.

Mr. FRANK. I am sorry. That is not good enough for me. We are here in a deliberative process and I am trying to express the sympathy I feel. But sloganeering like that does not help me. I am not a car. Don't put a bumper sticker on me. I am asking you a question and I want an answer. There is a problem here. It may lead us to a broader problem. Your argument appears to be that the investor community on which you have to depend, in particular an investor community because of the nature of your product that is not the broader one, does not understand this. We need to have more than just a bumper sticker.

Mr. Grady?

Mr. GRADY. Congressman Frank, I think it does beyond that. What clearly will happen if you move it into the income statement, it will reduce, of course, the reported profitability of the company, even though the operating circumstances of that company will not have changed, the cash will not have changed, the cash expenses will not have changed.

Mr. FRANK. No reality will have changed.

Mr. GRADY. But it will radically reduce——

Mr. FRANK. Okay. Who will be influenced by that?

Mr. GRADY. I think investors will be influenced by that.

Mr. FRANK. Okay.

Mr. GRADY. As we have discussed during the hearing, the method by which people will calculate how much that expense will be will be highly variable from company to company. It will make, in effect, the reported P/E ratios of all companies, which is how the comparing is done, less comparable.

I will give you a real world example. The way people calculate earnings will be just considerably more different from company to company because there are all these methodological issues.

Mr. FRANK. But can't you say, then, look, this is the way it used to be, and this is the reason for that volatility. It is there now, the reality is there now. Options are clearly not a nothing. They have some impact.

Mr. GRADY. The reality is there now and most investors, to your point, are sophisticated enough to look at the fully diluted share price and calculate their EPS.

Mr. FRANK. Are they able to make comparisons?

Mr. GRADY. The sophisticated investor will strip out the option expense and compare cash EPS, which means they will render GAAP irrelevant.

Mr. FRANK. Are you saying a sophisticated investor would disregard the existence of options in deciding whether or not to, you say, strip out. Please let me finish the question, Mr. Grady.

You are telling me that the sophisticated investor would simply ignore the existence of the options? I assume that is what "strip out" means.

Mr. GRADY. They would ignore it for purposes of comparing.

Mr. FRANK. Mr. Grady, please stop, because I think you are obfuscating, unintentionally.

Mr. GRADY. No, I am not.

Mr. FRANK. Then I may be, but here is the deal. I am an investor and I am trying to make a decision. When I make a decision based on, I do not invest in any real companies because we get enough people claiming we are guilty of conflict of interest, so fortunately I am free of that, but I am an investor and I am looking, you say, well, after the FASB thing, it will be hard to make comparisons. But how do I make the comparison now?

Presumably, if I am a sophisticated investor and I am trying to decide between one or another company and one has a certain amount of options and one does not, and another has options. How do I value those now? Or do I not take those into account in deciding when to invest?

Mr. GRADY. You do take them into account, as I said, in determining the share count for the company in the denominator of the earnings-per-share calculation. I believe that people will continue to do that.

Mr. FRANK. But is that easier to do now than it would be later? Why? Why is it easier to make those comparisons now than it would be if the accounting treatment differed?

Mr. GRADY. The ability to calculate the number of shares will be the same as it is now. What will be different will be the quality of the earnings being reported.

Mr. FRANK. I understand that. But you understand that those are just affected by the accounting. The reality has not changed, has it?

Mr. GRADY. The reality is being proposed to be changed, and that is that people have to take into——

Mr. FRANK. They do not have to. Investors are free to make his or her own decisions. The company is still there and those things are still there and the investor can still make the decisions based on——

Mr. GRADY. Here is what will change, I believe, in reality. The most common means by which investors compare stocks is price/earnings ratio. You will now have a wildly different set of assumptions that go into the "E" in a PE ratio.

Mr. FRANK. Okay. My last question is this, because here is what we are saying is that frankly the people who are getting more beat up here are the investors who do not come out of this looking all that smart.

Mr. GRADY. But I think——

Mr. FRANK. Excuse me, Mr. Grady, please stop interrupting. This is just not helpful. The point is this, what you are telling me is that if FASB's rule goes through, even though the reality of the company will not have been changed if they continue to give options, investors will look only at the P/E and will make bad decisions. They will make decisions on inadequate information. Inevitably, this has got to be something of a negative judgment on the investor community because you are saying if you do this, they will just look at the P/E and that will make this enormous difference to them, when in fact you were telling me it really should not, given that this is a perfectly reasonable thing to continue to do.

Mr. GRADY. May I make one comment?

Mr. FRANK. Sure.

Mr. GRADY. I believe that to avoid the confusion, which we were both just speaking about, what will happen is people creating the companies, people starting the companies, people running the companies will say, to avoid the confusion I will use more cash to reward employees and less options.

Mr. FRANK. I understand. But the confusion is on the part of the investor who is reading the situation.

Mr. GRADY. Which means less companies will be started.

Mr. FRANK. I understand that. The question is why that would be the case. It really does come down to apparently a lack of confidence that investors will be able to sort this out.

Mr. GRADY. Right. I believe this will make reporting more confusing, not less confusing.

Mr. SMITH. Let me add one thing. Reporting is one thing. Hiring employees is another. If you are out there, Mr. Frank, and you are trying to hire employees as a young startup company and you are competing against well-established big companies that have much better benefits, better pay, et cetera, what the heck are you going to offer them?

Mr. FRANK. Excuse me. You totally misunderstand my point. I understand that, that options are attractive. What I was trying to get at is, what about FASB would lead you to stop issuing options? That is the question. So your answer is totally irrelevant to what I was asking.

Mr. GRADY. It is the cost, the cost on the bottom line.

Mr. FRANK. I have gone over my time and I do not think this is going to be enlightening.

Chairman BAKER. If the gentleman would yield for just a minute, I appreciate the gentleman's sincere effort at this. I just want to make one small explanation if it might be helpful. It does change economic reality in this case. If there is a granting of an option at a fixed price, and going forward the price does not move in the money and the option is not exercised, the FASB requirement would require you to expense that in the current dollar disclosure, so you would have a negative impact on the corporate profit, which is not an accurate disclosure of true financial condition.

However, going forward if the option is exercised at a higher dollar price, I think argument can be made that contributions of those individuals who are engaged in the corporate structure as a result of the grant of the options, have increased value and therefore the dilutive effect on the residual shareholders is minimal, if at all. So it is not 100 percent accurate, but I think the negative effect of expensing when they are not exercised is far worse than the residual effect of expensing at the time of exercise, which is now required.

Mr. FRANK. I thank the Chairman. That is in the spirit of what I was saying. Again, it all comes down, unfortunately, to the way it is perceived. Let me just say one further thing, Mr. Chairman. I just want to now, in the absence of the Ranking Member of the subcommittee who had to leave, I just want to notify you that we are going to use our Rule 11 rights to ask for another day of hearings. A letter with the appropriate number of signatures will be delivered to you before the end of this hearing so that we can have another hearing.

Let me just say, this comes from people both for and against the bill. This is not a sign that people are against the bill. This is just an important subject and we will be asking for it. There is no reason that they should hold up any schedule of any action, so it is not to be taken as hostile to the bill.

Chairman BAKER. The Ranking Member had indicated to me his interest in that, and I said I have no such reluctance, but out of courtesy to the chairman I have not had a chance to visit with him about the schedule.

Mr. FRANK. That is why we thought we would use Rule 11, because that is an option to the chairman. He is a busy fellow. We do not like to bother him.

[Laughter.]

Chairman BAKER. We always appreciate your creative assistance in the conduct of the committee.

[Laughter.]

Mr. FRANK. Mr. Chairman, I cannot take credit for creating Rule 11. That somewhat pre-dates me.

Chairman BAKER. I recognize that and am thankful for that.

Chairman Oxley?

Mr. OXLEY. Thank you, Mr. Chairman. I certainly would not have any objection to another hearing on this matter. It is complicated and difficult, but very, very important in terms of our economic future in this country.

Mr. Grady, good to see you again. Welcome back to Capitol Hill.

Mr. GRADY. Thank you, Mr. Chairman. It is good to be here.

Mr. OXLEY. It is good to know that there is life after work at the White House.

[Laughter.]

You had emphasized in your testimony the issue of competition, particularly as the FASB proposal may very well, as I understand your testimony, put us at a disadvantage versus some of the Asian tigers, for example, that have learned some things, apparently, from our system and are quite aggressive in that area. I wonder if you would care to comment specifically on the competitiveness issue. Mr. Scalise and others that want to join in, I would be glad to hear from you as well.

Mr. GRADY. I think you can look in both directions, both to the east and toward Europe as well. I was struck by something that the Director of CBO said regarding CBO's study and saying that they did not see different effects in Europe versus the United

States, where IASB is now of course proposing expensing of stock options.

What is observable is that I believe the United States has outperformed the EU countries quite substantially, and I believe one of the principal reasons that has been true is because of the availability of risk capital, which has gone into startups, and because of the contribution of startups to U.S. GDP. What you now see is Europe has lower levels of venture capital investment, lower economic growth, and considerably higher unemployment. That has been the case for some time.

We did a study at the National Venture Capital Association to try to measure the contribution of venture-backed companies, mainly startup companies, to the U.S. economy. I refer to it in my written testimony, but I think it is important to highlight the results to the members. It showed that venture-backed companies in the year 2000 employed directly 12 million Americans and directly and indirectly, as Chairman Baker said earlier, 27 million Americans. Some of the other findings were that these companies accounted for $1.1 trillion in sales or 11 percent of U.S. GDP on far less than 1 percent of the invested capital in the country for the entire 30-year period measured.

So the job-creating leverage of these startup companies has been very high. The principal tool that they have used, as everyone on the panel has noted, has been to on the one hand pay people less cash, but by allowing them to trade-off units of ownership for cash compensation. That has been the model that has worked. People have wanted a piece of the rock. I do believe, as a number of witnesses and Mr. Smith have said, Taser is witnessing it and other companies are witnessing it on the competitive front, that people in both companies in Taiwan and China and elsewhere are advertising their willingness to give ownership to employees as a way of inducing them to come to work there.

Mr. OXLEY. So really one of the concerns, the latest buzz word around here, is outsourcing, and we are hearing all about that. In fact, this issue certainly cuts into that entire issue, does it not?

Mr. GRADY. I believe it does, because it will also raise the cost of creating the jobs here in the United States, as I was attempting to comment to Mr. Frank. I believe what will happen is that at the margin, startup companies will be required to raise more cash with which to compensate employees, which just means there will be less startups funded because there is only in effect so much cash to go around. So I think this would be adverse to the job creation prospects of the economy going forward.

Mr. OXLEY. Thank you.

Mr. Smith, why are so many CEOs opposed to expensing? Is it because it would lower the value of the options? From a CEO's standpoint, what is the major issue that you have with the proposal?

Mr. SMITH. I think Mr. Grady covered it pretty well. It is the valuation of the company. People look at price/earnings to justify purchasing or not purchasing a stock, the availability of capital in the equity markets. One of the things I pointed out before you came into the room, and that is we were able to attract some pretty significant board members on our company by using options. Without those, I frankly do not know how we would have gotten those people to come on and help us with the corporate governance we are now facing.

That is a real issue for small companies. You do not have a lot of cash. You have a lot of risk to offer people that come on the board. The trial lawyers love small public companies because their stock is pretty volatile and they generally get into a lot of stockholder lawsuits in which directors do not want to be involved. So I frankly am at a loss. This is going to be my last startup. I would be concerned about how you are going to get the right types of individuals to sit on these boards if you take away some of these incentives.

We just stopped giving them. We have already told our employees no more options. They all vest by the end of this year. That is it. If this legislation passes, the only people that are going to get them are going to be the four or five senior people at the top. I do not know what we are going to do in the future going forward.

Mr. OXLEY. That is interesting. It hearkens back to our hearings we had on securities litigation reform, which I think really did enhance our knowledge about what was going on out there. One area that has not been well discussed, and I am glad you brought it out, was the large potential for litigation in these areas, to the point where some of these trial lawyers were having computers that essentially spit out complaints based on a loss of value in the market. Quite extraordinary, and that ultimately led, as you know, to passage of that legislation, and I think I am right, the only veto President Clinton had overridden, with a strong bipartisan effort on both the House and the Senate.

So I think you have touched upon another interesting issue that is certainly important in this debate, that I had not considered until recently. I appreciate your testimony.

I yield back.

Chairman BAKER. I thank the Chairman.

Mr. Scott?

Mr. SCOTT. Thank you very much, Mr. Chairman.

It is the general feeling on this committee that you support H.R. 3574, the basically immediate expensing of the top five executives's stock options. Correct? And that the concern is that it goes no further, that there be no expensing of options for rank-and-file employees. In this legislation, it does not exactly, it is my understanding and I am a co-sponsor of it, but what we are saying is that no further expensing of these stock options until a couple of things take place; that there be an economic cost-benefit analysis study of different elements; and that the accountants come up with a more accurate way of measuring cost.

What say you about that? Is that enough to register safety on any concerns that we go beyond? I am not sure what I am hearing here, and especially from you, Mr. Smith. Did that satisfy you?

Mr. SMITH. Let me just say one thing. My mother had some ugly kids, but no dumb ones. What I have worked out is that we are not going to get this thing through. I think expensing any options is a bad idea, but I am practical enough to understand to get some change, to hold off this gigantic force to get options expensed, we are willing to concede to the five top people.

I think we do need a study because I think there are some real impacts people have not thought about, not only the lawsuits that are going to erupt, the cash that young companies are using from these employee options. The way it works is if an employee exercises their option, they pay the government taxes, but the company gets a credit for that. It keeps our cash and allows us to hire more people. I do not know whether anybody has even looked at that aspect of this thing.

There is an enormous tax base sitting out there of cash being used by young startup companies to fund their operations. If you take that availability of cash away and they now have to pay taxes to the federal government, you are going to start impacting these small companies's growth. So from those aspects, I would like to see nothing expensed, but being a practical person, as I said, my mother did not have any dumb kids, we are deciding this is the best option we can see to go forward. We think those economic studies will prove that out in the future.

I will yield to my other colleagues.

Mr. SCOTT. Professor Kruse, what percentage of companies that offer stock options offer them to a broad spectrum of their employees?

Mr. KRUSE. I do not have a ready answer to that off the top of my head what percent do. We have found that at least in a related survey of companies, we did find that about 3 percent of companies gave broad grants to employees, to more than 50 percent of their employees in the past year. But the number that may have done that in the years prior to that, we do not know. Still, 3 percent of companies gave grants in the past year and that is consistent with a BLS study as well.

Mr. SCOTT. And you believe the FASB rule would act as a deterrent to incentives for the rank-and-file employees?

Mr. KRUSE. Based on what companies are saying, that this is going to be something that causes them great concern, that they are likely to cut back on the broad-based plans and encourage concentration of executive options.

Mr. SCOTT. Mr. Scalise, you mentioned that stock options are granted to around 90 percent of high-tech employees. What posture would we be in with this rule in terms of the semiconductor industry especially, and its ability to compete with foreign companies?

Mr. SCALISE. I think it would have a major impact on our ability to compete. Again, getting back to your prior question, 100 percent of our companies grant stock options. As you pointed out, roughly 95 percent of those go to a broad base of employees outside of the executive ranks.

I recently completed a study for the President's Council of Advisors on Science and Technology dealing with manufacturing and innovation. This is one of the issues that we dealt with. I think what we have to recognize today is that we are truly in a new competitive environment out there, not only in manufacturing, but for people. I just gave you one data point there saying that roughly 5,000 of our good engineers, these are not just the rookies, these are the good well-trained engineers that have been in the business for a number of years, have now gone back to Taiwan. A number of them are going to China now.

So we are going to be greatly impacted if they can offer the stock option with the tax treatment they have, which is no taxable event; versus ours which is a highly taxed event as it currently stands. Then you have the other part of the problem which is dealing with the expensing issue, which makes for the volatility within the company, which the companies have to dampen if they are going to avoid some of the litigation that has been talked about here.

So it is a very complex set of issues that come together here. Suffice it to say that for the two reasons, the expensing and the volatility as associated with that, and the tax treatment we have versus the tax treatment of our competitors overseas, these are both working against us as far as maintaining our technology leadership going forward.

Mr. SCOTT. Thank you very much.

Chairman BAKER. Thank you, Mr. Scott.

Mr. Royce?

Mr. ROYCE. Thank you, Mr. Chairman.

I would like to begin by building on your last point, and maybe ask Dr. Smith, if we look at these proposed rules and let's say we take a hypothetical, and we have a company that has to expense $100 million of option grants. So the accounting rules would have that firm debit expense and credit paid-in capital. So now we look forward 1 year, 2 years, 3 years into the future, and let's say none of the options have been exercised because the firm's stock has declined in value during that time period.

So now what do we have? I would say we have a balance sheet that borders on being fraudulent at this point, and investors would be getting a false sense of the company's true financial picture at that moment. At the same time, we have passed Sarbanes-Oxley. Under Sarbanes-Oxley, we have dictated that you signed under perjury that the financials reflect the true operating income and expense and the correct balance sheet position of the company.

The question that I have, Dr. Smith, is, given our hypothetical, because you have now expensed that $100 million in option grants several years prior, are you now in violation of Sarbanes-Oxley? And more importantly, could some trial lawyers believe you are in violation of Sarbanes-Oxley?

Mr. SMITH. Let me just say one thing. The only employment this is going to impact is the trial lawyers are going to make more money and hire more trial lawyers. It is hard for me to guess, but you can bet they will sue. If you look at most of the cases out there, they never go to court. These lawyers are into the idea of settling with these companies and insurance companies outside of court.

So the answer is, anything like this that opens a door, they will definitely come in.

Mr. ROYCE. More slap suits?

Mr. SMITH. Absolutely. We may have been delivered a lawsuit today. Our stock dropped 32 percent yesterday and that generally brings them right out of the woodwork. That is the one company fear of most of us here, so this is just one more thing we have to deal with.

Mr. ROYCE. I will also ask you, we heard from the CBO director. Director Holtz-Eakin argued that expensing will help the economy because resources will be allocated more efficiently. Do you agree with that argument?

Mr. SMITH. Absolutely not. It is the big companies that benefit from this. These are not the people who employ and create the new jobs. They employ lots of people, but they are not the growth gazelles that really provide a lot of employment. Those are coming from young startup companies like us. The big companies will benefit because they have no volatility in their stock. They give very few options out to people. The penalties will go to the people like us who are creating the jobs, who are small and have the very volatile stock. So I absolutely take issue with that, and I do not know anybody at the CBO that ever started a company or ever gave out a stock option or ever received a stock option.

Mr. ROYCE. I am going to ask Mr. Grady to respond to that question as well. The other suggestion that was made by the CBO director was that the venture capital community will fill the void. I would just like to ask Mr. Grady, it seemed earlier that you disagreed with that argument. I would like to hear your reasons.

Mr. GRADY. I do disagree because what will happen is the venture capital community will have to use more cash to compensate employees, which means we will create fewer companies with fewer employees, by definition.

On the first question of the efficient allocation of capital, I believe it will not increase the efficiency because it will create some of the anomalies that you have suggested. Your first question was not merely hypothetical. For example, Intel Corporation, and maybe Mr. Scalise wants to comment on this, I believe reported that they would have taken charges if expensing were a requirement, into the several billions of dollars, more than $2.5 billion, for options granted in 2001 and 2002 or 2003 that expired without being exercised; that were never in the money and that therefore basically never existed. Under this proposal, the accounting for those options that never existed, those shares that never existed, would be identical to the case in which Intel had spent $2.5 billion or $3 billion of cash. Clearly, that is not an optimal or even accurate result.

As I said in my earlier statement, that is the problem with being required to value the options on grant date. You could switch it and say, gee, we will value them on exercise date or you could use this intrinsic value method that I mentioned. That creates its own anomalies, because if you use the intrinsic value and say a stock comes public at $20 and the stock trades down, but you recorded a value the day the company came public at $20 and the options had a certain assessed value.

If the stock went down, you would actually decrease the value of those options. So what you would be saying is, because the stock went down you are judging that company now to be more profitable.

Mr. ROYCE. We have an opportunity for a real-world response if we could go to Mr. Scalise and just let him respond in terms of the actual difficulty we would be putting a firm like Intel into.

Mr. SCALISE. I think it would be significantly more difficult. Your mention of the Sarbanes-Oxley Act is really critical here, because these two do come together. When you look at the lack of transparency, the lack of comparability, and then the volatility that results from that, and then the requirement to attest to all of these documents when in fact you will create expenses on issues that never really occurred in the final analysis, as just pointed out by Mr. Grady here, it is very complicated and it is very interrelated.

It is going to create a lot of hesitation with regard to putting out more stock options because they are not going to do it. They are not going to want to increase the volatility and increase the risk of more and more litigation, because as we all know we have folks just sitting out there waiting to drop that next lawsuit.

Mr. ROYCE. Thank you, Mr. Chairman.

Chairman BAKER. I thank the gentleman.

Mr. Sherman?

Mr. SHERMAN. Yes, as I count, we have six panelists who are in favor of the bill. My guess is that that is reflected up here as well.

We can compete with China to have the loosest accounting standards so our companies can report the highest income, no matter how much money they spend on this or that, report a lot of income. Or we can compete with Europe to have the tough and reasonable accounting standards uninfluenced by what would be viewed at least by the public in a highly publicized first-ever intervention to provide looser accounting standards to encourage what is viewed as executive compensation. I think we need to compete with Europe for capital by showing that we have the best accounting standards.

What flabbergasts me is that this bill, if I hear Mr. Grady and others correctly, would have the effect of helping high-tech companies like the ones based in my state compete for capital against these lower-tech companies that are most associated with some of the other regions of the country. I have folks from other regions of the country supporting the bill and trying to help high-tech companies in my state get capital. I thank them.

Mr. Smith points to this big practical problem. He could not afford to adequately compensate board members. The company could not afford to do that without the stock options. You know, now and then I hear from one of my constituents that board members are not being adequately compensated, or the company cannot afford to compensate board members. But I hear more often that the company cannot afford to provide health care.

So if we want for the first time ever to tell the FASB to do something because we want to encourage companies to do something, why don't we tell them that what you pay for health insurance should never be listed as an expense? Or at least provide them with an avenue, if you give a 30-year promissory note to the health insurance company, you do not have to list it as an expense. Give stock options to a health insurance company; provide coverage for your employees, you do not have to list it as an expense.

Why have we decided that the first time Congress will demand a departure from regular accounting is to encourage companies to do something we think is vital. Stock options, not health care.

Mr. Hassett points out that it would invite lawsuits if we tell companies they have to expense stock options, but we do not tell them how. And Mr. Grady echoes this. I could not agree with you more. But Mr. Hassett, how is it that we have not had a lot of lawsuits already because we have a requirement that this information be disclosed in footnotes and we have no real standards to tell companies how to put it in the footnotes. Don't trial lawyers read footnotes? I know they are real small, but you can blow them up and show them to a jury.

Mr. HASSETT. Here is the state of affairs that concerns us. When we put the account for options into earnings, we say, well, it used to be we thought we were making $8 this year, but now we are going to put in the expense for options and it is $7. And then we run for a few years, say, at $7 as earnings every year. And then at the end of that period, people vest and realize, and it turns out that when we said that our earnings were $7, which will be true for probably half the companies, we were incorrect because it was a prospective figure.

Mr. SHERMAN. I understand the incorrectness.

Mr. HASSETT. The point is that it is in the earnings statement.

Mr. SHERMAN. So you are saying that you cannot go to a jury and say, I am an investor; I thought that their adjusted earnings adjusted for the expense of compensating people with options was such and so, as disclosed in their footnote, and it turned out to be such and so. I think we have some lazy trial lawyers out there that are not taking advantage of the vaguenesses of our current accounting standards.

Mr. HASSETT. May I respond, Mr. Sherman?

Mr. SHERMAN. Yes.

Mr. HASSETT. Thank you. I think that the current state of the accounting rule suggests that we are not so sure precisely whether it is $5 or $4 or $3 and that we are leaving it in the footnotes. For the shrewd investor, it is his or her job to figure out what he thinks they are worth when he is deciding whether or not to buy the stock. I think that is the appropriate state of affairs. I think when we put it in the earnings statement, we are giving people the false impression that we know exactly the value.

Mr. SHERMAN. You are making a policy argument. I was just wondering why creative trial lawyers are not making the counter-argument.

Mr. HASSETT. I think because the ambiguity is there.

Mr. SHERMAN. Let me go on. This bill is being put forward as protection for broadly based stock options. You can put a lot of lipstick on a pig. Zero volatility for the options given to the richest executives in America, and you put that in a bill and you say you are trying to help secretaries? The number six guy at GM; the number six guy at Intel are somehow struggling manufacturing workers?

If the bill was well crafted to achieve its alleged purpose, it would deserve a lot more support than a bill, a huge portion of the benefit of which is going to go to the number six guy at General Motors and the number one guy at Intel whose options will be valued at zero volatility.

We have heard discussions of employee stock ownership plans, ESOPs, none of which are affected by the FASB pronouncement that we are here to discuss. In fact, those plans are going forward. They are big in our economy and they do not get any favored accounting treatment, nor is anybody arguing that they should get a favored accounting treatment.

Mr. Kruse tells us that 79 percent of those who hold options make under $75,000. Let's say in your survey there was a company, because I have seen a company like this, 100,000 options held by each of the top two guys. Another 100 employees, all with incomes under $75,000, each get about 50 or 100 options. If you were surveying that company, wouldn't you conclude that 98 percent of the option holders are people who make under $75,000, if that was your whole population of the survey?

Mr. KRUSE. That is absolutely true.

Mr. SHERMAN. So what we do know is that there are a lot of working-class folks and middle-class folks who have stock options, but there may not be a lot of options in the hands of working-class folks.

Mr. SMITH. Let me answer that one because I have a practical application.

Mr. SHERMAN. Your company is great.

Mr. SMITH. Forty-five percent is going to the top; 55 percent goes to the working people below that.

Mr. SHERMAN. Your company is great, but that does not tell us about the economy overall. If you were running all these companies, things might be different.

Mr. SMITH. GM does not tell us about the economy overall either. It is the small companies that are providing the jobs. The guys you are going to penalize are the job-creators. That is the reason we are here today.

Mr. SHERMAN. Mr. Smith, I just want to comment. Not every small company is giving stock options. Your beauty shop, no stock options. Your local dry cleaner, no stock options. Lots of small companies. Your machine shop, very rarely do they give stock options.

So to take the idea that all the jobs created by small business are driven by stock options, they are driven by other things.

Mr. SMITH. How about a few facts here? The facts are the job gazelles, the small growth companies that are providing the jobs are not the hairdressers and not the ones you mentioned. They are companies just like us. Those other people that are giving the jobs in this economy——

Mr. SHERMAN. Mr. Smith, it is my time. I did not even ask you a question. Your gazelle-like feistiness is appreciated. But the fact is that is we as a Congress decide to contort the accounting rules for the purpose of pulling capital out of the old economy and putting it into the kinds of companies that Mr. Smith thinks should get the capital, that is a whole new economic planning role for this Congress. I do not know whether it is better to see stock purchased in Proctor and Gamble or in Mr. Smith's company. I know he thinks that his company is the best way for our society to allocate its capital.

I yield back.

Chairman BAKER. Thank you, Mr. Sherman. I let you go on well beyond time in recognition of your position on the issue, but for members's purposes, I am going to try to recognize as many as we can before adjourning. We have a set of five recorded votes which would disrupt the committee process significantly.

So Mr. Shadegg, if you have a comment?

Mr. SHADEGG. Thank you, Mr. Chairman. Let me begin with one question.

As I understand the FASB proposal, they do not say how to do this. They say you simply have to do it. So let me begin, since we can obviously make it clear as the questioning has just suggested, I will ask each of you quickly, and I would like you each to answer, is there a single agreed-upon method by which this ought to be done that will make the reporting of all companies parallel or comparable for stock evaluators? Just yes or no.

Mr. SCALISE. No.

Mr. GRADY. No, there is not, and especially not for private companies.

Mr. SMITH. No.

Mr. HASSETT. No.

Mr. HOLTZ-EAKIN. No.

Mr. THOMAS. No.

Mr. KRUSE. No.

Mr. SHADEGG. I think that kind of sums up my deep concern. Mr. Grady, my friend Mr. Frank on the other side I do not think ever let you get across that point. I am going to tell you what I think your point was, and then you tell me if I am right. I think your point was, look, yes there are footnotes now; yes, people can evaluate this information; yes, sophisticated investors can look at it. But if you compel it to be a much more prominent factor in the reporting of the company's performance and in this calculation of P and E, given that nobody has agreed upon the right way to do it, then we are going to have inconsistent results and it could lead to much greater abuse of investors than what we currently have. Is that the essence of your position?

Mr. GRADY. I would agree exactly with that statement.

Mr. SHADEGG. I just think this is a huge deal. We just heard a comment about how we could create the loosest accounting system in the world. I would suggest quite frankly I think FASB is proposing that we make the accounting system looser than it is right now. I understand IASB has said we are going to do this in Europe. It seems to me, first of all, I am aware that in some countries in Europe right now they require stock expensing and in those countries there are essentially no options or option expensing, and essentially there are no options.

It seems to me perhaps what we ought to do this time, if IASB has decided this is a great idea, why don't we let Europe go first and watch them and see if in fact it does not damage them. My concern, given a world market, is that if we do it and some others do not do it, we could be putting ourselves at a dramatic competitive disadvantage which I would rather not do at this particular point in time.

Mr. Holtz-Eakin, I know that you did the study and the analysis that looked at how stock options would affect both stock prices and the company's access to capital. Is that right?

Mr. HOLTZ-EAKIN. We did a study on the accounting of employee stock options.

Mr. SHADEGG. Right. Here is the question I want to know. How did you go about evaluating the question I have raised, which is, how many companies would continue to offer stock options and to what extent does your report give us the answer to that question?

Mr. HOLTZ-EAKIN. The report actually does not address the individual decision by firms to offer options versus other forms of compensation.

Mr. SHADEGG. So it does not look at the issue of whether——

Mr. HOLTZ-EAKIN. It looks at the accounting of those two activities.

Mr. SHADEGG. So it kind of assumes a static situation and says, if these companies are offering stock options now, this is how they are performing and they are not expensing them. If they continue to offer them, here is what would happen under that static kind of analysis. It was not looking at the question of whether or not they would be disincented from continuing to offer stock options.

Mr. HOLTZ-EAKIN. I think a fairer way to say it would be that it looks at the relative treatment of stock options as employee compensation versus other forms of compensation. It puts them on a level playing field and examines the accounting treatment in that setting.

Mr. SHADEGG. Given the great concern expressed by Mr. Smith and others that the net effect of this rule is going to be to disincent companies from offering stock options, and indeed from my perspective since I like startup companies and I like innovation and I like new people coming into the market and I think that is where America leads the world, wouldn't you agree that that is an issue we should look at before adopting a change in policy?

Mr. HOLTZ-EAKIN. I think it has been a bit frustrating to hear the way the issue has been characterized today because the key issue here is to remember that the income statement is designed to display in a fair fashion the net income, the matching of costs and the revenues generated by a firm for purposes of financial disclosure. It is clearly the case that stock options could still be a part of that employee compensation.

Mr. SHADEGG. Let me go back to Mr. Frank's style. You are not answering my question. My question was as a policymaker, not can they do it differently, my question was shouldn't we look at the effect of the policy not just on what will it do to stock prices, but rather on the incentives it would create to continue or discontinue engaging in the process of offering options?

Mr. HOLTZ-EAKIN. It depends on the question you want answered. If the question is, what will produce broad economic performance in the United States, I do not think that is the central question. If the question is, how many stock options will be granted in the United States, it is a very central question.

Mr. SHADEGG. Since I think how many are issued affects our economy and at the end of the day everything I look at I have to put at least through that filter, it seems to me to be of grave concern.

Mr. Chairman, I know you want to get to a number of other witnesses. I strongly feel that with the concerns that have been expressed here by all of the witnesses, before we leap off into this abyss, we need to look at it more carefully. It is odd to me. It seems to me strange that the IRS would put out a regulation that says we want every taxpayer to report X, but quite frankly we do not know how you are going to value X. I have trouble with a policy that says we are going to solve this problem; we are going to tell you to address this issue, but we are not going to give you a uniform method for calculating it, and we think we are bringing more certainty to the market. That is just a grave concern on my part.

I yield back the remainder of my time.

Chairman BAKER. Mr. Miller?

Mr. MILLER OF NORTH CAROLINA. Thank you, Mr. Chairman.

Mr. Smith, I know that you expressed at the beginning a frustration that no one who seems to be involved in this debate on our side knows anything about stock options. I admit that I never have had one, but my brother works for a bank. He has described to me what he does. At the end of it, I knew he worked for a bank.

[Laughter.]

He has some fairly impressive titles, but I also know that banks pass out titles instead of compensation. I hope we never have to value that.

[Laughter.]

I am trying to figure out how this works and whether it really is going to provide any kind of useful information to middle-class investors. Let me try to get a feeling for how this works. My understanding is a mid-level employee may be given 3,000 options. The market price of the company now is $55, and one-third or 1,000 are exercisable in a year, say, at $60; the next one-third a year later at $65; the next year, the last 1,000 at $70. They expire if not exercised within 5 years of when they vest and they cannot be transferred and they are forfeited if they are not exercised at the time the employee leaves the company. Is that generally the way it works? Kind of, Mr. Grady?

Mr. GRADY. That is generally the way it works. The only slight correction I might make is that typically the strike price on those options would be the $55 at which they were granted. They probably might choose to exercise them if the stock went up to $60 or $70 a year later; and if the stock went down to $40, they would not exercise.

Mr. MILLER OF NORTH CAROLINA. But if they have an option at $60, they would rather buy it through the market rather than by exercising the option.

Mr. GRADY. Because it goes below, yes, sir.

Mr. MILLER OF NORTH CAROLINA. But it has some value, but if it is not traded, would you value it by what? If the company has analysts and they project a 10 or 15 or 20 percent stock price per year in the next 5 years. Do you look at that? If there are no analysts following the company, do you look at what the board of directors or the management forecasts are for growth of earnings? How do you value something that can be exercised in the future?

Is there any understanding at all whether these will be valued at the time of exercise or when they vest, when you can exercise them, or at the time of their issue in the first place?

Mr. GRADY. The exposure draft suggests valuing them at the time of grant, when they are issued in the first place, when their value is frankly highly speculative.

Mr. MILLER OF NORTH CAROLINA. So even when you are being granted something that is only at $70, that you can exercise at $70, even though the stock is trading at $55, you have to establish some value for that and declare it now.

Mr. GRADY. Yes. You have to estimate what the value would be.

Mr. MILLER OF NORTH CAROLINA. Okay. If stocks are not exercised in the next year or the year after that, is there any requirement that the company go back and true up the cost because the stock went up or down?

Mr. GRADY. Generally, no. For public companies if they value them at the time of grant, that is it. Now, there are different methods. Some have said intrinsic value would be allowed for private companies where you would go back and true up each quarter. The FASB actually seeks comment on whether instead of using grant date as the measurement period, you should use exercise date.

As I mention in my testimony, while that would get around the problem of how hard it is to value the options at grant date, it creates a different problem which is if you require them to be expensed on the exercise date, what you are in effect doing is penalizing the most successful companies and helping those whose stock price has languished.

Mr. MILLER OF NORTH CAROLINA. I think most of the testimony today has been about the effect on the economy of encouraging or discouraging, or to use the current noun-verb, incentivize or incent or disincentivize or disincent. But just looking at this from the standpoint of middle-class average investors, is this going to provide them more useful information than a footnote telling them how many options are out there and what the terms are under which they can be exercised.

Mr. GRADY. I believe it will provide them with less reliable information, far less reliable information for the investor for all the reasons we said in our testimony.

Mr. MILLER OF NORTH CAROLINA. Alright. I am probably the last one to have anything. Mr. Smith, I want to assure you that I have lived my brother's experience. My brother and his wife and my wife and I have a beach cottage together. When the stock of his company is doing well, he wants to go in together and reupholster the furniture and buy a DVD for the cottage. When the stock is not going well, he wants to sell.

Mr. SMITH. My comments have related primarily to the people testifying, not the people sitting on that side, obviously, the policymakers. I am more frustrated by the fact that like yesterday in the Senate, all the people that were testifying basically there were no business people. They were people having FASB, prior Federal Reserve chairmen, and all those sorts of folks. Great folks, but never in my opinion ever started a company.

Chairman BAKER. The gentleman's time has expired.

I will get Mr. Lynch in, if I can.

Mr. LYNCH. Thank you, Mr. Chairman.

I want to thank you, Mr. Chairman, for your good work and the panel for helping us out. I apologize for having to rush out here at the end. Prior to coming to the Congress, I was actually an iron worker for about 20 years, so I am similar to some of the production employees you have been talking about earlier today. I also was a former union president of the iron workers. So I spent a considerable amount of time working toward greater corporate responsibility, greater corporate accountability, transparency, and those issues.

That much being said, I have to say that I have some very, very, very serious concerns about this FASB exposure draft that is under consideration today. I think it is a real mistake. It has been my own experience that the granting of stock options has given a lot of opportunity for rank-and-file employees to own a piece of the rock, as has been said earlier here today.

It does in fact incentivize the workplace for many of our workers, if they know that if they work their tail off that they are going to help the company succeed, and then by doing so they themselves will be enriched. That is a good thing for America and I think it is a good thing for our corporations here.

Again, Gillette Safety Razor Corporation is in my district. A lot of the young fellows and women who went to high school with me, went to work. Some husbands and wives in the same corporation for Gillette. They have a great stock purchase program at Gillette. A lot of the folks that I went to high school with went to work on the assembly line and now they are looking pretty closely at retirement. Some of those people when Gillette was at their high end were millionaires, based on the amount of stock that they had purchased in their own company. Good hard workers. I do not want to see that opportunity denied from rank-and-file workers. I think that it would be a mistake to adopt this rule that would basically kill that whole process.

I know especially in the high-tech area, this is an important tool in bringing bright young employees into the workplace. I do have one question, and then I am going to run out. I know that we have talked about H.R. 3574, which would basically expense the options granted to the top five employees. In thinking about this problem in a different way, would it be better, and this is for the entire panel, and you might have to holler your answers as I run down the hallway, would it be better to look at some fixed percentage of the stock options granted each year and expense those some small percentage, so that it is not just the top five? Because the top five companies, as Mr. Smith has pointed out, in a small corporation to force expensing on that small group may have a detrimental effect on the operation of the corporation itself. I just wanted to get that out there. I think it is a great suggestion in terms of a compromise, but there might be a better compromise out there.

I want to thank you for coming here. Mr. Chairman, I want to thank you for your enormous patience.

Chairman BAKER. I thank the gentleman.

Did anyone care to respond?

Mr. HOLTZ-EAKIN. The key for fair portrayal of net income is the value of options granted, not the number of people that you choose to expense, or to the extent that you have revealed the value of options granted, you will become closer to net income as measuring the economics of the corporation.

Mr. LYNCH. Right. I understand that.

Mr. HOLTZ-EAKIN. A fixed fraction of the value reveals the value of options granted. That would be tremendous.

Mr. LYNCH. Okay. Thank you. Thank you, gentlemen.

Chairman BAKER. Let me express my appreciation to each of the witnesses. We certainly do appreciate your participation. This obviously is a difficult subject and we are doing our best to achieve the best public policy.

There being no further members to be recognized, I do now adjourn this meeting of the Capital Markets Subcommittee.

Thank you.

[Whereupon, at 12:40 p.m., the subcommittee was adjourned.]

THE FASB STOCK OPTIONS PROPOSAL: ITS EFFECT ON THE U.S. ECONOMY AND JOBS

Tuesday, May 4, 2004

U.S. HOUSE OF REPRESENTATIVES,
SUBCOMMITTEE ON CAPITAL MARKETS, INSURANCE
AND GOVERNMENT SPONSORED ENTERPRISES,
COMMITTEE ON FINANCIAL SERVICES,
Washington, D.C.

The subcommittee met, pursuant to call, at 2:05 p.m., in Room 2128, Rayburn House Office Building, Hon. Edward R. Royce presiding.

Present: Representatives Shays, Royce, Hart, Sherman, Moore, Frank (ex officio) and Hinojosa.

Mr. ROYCE. [Presiding] I would like to call this meeting of the capital market subcommittee to order.

This afternoon we are going to convene for the purpose of reviewing the pending Financial Accounting Standards Board employee stock option expensing proposal, and we are also going to be looking at the potential effects its adoption may have on job creation and on the U.S. economy.

In previous hearings on this subject, I have expressed deep concerns about the potential economic consequences of FASB's proposal to require the mandatory expensing of employee stock options.

Like other supporters of Chairman Baker's legislation, H.R. 3574, I believe that broad-based stock options have played an important and positive role in our economy. Stock options enable emerging companies which often do not have a tremendous amount of excess cash or a tremendous cash flow to attract talented employees that would otherwise not work for such innovative firms.

Some people claim that issuing stock options represents an expense to a firm. However, stock options do not represent a cost to an entity. No cash is ever disbursed from the company's treasury. Existing shareholders may see their ownership diminished through dilution, but current accounting standards already require potential dilution to be fully disclosed.

In the not-so-certain case that employee options are actually exercised and the employing company then receives cash, employees who accept options are taking a well-known risk. There are no guarantees a firm will succeed and its stock price will rise.

We hear about the successes in business, but we should not forget there are far more failures. Creative destruction leaves a wake of failed ideas.

The specific purpose of today's hearing is to explore the economic impact of FASB's proposal. Economic behavior has already changed because of this proposal. Many technology firms have already announced that they will no longer issue employee stock options. As a result, many firms have not been able to attract needed employees. Whether an individual is risk-averse or that individual is risk-taking, or even risk-loving, he or she is not likely to leave their job with a large, mature firm to go to a start-up for a compensation package containing less cash and no stock options.

If one accepts the premise that FASB's proposal will end broad-based stock option plans as we know them today, then we should think about the potential long-term negative consequences for our economy. Firms like Intel, Microsoft, Cisco and Yahoo all used stock options at their early stages to attract their employees. Other nations in Asia are now trying to incubate an environment like the one that we had here.

Would these firms have reached their amazing levels of success had stock options not been an available tool for recruitment? Will this proposal inhibit the development of the next Intel? Established firms will survive and prosper under any new rule issued by FASB, but I think some of us are concerned that new firms may not develop as a result, and I believe that it is important for Congress to raise these concerns.

We are very fortunate to have Mr. Herz and Mr. Batavick here today to help deal with these issues, and I hope that in your opening remarks you will address such questions as has FASB field-tested valuation models? Has FASB considered the economic consequences of mandating expensing? Has FASB considered that mandatory expensing could give foreign-based firms a competitive advantage in attracting employees? Is FASB concerned that its proposal could make financial comparability between firms more difficult? And lastly, is FASB still open to considering other nonbinomial methods or models for this approach?

I look forward to hearing answers to these and many other questions, and I would like to turn to my California colleague now, Mr. Brad Sherman, for any opening statement he might like to make.

[The prepared statement of Hon. Edward R. Royce can be found on page 164 in the appendix.]

Mr. SHERMAN. I thank my friend and colleague from the Los Angeles area. I want to commend Chairman Baker for having hearings where at least we finally hear from the FASB, since we have had so many hearings criticizing their work or their intended work. It would have been nice if the Chairman had gone one step further and scheduled these hearings at a time when most of our colleagues would be able to attend, and that these hearings could be as widely attended as the hearings bashing the FASB were. Of course, those were scheduled at a time when there could be votes on the floor. These are scheduled many hours before the first vote of the week, and it would have been nice, I guess, if the Chairman had at least scheduled these hearings at a time that was convenient for him to attend.

I have signed letters for a long time, as one of the few CPAs in Congress, saying let the FASB do its job. My problem is the FASB has not been doing its job in two areas, both directly related to high-tech firms principally, although—stock options go way beyond high-tech.

The first is stock options where for—going back to the APBs, let alone the FASB announcements, you have punted on this issue with a unique approach where you say, this is the right way, but you are free to do it some other way.

Where are the plaintiff's lawyers when you need them in that?

The second area is in research, where you and I have talked, Mr. Herz. You know that demanding the write-off of research is very harmful to our economy and is wrong accounting and has been, and that there isn't a single accounting theory book I can find published in the last century that would form a basis for the immediate write-off of research; and, yet, what we have here is, in some bizarre way, compensating errors. You don't make high-tech firms write off their executive compensation, but you do force them to treat every research project as if it is a black hole that produces no asset.

Now you are undoing one part of the problem without the other. It may very well be that we should wait to deal with one issue until you can deal with the other. Correcting one of two errors where there are compensating errors may give you a worse appraisal of how the high-tech sector is doing than leaving the matter alone until you can deal with both.

But let me put some dollar figures to contrast the size of these two. Stock options, if expensed last year, total expense would have been $47.6 billion. Some roughly $10 billion of that was expensed as companies voluntarily decided to expense stock options, but roughly $38.6 billion, to calculate it in a variety of different ways, would have been expensed had this provision been applicable last year.

In contrast, on the research side—and I think this number is way too low, but the number I have been given by the National Science Foundation is $176 billion, and I would suggest that the private sector is probably doing a lot more research than that.

So the research is at least triple in importance, perhaps a factor of 5, a factor of 10. And so when you go to determine what are the net results of our high-tech firms as compared with firms that don't do much research and may not do much in the way of stock options, you have these offsetting errors. The one you are not—the one we are not dealing with, the one you haven't dealt with yet, is at least five times as big and would cause more investment in companies that do research.

Now, we are told that stock options aren't an expense. Let's apply this to every use of stock options other than compensation. Well, first we are told stock options are not cash. Well, you could issue shares of stock, and that would not be cash either, and I won't bother to ask this as a question, because we all know the answer.

If you issue a bunch of shares of stock to compensate your employees, you have to list it as an expense even though it cost you no cash. The sole effect is to dilute the shares outstanding. You have to list it as an expense. You issue stock to your lower-level employees, to your upper-level employees, to your board members an expense.

If you were to issue shares to the best charity in our country, you would have to list it as an expense. If you were to issue shares to an insurance company to provide health care for your employees, an expense. And if you did options, if you gave options to a charity, you gave options to a health insurance company, you gave options to a special fund that was rebuilding Iraq, it is on that we have decided that the only thing that is so important that we as a Congress should interfere with the FASB and interfere with the basic rules of accounting theory is not in the area of charity. We could get more charitable contributions if we just decided charity never has to be listed as an expense, or if you use stock or you use options to make a charitable contribution. We could have more health care for employees if we just tweaked the accounting rules and said cash or stock or options used to pay for health care doesn't have to be listed as an expense. But health care for our employees, charity paid for by the corporate sector, these do not attract the attention of Congress. The only area where Congress wants to tweak the employees is in executive compensation.

Now, we are told that it is broad-based. We were told that a lot of low-level employees get some options, but almost all the options are going to some people who are at the top of corporations, and it is that reason that the bill itself is written to define broadly based as, well, you are just not one of the top five employees, so if you are the number six person in Intel or the number six person at Disney, you are a poor, struggling secretary, I don't think so.

We are told about competitiveness. Well, we can compete for capital around the world with two approaches. One is the European approach, and it has always been the American approach. That is, have tough accounting standards, do the best job of enforcing them, give investors the most accurate possible picture according to accounting theory. You guys haven't done a good job on research in stock options, but on everything else that has been our proposal. That is the European approach.

The other way to compete is to emulate what I would call the Bangladesh model. That is to say, let companies report what they want. They will report high earnings, and everybody will want to invest.

I would suggest nobody in this room has chosen to invest in whatever stock market can give them the loosiest, goosiest, rosiest accounting picture possible, but rather they turn to those stock markets which have the toughest standards.

So I look forward to questioning my friends at the FASB on whether their exposure draft really does do the job, and I have got some severe problems with it, why they have decided to take an industry that is punished unfairly by your rule on research and punish them fairly by correcting your multiyear problem on stock options, and to proceed with these hearings. But I would say that before we tweak the accounting rules to encourage executive compensation, we ought to tweak the accounting rules to encourage health care coverage for rank-and-file employees.

Now, I do have—I would like unanimous consent to insert in the record a letter from the SEC Chairman to the Ranking Member of the subcommittee Mr. Kanjorski dated May 3rd in which he states that the process established by the FASB to consider the pending stock option proposal should be allowed to run its course. I wonder if there is any objection.

Mr. ROYCE. Without objection.

[The following information can be found on page 210 in the appendix.]

Mr. SHERMAN. I yield back.

Mr. ROYCE. If they are so ordered.

If there are no more opening statements, I would like to——

Mr. SHERMAN. There may be some.

Mr. ROYCE. All right. Let me turn to Mr. Shays and——

Mr. SHAYS. I would be happy to defer to the Ranking Member.

Mr. ROYCE. We will go to our Ranking Member.

Mr. FRANK. I want to be brief, because I just want to, first of all, make clear the Ranking Member of the subcommittee Mr. Kanjorski had requested this and thought it was very important, but a resident of his district was killed in Iraq, and he is understandably at that funeral. So I want to make clear that his absence is not anything that was avoidable, and this remains a very important subject to him, and I appreciate the fact that we are going ahead with the hearing at his request.

And secondly, I want to say I am torn, as I have said before. I am very reluctant to see us interfere with the FASB, partly because while the previous speaker is an accountant, almost nobody else around here is, and we as Members of Congress inevitably have to deal with subjects where the subject matter is very difficult for lay people. I am loathe to get us into more of these.

Of all the roles I do not wish to play, it is being the appeals board to the FASB. Indeed, I think one sure way to cut down on campaign spending would be if Members knew that the consequence of winning a congressional seat and spending all that money was that you got to be the superappellate board on the most arcane accounting issues, I think that would be a severe disincentive.

On the other hand, I have listened to some people for whom I have an enormous amount of respect in an industry which is very important to us, both because of the inherent good it does and because of the contribution it makes to our economy in various forms of high technology, and I am struck by the virtual unanimity of their concern. And so one of the things that I am going to hope that Mr. Herz can address is who is getting hurt by this.

Obviously there are technical questions to be resolved about what is or isn't the appropriate accounting, but accounting is, after all, the—a functional discipline. It is not an abstract one. We use accounting so we can better understand reality, and I do have a question as to whether or not—and maybe this isn't within FASB's jurisdiction—but is it the view of the Board and others who are advocates of this change that there are now investors who are being misled? Are there people who invest in these companies, and because options are not expensed but are listed elsewhere—obviously, I think we all agree, if people were giving the options and weren't telling you, that would be a terrible problem, but that is not what is currently allowed.

So the question is are there people now who are being misled into investing, because while the information is being presented, it is being presented in a form different than you think accounting principals require? And that is really, I think, a very important question for us, at least within the FASB.

I continue to believe myself that the damage that I have seen done by options has come in the perverse incentive in some case options have given the heads of some corporations, in many cases not high-tech corporations, who give themselves options, cash them in after the stock price has been driven up, and shortly thereafter the stock price tumbles, partly because some of the things that drove the price up weren't very good things for the long term. That is an abuse. I see it. I think we should try and deal with that and ask the SEC to help.

But that is the central question, because I accept what I hear from a large number of people in the high-technology area that this will be damaging to them, and I want to know what harm are we undoing.

So the last thing I would say is that it is also the case obviously that I guess there are very few—we know the perception and reality intermingle. This appears to be a case where perception is everything, because the reality is not being changed. The reality of options being granted won't change. Apparently a lot of people on both sides of this issue think in enormous-amount terms on how they are described, and I would hope that we could address the implications of that. Thank you, Mr. Chairman.

Mr. ROYCE. Thank you.

Mr. ROYCE. Mr. Shays.

Mr. SHAYS. Thank you. I just want to disclose the fact that FASB is in the 4th Congressional District of Connecticut, so I may be unduly influenced by that; to say that we are grateful FASB is in the Fourth Congressional District, we appreciate the good work the Board does, even if some of its members are not enlightened enough to live in the 4th Congressional District. And I would say to you that in my judgment, a tie goes to FASB.

Mr. ROYCE. Mr. Moore.

Mr. MOORE. Thank you, Mr. Chairman. I just want to thank the Chairman, the Ranking Member for convening this hearing. I want to also extend my appreciation to the witnesses for appearing. I look forward to your testimony. We will have questions. Thank you very much.

Mr. ROYCE. Any other opening statements from the Members?

In that case we will go to an introduction of our witnesses. First we have Mr. Robert H. Herz. Mr. Herz was appointed Chairman of the Financial Accounting Standards Board effective July 1st of 2002. Previously he was a senior partner with PricewaterhouseCoopers.

Prior to joining the Financial Accounting Standards Board, Mr. Herz was PricewaterhouseCoopers' North American theater leader of professional, technical risk and quality, and a member of the firm's global and U.S. Boards. He also served as a part-time member of the International Accounting Standards Board. Mr. Herz is both a certified public accountant and a chartered accountant.

We are also fortunate to have here his colleague Mr. George Batavick. Mr. Batavick was appointed to the Financial Accounting Standards Board effective August 1st of 2003. Prior to joining

FASB, Mr. Batavick was most recently the former controller of Texaco. In this post he had companywide responsibility for strategy and policy matters covering all aspects of accounting and financial reporting, special studies, internal controls and tactical plan coordination.

Welcome back, Mr. Herz. You have the floor, and I would ask both of our witnesses—you will be recognized for a 5-minute summary of your testimony. Your written statements will be made part of the record. Mr. Herz.

STATEMENT OF ROBERT H. HERZ, CHAIRMAN, FINANCIAL ACCOUNTING STANDARDS BOARD

Mr. HERZ. Thank you, Representative Royce and members of the subcommittee. George is with me because he heads up our Small Business Advisory Committee, and he will be talking about some of that activity.

We are pleased to appear before you today on behalf of the FASB. We are very happy to participate in this hearing, particularly since H.R. 3574 or any similar legislation if enacted would preempt and override our ongoing public due process to improve the accounting and financial reporting for equity-based compensation.

We have some brief prepared remarks, and we would respectfully request that the full text of our testimony and all the supporting materials be entered into the public record.

Mr. ROYCE. Without objection.

Mr. HERZ. As you know, our ability to conduct our work in a systematic, thorough and unbiased manner is fundamental to achieving our mission of improving accounting and financial reporting standards in this country. Those standards are essential to the growth and stability of the U.S. economy because investors, creditors and other consumers of financial reports rely heavily on credible, transparent, comparable, unbiased financial information to make their investment and credit decisions.

Now, because the actions of the FASB affects so many organizations, our decision-making process must be open, thorough and as objective as possible, and therefore, our rules of procedure require a very extensive and public due process.

We issue proposals for comment, and then after that, when we get the comments, we hold roundtables, we actively redeliberate all the key issues. Those redeliberations often do result in significant changes and improvements to the proposals.

The Board makes final decisions only after carefully considering and analyzing the input of all interested parties. We do our best to try and balance the often conflicting perspectives of various parties and make independent, objective decisions guided by the fundamental concepts and key qualitative characteristics of sound, fair and transparent financial reporting.

In March of 2003, at a public meeting, we decided to add a project to our agenda to address issues relating to improving the accounting for equity-based compensation. The project was in response to the high level of public concern expressed by many individual and institutional investors, financial analysts, creditors, major accounting firms, many study groups and many other parties, including many Members of Congress, about the need to improve the accounting for equity-based compensation.

Many believe that the existing reporting for equity-based compensation results in significant distortions in the reporting of earnings, operating results and operating cash flows, distortions that they believe cannot be remedied solely by improvements in disclosures. So the ultimate goal of our project is to develop a standard that results in reporting that more faithfully reflects the underlying economic effects of equity-based compensation and that brings about greater comparability of reporting.

The project also provides an opportunity to achieve greater international convergence of accounting standards, an objective that we have been specifically encouraged to pursue by the Sarbanes-Oxley Act, by the U.S. SEC and by many other parties.

On March 31st of this year, we issued by a unanimous vote a proposal for public comment to improve the accounting for a wide range of equity-based compensation arrangements. That proposal is a result of a very extensive public due process. The process included the issuance of a preliminary document for public comment, the review of over 300 comment letters and over 130 unsolicited letters, review of research and consultation with many, many parties.

Based on our extensive public due process to date, the Board believes that the proposal would significantly improve the financial reporting for equity-based compensation arrangements. By creating greater transparency, completeness and a more level playing field in the accounting for different forms of equity-based compensation, we believe that the proposal would enhance the comparability of reported results between enterprises that choose to compensate their employees in different ways.

The proposal would achieve it through a number of provisions, including eliminating the existing exception for so-called fixed-plan employee stock options, which, as Representative Sherman indicated, are the only form of equity-based compensation that is not currently required to be reported as an expense in the financial statements.

The proposal also includes provisions that we believe would improve the transparency of the effects of equity-based compensation on reported cash flows and that are aimed at addressing what many believe have been significant distortions in the reporting of operating cash flows by companies that make significant use of employee stock options.

The proposal reflects the view that all forms of equity-based compensation should be properly accounted for as such, and that the existing exception for fixed-plan employee stock options results in reporting that not only ignores the economic substance of those transactions, but also distorts reported earnings, profitability and other key financial metrics.

I would note in contrast that this distortion again, as Representative Sherman indicated, does not occur when the same company uses stock options or similar instruments such as warrants for purposes other than compensating employees; for example, in acquiring goods or other services, or in financings or M & A transactions. In all those cases the current accounting has long required that the options or warrants be properly valued and accounted for in the financial statements.

In the public company arena, the proposal would bring about greater comparability between the now over 575 companies that have voluntarily opted to account for the cost of employee stock options and the many others that have not done so.

It would also be responsive to the growing number of companies, including a number of major technology companies, whose shareholders by a majority vote have approved nonbinding proxy resolutions mandating expensing of all employee stock options. Managers of a number of those companies have indicated that they are awaiting completion of our project in order to respond to the demands of their shareholders.

The proposal would also result in substantial convergence in the accounting for equity-based compensation between our standards and international standards that are followed in over 90 countries around the world.

I would also note that in Canada, who often follows the lead of the U.S. in improving accounting standards, they felt they could not wait on this topic and decided to mandate expensing of all employee stock options beginning in January of this year, and I understand that implementation of their new standard is going very smoothly.

Finally, with regard to the potential economic consequence of our proposal, many economic experts that have addressed the issue of the accounting for employee stock options, including Federal Reserve Chairman Alan Greenspan, former Federal Reserve Chairman Paul Volcker, Nobel Prize-winning economists Robert Merton, and Joseph Stiglitz, and groups like the Financial Economist Roundtable, the Republican staff of the Joint Economic Committee of the Congress, the Conference Board Commission on Public Trust and Private Enterprise co-chaired by Pete Peterson and John Snow, major investment banks, and the Congressional Budget Office have all indicated support for mandatory expensing of employee stock options.

Indeed, many of these experts have also indicated that mandatory expensing could have positive economic consequences because of the improvements in capital allocation that would result from having more credible, comparable and transparent financial information, not to mention helping to continue to shore up public confidence in financial reporting.

Now, we recognize that one size may not fit all, so I am going to hand over to George in a second who will discuss the several special provisions contained in our proposal relating to small businesses and start-ups, as well as other matters relating to our continuing work and due process on this topic.

I would like to assure you that we recognize the importance of small business and start-ups to job creation, to entrepreneurship and to our Nation's economy, so we also understand that any standards we prescribe that apply to small business must not only be conceptually sound, but also must be operational and cost-effective.

Mr. ROYCE. Mr. Batavick.

STATEMENT OF GEORGE J. BATAVICK, BOARD MEMBER, FINANCIAL ACCOUNTING STANDARDS BOARD

Mr. BATAVICK. Thank you, Mr. Royce, and thank you, Bob, and good afternoon everyone. Before I outline the special small business provisions contained in our proposal to improve the accounting for equity-based compensation, I would first like to provide some brief background on small businesses and financial and accounting reporting standards.

First, there is no Federal law requiring nonpublic enterprises to use FASB standards. Thus, for most small businesses, the use of our standards is primarily a private choice. For some small businesses, that choice may be influenced by whether they have plans to become a public enterprise. For other small businesses, the decision to follow FASB standards may be influenced or controlled by their current or potential lenders-suppliers, other contracting parties or State regulators. To the extent that one of these parties requires that the financial reports of small businesses comply with our standards, that requirement presumably reflects the party's opinion that our standards result in better, more transparent information for their respective purposes.

Second, it is also important to note that the FASB has long recognized as part of our public due process procedures that the cost of complying with our standards can fall disproportionately on small businesses. In recognition of that fact, the Board actively solicits and carefully considers requests from users, auditors and preparers of the financial reports of small businesses to provide for special provisions to alleviate the costs of implementing our standards. Those requests come from our continuous and ongoing due process and deliberations throughout the life of the project.

If you are following our project on equity-based compensation, and you wanted to keep up on what was happening, all interested parties, including small businesses, can take advantage of our free weekly action alert, which is by e-mail. We discuss current agenda items and past Board decisions. Interested parties can also attend our Board meetings, call in or listen to our free Webcast of our meetings on the day of the meeting, with replays of our meetings available 1 week thereafter.

Our meetings also get extensive news coverage by the top news agencies, and our free Web site includes up-to-date summaries of all equity-based compensation issues discussed in our tentative decisions.

We actively seek input from various State CPA societies, and membership in turn brief their clients, in many cases small businesses, on the status of this and other Board activities.

In addition, liaison meetings with various groups having small-business representation and Board member and staff speaking engagements provide additional means of receiving valuable input from the small-business community.

With respect to this proposal on stock-based compensation, it is our understanding that although the use of employee stock options is present at some small businesses, particularly start-ups and venture capital-backed enterprises that plan to become public enterprises, the vast majority of small businesses, over 95 percent, in the U.S. do not grant employee stock options.

As indicated earlier, however, for those small businesses that are affected by our proposal, the proposal includes several provisions intended to alleviate the cost of implementation. First, the proposal includes a special provision that would permit most small businesses, including all that are not public, to measure compensation costs using a simpler, less costly intrinsic value method rather than the fair value method that would be required for most public enterprises. Under the intrinsic value method, the amount of compensation expense required to be reported would generally be equivalent to the amount of the income tax deduction for stock options.

Second, the proposal includes a special provision that provides most small businesses that are nonpublic enterprises with a simpler, less costly prospective transition to the new requirements.

Finally, the proposal includes a special provision that provides that the effective date of the proposed standard for nonpublic enterprises would be delayed for 1 year until 2006.

I also would like to note that the proposal includes a notice for recipients that highlights and describes all these special provisions. The notice requests that respondents to the proposal indicate whether there are other special provisions for small businesses that might be appropriate and whether any or all such special provisions should be extended to public enterprises that are small business issuers under the Federal securities laws.

The Board currently plans to discuss the proposal, special provisions and other issues about the proposal with representatives of small business at the inaugural public meeting of our Small Business Advisory Committee next week, May 11th. Our request for agenda items for this meeting showed interest in this proposal. We also plan to hold public roundtable meetings in June with valuation and compensation experts, and users, auditors, preparers of financial reports to discuss a broad range of issues about the proposal.

Following the end of the proposal's comment period in June, the Board plans to redeliberate at public meetings issues raised in response to the proposal. Those redeliberations will include very careful consideration of the ongoing input received from all parties, including ongoing input from the members of the Small Business Advisory Committee. Only after carefully evaluating the input at public meetings will the Board consider whether to issue a final standard.

The Board's current plans are to complete its deliberations and be in a position to issue a final standard in the fourth quarter of this year.

On behalf of myself and Bob, I would again like to express our deep appreciation for inviting us to participate in this hearing. All the information we obtain in connection with this hearing will be carefully considered.

In conclusion, let me assure you that you, the users, auditors and preparers of financial reports, including small business financial reports, can have confidence that the Board will continue to actively reach out and solicit input in response to our proposal. That input will be carefully considered in an open, thorough and objective manner. Our ultimate goal is to develop an accounting standard that will faithfully report the underlying economic effects of equity-based compensation transactions and thus significantly improve the transparency and integrity of financial reporting in the United States.

Thank you again, Representative Royce and other subcommittee members. Bob and I would welcome the opportunity to respond to any questions.

Mr. ROYCE. I thank you, Mr. Batavick.

[The prepared statement of Robert Herz and George Batavick can be found on pages 172 and 175 in the appendix.]

Mr. ROYCE. Let me begin by asking a question of Mr. Herz.

Mr. Herz, in a letter to the Financial Accounting Standards Board dated December 29th of 1993, Coopers and Lybrand contended that using option pricing models results in unreliable information and would have an adverse impact on the comparability and usefulness of financial statements, and your name and number are provided as contact information to discuss this letter. I wanted to ask you how you reconcile your position in this letter with your position today. We are assuming that the letter would not have provided your contact information without your endorsement of the arguments that are made there, which are some of the arguments that we have heard on the Hill over the last month again replayed as we have discussed this issue.

Mr. HERZ. Well, I don't remember the particular memorandums. I obviously take good faith that that is it.

Mr. ROYCE. Well, don't take it on faith. It says, if you have any questions regarding our comments, please contact Ronald Murray or Bob Herz at this number, or David Lookate.

Mr. HERZ. Right. I think that, you know, at that time I did believe on the face of it without a lot of investigation, I just had come into the national office of Coopers and Lybrand, and from the practice that, you know, those were the views. Those were the views that we were hearing from many clients at the time.

I have now had the benefit of an intensive look at this subject, both on the International Accounting Standards Board and also at the FASB, I mean, an intensive look at it, and you live and you learn. I don't believe that those arguments, as far as at least the valuation, hold water. Will they have an impact on emerging businesses? Well, we have got special provisions in our proposal, A; and, B, yeah, there are economic consequences in terms of better information that arise from changing accounting standards.

Mr. ROYCE. Well, let me ask you a question about that intensive look, and I may be wrong on this, but to my knowledge, as far as the Board is concerned, I don't think that you field-tested valuation models when it comes to trying to determine this new methodology. I don't know that you have taken various valuation models by a cross-section of companies so the significant data would be collected on the accuracy and reliability of these different valuation models. And I was going to ask you, are there any studies that you have relied on that show specifically that the binomial method values employee stock options accurately?

Mr. HERZ. Well, we have done a lot of work on the valuation area. We have convened a group of expert panel called our Options Valuation Group, which are experts in valuation compensation, equity derivatives, which a stock option is. Our staff and the Board met with them a number of times. We did have field visits to a number of companies that included a cross-section of companies across industries and sizes of companies, both public and private. We have reviewed the results of research studies on data that exists.

Let me step back, though, that——

Mr. ROYCE. Let me explain where I am going with this so that you better understand my point. Your spokesman Cheryl Thompson defended the decision not to field-test valuation models by telling the press that the ultimate field test has already taken place. She added that public companies have been performing this field test for 7 consecutive years, so the test sample is huge. It involves thousands of companies.

I believe I am correct in assuming that Ms. Thompson is referring to the use of Black-Scholes in footnote disclosures over the past number of years. I suppose that one could argue that it makes sense if the exposure draft required all companies use the Black-Scholes model, but what we are now doing is urging companies to use something different, which is the binomial method. And so my question here is why not conduct field tests on the accuracy of that particular model?

Mr. HERZ. Well, the—first of all, there are now 575 companies that are expensing in their income statements. Some of those use the binomial model, and we have talked to them.

Secondly, it is a misnomer to call them completely two different models. They are basically related. They are derived from the same financial economic theorem. The binomial model is really opening up the Black-Scholes model. The Black-Scholes is kind of a hard-wire model that you put in one set of assumptions, and you get a result. The binomial works off of exactly the same theory, but you can peer into the hard-wiring and look at it period by period, and you can make adjustments for better data period by period.

Mr. ROYCE. Well, you make the point that 576 firms, in your words, have——

Mr. HERZ. Can I——

Mr. ROYCE.—expense—let—let me just ask you, do any of those companies have broad-based stock option programs? Because there are thousands and thousands of companies that have not embraced this, that do have broad-based stock option programs, and that is where we are focused. And I will let you respond to that, and then I have one last question before we go to my colleague here.

Mr. HERZ. Well, there are a number of companies with broad-based plans that have gone to expensing, like Netflix and Home Depot and Wal-Mart and the like.

My other point I was trying to make is that the binomial model is regularly used on a daily basis to value equity derivatives and other derivatives. It is a model that works.

Mr. ROYCE. My last question is this, and I realize the Financial Accounting Standards Board is pretty far down the path on this proposal, but that said, just yesterday I learned of a new proposed method of expensing options that works very differently than Black-Scholes and works differently than this binomial method and that you have articulated, and I was going to ask what your opinion would be in terms of being open to consider this new proposal for expensing at this point in the process.

Mr. HERZ. Oh, we are open—we get suggestions almost daily, so——

Mr. ROYCE. So what would the process and the timetable be——

Mr. HERZ. The process is they should send us something in writing, and then we will have a look at it, and we will meet with them. And we have done that with many different parties. And we also, when we get something like that, consult with our panel of experts also.

Mr. ROYCE. Thank you, Mr. Herz.

We will go to Mr. Sherman.

Mr. SHERMAN. Thank you, Mr. Chairman.

Mr. Batavick, your testimony provided really useful, personally, information. Right after these hearings I am going to go out and sell all the stock in the company that makes Ambien. That stock is going to crash once everyone becomes aware that replays of FASB meetings are available for free.

It is rather absurd for you to say that small businesses don't have to use FASB pronouncements in preparing their financial statements if they choose not to go public. Every bank wants statements prepared under Generally Accepted Accounting Principles, and FASB pronouncements cannot be ignored in determining what is generally accepted. And, of course, our State corporate laws make certain dividends illegal unless certain capital—certain amounts of capital are available calculated under GAAP. So you understate the importance of your Board if you say that you are not legally binding on nonpublic companies in this country.

Speaking, though, of small businesses, the binomial method, as I understand it, could be expensive to use, could involve many thousands of dollars of accounting fees. Let's say you had a small company, you used Black-Scholes, and you came out with, say, half a million dollars of stock option compensation expense. But that half million was material. Is there anything in the exposure draft that says in order to help you save on accounting fees, as long as your Black-Scholes number is under half a million, you can use binomial; or does the exposure draft say if you are tiny, then whatever amount that is material to you, you have to go spend the money on the accounting fees to use the more sophisticated approach? Do you allow a less expensive calculation method for small companies?

Mr. BATAVICK. Right now we are not requiring one method over the other. What we are saying is the fact that we have a Black-Scholes method, we also have the binomial method, and the statement we make in the proposal is that in certain circumstances that may be preferable, but it is also based on if you have the information available to——

Mr. SHERMAN. I would hope that—and I will get to this in a second. I think it is a tragic flaw in your exposure draft that you provide so little guidance as when to use one method or when to use the other and——

Mr. HERZ. Could I just interject, if I might?

Mr. SHERMAN. Yes.

Mr. HERZ. In our proposal if a small business is a private company, they don't even have to use option pricing models. They can elect not to use option pricing models.

Mr. SHERMAN. Yes, but many of—if they are not someday going to be public, nobody may want the stock options anyway. Stock options are generally used for companies that intend to go public. I realize there may be some exceptions to that.

Mr. HERZ. We don't say if you are going to go public. If you are private, you——

Mr. SHERMAN. You don't have to. I would hope that GAAP would mean the same thing, that we would take the—I know you can propose vague standards. That is what you have done the last 30 years. You said you can expense them or not expense them, your choice. Now you are going to say, well, by Black-Scholes, binomial, or if you are not public, some other guesstimate.

I would hope that you would provide real guidance to the profession, that people reading financial statements are not going to have to look at the footnotes and try to guess what was done and how to make two statements comparable. The whole idea here is you should be able to compare Coke and Pepsi, not the taste test, the financial test. And for a while there, one was expensing and one wasn't. Now we are going to have one binomial and one Black-Scholes and then some small beverage company using a third method or no method at all.

I would hope that if you are in the standards-writing business, you would write standards, not guidelines, not guesstimates, especially when those who oppose what you are doing have said this could be a fertile area for lawsuits.

Now, I realize there are other areas of accounting where a judgment is required, but here you are talking about executive compensation, the juiciest thing to bring before a jury. You are inviting lawsuits when you take that juicy area and you don't provide guidance.

I would hope that guidance would factor in availability of information, would factor in cost of calculation, and would then say, okay, apply Black-Scholes. If you meet these standards of materiality, if you meet this dollar figure, then you have got to go use the binomial, and here's how you ought to use it.

Let's see. My next question, though, is why don't you delay this whole thing until you get the research thing right, and are you concerned that you are now going to have—eliminate this compensating error, and you are going to adopt an accounting system for this country that discriminates against our high-tech sector?

Mr. HERZ. Let me go back to a few other points you made and then go to the R&D point.

I think if you look at our exposure draft, there is plenty of guidance on valuation. It may not be hard-wired guidance. It is guidance that fulfills what we have been told to do in objectives-oriented standards by the SEC in the report they issued to you last summer, to Congress on Sarbanes-Oxley. It is much more detailed, for example, than in many other areas of valuation. I——

Mr. SHERMAN. As is executive compensation. Two accounting firms should come up with the same answer. If they don't, there is going to be lawsuits, and if there is going to be lawsuits, that is a strong argument for us to pass this bill.

Mr. HERZ. If you look at our notice to recipients, there are several questions specifically on that point, how hard-wired, how prescriptive would you like us to get, models, assumptions. Now, we have already gotten some responses that say we have already provided too much guidance. So there is a diversity of views. I——

Mr. SHERMAN. Well, of course. The people who don't want to expense options want as much looseness as possible so they can state as low a number as possible.

Mr. HERZ. But one of those responses is from a major audit firm. Okay? So——

Mr. SHERMAN. But they tend to agree with their clients. Surprise.

Mr. HERZ. I don't know if their clients feel that way. I mean, the point is there is a diversity of view. We have asked the question specifically because we recognize that sensitivity. We can hard-wire everything if that is what people want.

Mr. SHERMAN. Or that one accounting firm could compete under the slogan, we use the play in the joints to understate your executive—to minimize the statement of your executive compensation. It would be a whole new slogan.

Mr. HERZ. I think one of the benefits of the Sarbanes-Oxley, the auditors are doing more robust audits, I believe. The SEC is certainly reviewing a lot more, and this is an area they would intend to review.

On your R&D question—and, you know, you and I have had discussions. I personally agree with you, but thousands don't. And I will tell you there is good news on that front, or potentially good news on that front, in that we met with the International Accounting Standards Board, like we do every 6 months, and we, subject to our own agenda processes, agreed to look at the area of both R&D and more broadly intangibles.

Mr. SHERMAN. But, Mr. Chairman, shouldn't you stop all work on this stock option thing, which is going to hit high-tech hard—and they are already screaming—when you are already hitting them? And fairly, I might add, but you have been hitting them hard and pounding them hard, much harder unfairly. Shouldn't you abstain from correcting this mistake until you can deal with that mistake, or do you think you should just pound high-tech when they are right on the accounting and when they are wrong on the accounting?

Mr. HERZ. Well, again, the issue of R&D, you and I may agree personally. There are many who don't, so——

Mr. SHERMAN. Is there any accounting theory textbook, that supports the idea of expensing every research expenditure done in-house no matter how valuable the results are and no matter how provable the value of those results are?

Mr. HERZ. The accounting rationale is that it is not sufficiently measurable.

Mr. SHERMAN. You can't measure—yes. That is—you know how—let's put it like this: There is no accounting theorist I am aware of anywhere in this country that would come to the conclusion that you should write off all R&D.

Mr. HERZ. I would ask the—in response to your suggestion, which, you know, I agree with—as you know, I agree with not only capitalizing R&D per se, but I think the whole area of intangibles that are big-business value drivers is something that is missing off of contemporary balance sheets.

I will tell you, though, the history of this issue

being—the last time, I understand, it was raised by the FASB a few years ago, the biggest opponents of it were the high-tech firms.

Mr. ROYCE. Mr. Frank.

Mr. FRANK. Mr. Herz, in the full text that you gave us, and I appreciate it, on page 27, you address towards the end the objections, and you list four of them. The last one is you phrase the objection as mandatory expensing of employee stock options will have negative economic consequences.

To me that is the nub of what we are here for. We are not the plutonic board of perfect accounting. We get involved where there are negative economic consequences, and I have to tell you, I don't—I think if I were a judge and this was the argument, you would lose on summary judgment. I mean, you make a lot of good arguments, but there is none.

You kind of implicitly—and that may not be controlling, but this is so you will understand the dilemma. Implicitly, in the beginning of the second paragraph of that page, the Board's operating precepts require it to consider issues in an even-handed manner without attempting to encourage or to discourage specific actions. That does not imply that improved financial reporting should have no economic consequences, but it seems to me to be a concession that—not a concession, a statement that you are going to go ahead and do this, and that is the dilemma many of us have, because I certainly agree on the accounting—let me ask you, to go back to the question I posed, other than aesthetically, who is getting hurt now by the current accounting firm options? Who is the victim?

Mr. HERZ. Well, I think this all kind of relates together.You know, our mission is to improve financial reporting——

Mr. FRANK. I understand that, but if that is the answer, okay, but is somebody being hurt now by the current situation?

Mr. HERZ. Well, certainly the people who were surveyed the financial analysts, surveys of investors, tech investors, all say they want it in the score because it is not transparent right now. They don't—they pick up numbers from databases. The CBO said that it would be more transparent——

Mr. FRANK. Please, I don't need you to tell me what the CBO said. I rarely pay attention to them. And transparency is a means, if not the end. And if the answer is it is wrong and it doesn't make a difference if anybody is getting hurt, then okay. But as far as transparency, let me say this: The information is there now, isn't it? It is just not—if I were going to invest in a company, which I—we get enough ethics from—so I don't address individual companies. But if I was going to invest in an individual company, I or somebody I was paying to help me do this would read the footnote. So let me put it this way: If I were going to invest in an individual company, would I get more information about what is actually happening one way versus the other?

Mr. HERZ. You're going to get more information the way we are proposing it

Mr. FRANK. What information would I get from you that I don't now get? I would get the fact that the options would be—would I not now get the fact that the options were being granted and how many there were? Would I not know that?

Mr. HERZ. You would know that, but you would not know things like operating margins, return on equity, all those things that are just—by not running it through the financial statements, you are not getting the full accounting

Mr. FRANK. You are saying that I would be—that the investors can't do that themselves. I get everything else and then I get the options, and I wouldn't be able to, myself, figure out or decide for myself to what extent the existence of the options added to or detracted from the value of the investment?

Mr. HERZ. If you were a sophisticated investor and you took the footnote, you would be able to get part of that information, not all of it

Mr. FRANK. What wouldn't I be able to get?

Mr. HERZ. You wouldn't be able to get things like gross margin, you wouldn't be able to get operating results, you would have to recompute——

Mr. FRANK. Well, those are things to which there is some element of uncertainty, though; right?

Mr. HERZ. Well, they are things that if you do the accounting properly, they are just there.

Mr. FRANK. Well, but isn't there some element of uncertainty there? I mean, I was struck when you told Mr. Sherman that the obstacle to dealing with research differently is that it is hard to measure. Is it a lot easier to measure than the options, or a lot harder?

Mr. HERZ. No, the options are much easier to measure than the early stage of research

Mr. FRANK. And you couldn't just make available to people what the measurements are and let them do it themselves?

Mr. HERZ. We have been doing that

Mr. FRANK. Okay, we have been doing that. Who has been hurt? Have you gotten any complaints? Is there anyone we know of that?

Mr. HERZ. Yes.

Mr. FRANK. No, I know they said we would rather. Did anyone say I was misled?

Mr. HERZ. Yes.

Mr. FRANK. I invested unwisely?

Mr. HERZ. Yes, we have lots of letters from individual investors.

Mr. FRANK. Well, I have read your comments and the samples you gave. None of them say that. You gave one set of samples. You didn't give the other. You gave people that said, oh, these greedmongers, they are terrible. You have people saying it would be more desirable. But surely you understand the difference between a general assertion that it would be desirable and an assertion that an individual was hurt.

Does anybody anywhere—I will make a plea. There are other people here from the SEC; would anyone bring forward to me some individual who was misled because the options were not expensed? Do you know of any claims of that sort, Mr. Herz?

Mr. HERZ. Yes.

Mr. FRANK. Where are they, Mr. Herz? They are not in your statement. Point them to me. Which one did I miss?

Mr. HERZ. I don't know, we have got hundreds and thousands.

Mr. FRANK. Well, you picked some out. None of the ones you picked out say that. None of the ones you picked say "I was misled," and I am reading them. I strongly recommend people like me will stay away from the market as long as they are passed out like funny money

Mr. HERZ. Can we follow up with you?

Mr. FRANK. Yes. Okay. And I am surprised we haven't heard reports because this is the issue.

Mr. HERZ. I think an important point is that it is a well-known, well-accepted thing in accounting, that disclosure doesn't cure bad accounting. And we get requests all the time for just put it in the footnotes. When we were going through the improvements——

Mr. FRANK. Sir, you do realize this is totally irrelevant to my question? If you want to give more general statements about why you should do this, okay. And that is part of the problem you have got.

I thank the Chairman for the indulgence. Here is the problem you have got, and I don't want—I am not a co-sponsor of the bill. I am really torn here. But I have people telling me this is going to cause a problem. I mean, I have a technical intellectual argument. Clearly these are not free. I understand that. How you account for them there is a question.

But a lot of people are saying, look, this is going to cause a problem; and they are going to cause a problem again because of the way the market will perceive this. And so as a public policymaker, not as an accounting technical specialist, I say, okay, well, if there is a potential for the problem here, what are we solving? What are we solving? What problem am I solving other than an intellectual failure?

Frankly, if I was going to go around this city and resolve every intellectual failure, I would be a wreck. So I am looking for some public policy break. And, yes, I would appreciate it, please follow up with me, because I think that is why you are here. You are not here because people differ with you technically on the accounting. As was implied in the question from Mr. Sherman, no one cares about that. That is your job, and we are glad you have it and are ready to do it.

The issue here is, is there some real economic harm that could come? And that is the area I think in which further help from you would help your cause, and so that is it.

Yes, I yield to my colleague from California.

Mr. SHERMAN. I would say the one obvious harm is that those companies that choose not to use stock options are at a disadvantage in attracting capital as opposed to those who do.

Mr. FRANK. Okay. But I would say again, because people in the market don't understand this, it all comes down—to some extent I have to say I feel a little bit good about this in one sense, having been for years told, listen—well, let me say there was a former majority leader of this institution who used to say government is dumb and markets are smart. Well, these markets ain't the smart ones. These are the markets that are confused because of the accounting.

So I am just a little glad to say that. I agree. But that is the issue; it is not the investor being misled, it is the competitive disadvantage to the other people.

I am sorry. Did the other gentleman from California want me to yield?

Mr. ROYCE. No, I was just going to make the point that it is easier just to point out the intellectual failures in this city than in the market.

But we are going to go to Mr. Hinojosa.

Mr. FRANK. Thank you

Mr. ROYCE. Mr. Hinojosa, you also had an opening statement you wanted to make, and at this point we will give you that opportunity, and then, please, go to your questions.

Mr. HINOJOSA. I will submit my opening statement in writing.

Mr. ROYCE. Without objection.

[The prepared statement of Hon. Rubén Hinojosa can be found on page 81 in the appendix.]

Mr. HINOJOSA. I would like to make a statement and ask a question or two. Thank you, Chairman Royce.

I am very pleased that the subcommittee had the opportunity to hear the views of the Financial Accounting Standard Boards, or FASB, on its proposal to expand stock options, especially since you are the entity that will be directly impacted by the legislation I have co-sponsored and supported thus far, H.R. 3574, the Stock Option Accounting Reform Act.

I am aware of the allegations that have been made, that FASB has been hiring lobbyists, or, rather, actually having registered lobbyists on staff who have been encouraging Members of Congress to support its proposed legislation, thus calling into question the longstanding perception of FASB as an independent agency. Certain individuals have come to my office recently to express concerns about particular aspects of H.R. 3574. And after listening to you make your statement and the questions that the Chairman and others have asked, I will reread through today's testimony and have my staff obtain a copy of it to determine if those concerns were addressed, as well as having them follow up with FASB.

Mr. Batavick, what is your background?

Mr. BATAVICK. Most recently, I was the retired comptroller of Texaco, Inc. We were acquired by Chevron a few years ago, and because of that I left the combined company. Prior to that I was with Getty Oil Company. That was acquired by Texaco. And before that I was in public accounting.

Mr. HINOJOSA. Those are very good companies, very large, and I just cannot understand how you can be speaking so much for the small businesses unless you ran small businesses before you went to Texaco.

Mr. BATAVICK. Actually, when I was going through school, I worked two summers at a public accounting firm that only did the accounting for small businesses. I did both accounting as well as auditing. Also, when I joined Getty Oil Company, most of our service stations are not owned by the company themselves, they are owned by small businesses. And I worked very closely with those small businesses during my early years.

Mr. HINOJOSA. Well, Mr. Chairman, and Ranking Member Barney Frank, and Congressman Sherman, again thank you for calling this important hearing and I look forward to working with you.

Mr. ROYCE. Thank you. Mr. Herz, you wanted to respond?

Mr. HERZ. Yes, I wanted to respond to the question about lobbyists. I want to be very clear on this. We have not asked any firm to lobby for us with respect to our proposed standard to improve the accounting for equity-based compensation.

Our Washington, D.C. Representative, Jeff Mahoney, since 1996 has provided information and responded to questions about the FASB and its activities from staff and Members of Congress, Federal Government officials and other interested parties in Washington, D.C. He also works hard to keep interested parties informed. And, yes, we do speak our minds when there is proposed legislation that would intrude upon our independence and upon our ability to do our work in a thorough, open, and objective way.

Jeff also arranges for me to meet directly with Members of Congress, Federal Government officials, and other interested parties to provide them with timely information on our activities.

Because our communications sometimes entail lobbying contacts, as defined in the Lobbying Disclosure Act, relating to proposed legislation like this one, relating to our mission and activities, Jeff and I, and my predecessor since 1998, were registered under the Lobbying Disclosure Act on behalf of the Financial Accounting Foundation, our parent group.

Basically, the history of this is that when Chairman Baker introduced a bill in 1998 relating to accounting for derivatives, many Members of Congress solicited the views of Mr. Mahoney and our then-chairman Ed Jenkins. They consulted with legal counsel who advised them to be safe, to register as lobbyists. When I came on board they registered me as a lobbyist. That has nothing to do with this particular matter in question.

In fact, I think it is a little bit like the pot calling the kettle black. We have all read all the stories, and in a Senate hearing last week one of the Senators used the term high-tech lobbyists swarming all over Capitol Hill. We did not start anything here in Congress. It is your purview. We welcome the inquiry and all of that, but we try to respond to the questions of Members about the proposed legislation. But that is all.

Mr. ROYCE. Mr. Herz and Mr. Batavick, we want to thank you both for appearing before our panel today. Let me also note that some members may have additional questions for both of you which they might want to submit in writing. If we can give them 30 days to submit those questions, and within those 30 days if you would complete your response for the record, we will collect those from you.

Again, we thank you both for making the trip here to testify today. This hearing is adjourned.

[Whereupon, at 3:17 p.m., the subcommittee was adjourned.]

APPENDIX

April 21, 2004

Opening Statement

Chairman Michael G. Oxley
Financial Services Committee

The FASB Stock Options Proposal: Its Effect on the U.S. Economy and Jobs

Subcommittee on Capital Markets, Insurance, and Government Sponsored Enterprises

April 21, 2004

Good morning. Today, for the third time this Congress, we will discuss stock option accounting. The number of hearings this Subcommittee has held demonstrates how important this issue is. I applaud Chairman Baker for his good work on this subject. In light of the Financial Accounting Standards Board's recent proposal, it is particularly important now.

The question of whether stock options should be expensed has been debated for many years.

Some, like the former Chief Accountant of the Securities and Exchange Commission, Walter Schuetze and numerous experts in accounting, believe that the FASB's position that the issuance of employee stock options creates an expense is simply improper accounting.

Mr. Schuetze observes that the issuance of a stock option to an employee does not change the market capitalization of the corporation, as measured by the market value of the outstanding shares and the value of the outstanding option. Thus, there is no expense. If there had been a true expense, which he defines as the "using up" of an owned asset or the decline in the value of an owned asset, then the market value of the outstanding shares and option should have declined, but that is not the case.

Others, like FASB, as evidenced by its recently released proposal, take the contrary view, arguing that employee stock options do constitute a corporate expense. FASB's position is that all employee stock options have value – which employees purchase with the services they provide. Because they have value, FASB asserts, when stock options are given to employees they give rise to compensation costs that are properly included in measuring an enterprise's net income.

Some point out that the grant of an employee stock option is an opportunity cost to the issuer. They argue that if a company were to grant stock, rather than options, to employees, the company's cost for this transaction would be the cash it otherwise would have received if it had sold the shares at the current market price to investors. But this situation is not analogous to that of the issuance of employee stock options.

Not only are employee stock options issued exclusively to employees of the issuer, but each employee stock option is written for a specific individual. Thus, there is, by definition, no market into which these options can be sold.

Another significant problem is the accurate valuation of stock options. While there is a diversity of opinion on the merits of requiring the expensing of employee stock options, there is uniform agreement on at least one aspect of this debate: it is extremely difficult to value those options. This gives rise to concerns that strike at the heart of financial statements: what use are they if not for purposes of comparing one company's statement against another's?

The FASB itself recognizes that there is no options-pricing model that gives an accurate assessment of the value of options across all enterprises. The Black-Scholes model has been shown to have significant deficiencies for purposes of valuing employee stock options. The Binomial method has similar problems. FASB's solution is to provide no guidance as to what method a company must use to calculate value.

The lack of a uniform, reliable valuation method creates problems of comparability among companies, accuracy of the financial statements themselves, and, as one of our witnesses today suggests, even opens up the possibility of manipulation of earnings by management. These are concerns that merit further consideration.

But, as Craig Barrett, the CEO of Intel, has observed, whether or not stock options should be expensed is not just an accounting issue. It is also an economic issue. And that is the focus of today's hearing.

Preserving the independence of the Financial Accounting Standards Board is a consideration. That's an issue of process and jurisdiction, and certainly the members of this panel have a great respect for FASB's expertise. However, some issues go beyond that of accounting and enter the mainstream of economic policy. If it is true that the adoption of FASB's employee stock option expensing rule would cause significant and serious damage to job creation, then it becomes an economic policy issue and one that Congress should certainly review.

Dozens of chief executives have publicly stated that their firms will reduce or eliminate options if the FASB proposal is enacted in order to avoid the negative impact that expensing will have on earnings per share (and, in turn, the company's share price). If this is the case, then shareholders and our economy as a whole will sacrifice some measure of economic growth.

The venture capital community has been quite outspoken on this issue. One of our witnesses today discusses the great extent to which venture-backed companies rely on stock options to attract and retain talent. He also points out that in over 70 percent of venture-backed companies, stock options were awarded to all employees, not just the top executives. These companies are a significant component of our economy. He cites statistics illustrating that venture-backed companies directly or indirectly accounted for 27 million jobs in 2000, and had sales constituting about 11 percent of the GDP.

These are compelling figures. If the FASB proposal will undermine job creation and economic growth, then it calls for closer scrutiny by Congress.

The Congressional Budget Office study concluded that expensing employee stock options will not have a significant effect on the economy. The study argues that the information has already been disclosed in footnoted financial statements and thus is reflected in the stock price. We will examine today whether this analysis is correct.

While there are many informed experts on both sides of this issue, there are some aspects of this debate on which there is agreement. First, expensing employee stock options is not a silver bullet for achieving better corporate governance. And second, the importance of transparent, accurate financial statements cannot be overstated.

I look forward to hearing from our esteemed panel of experts today as we consider the far-reaching implications of FASB's proposal.

###

April 21, 2004

Opening Statement by Congressman Paul E. Gillmor
House Financial Services Committee
Subcommittee on Capital Markets, Insurance, and Government Sponsored Enterprises
Hearing entitled, "The FASB Stock Options Proposal: Its Effect on the U.S. Economy and Jobs"

Thank you, Mr. Chairman, for holding this hearing and allowing our Committee an opportunity to discuss the Financial Accounting Standards Board's (FASB) recently released Exposure Draft on their proposal to require firms to recognize the fair value of employee stock options as an expense.

I also anticipate that at today's hearing, we will discuss the Congressional Budget Office (CBO) Paper released on April 4, 2004 entitled, "Accounting for Employee Stock Options," and its important findings. As the CBO Paper details in its summary,

> If firms do not recognize as an expense the fair value of employee stock options, measured when the options are granted, the firms' reported net income will be overstated... Although complicated to calculate, the fair value of employee stock options may be estimated as reliably as many other expenses.

The CBO Paper goes on to address the subject of today's hearing, the effect of FASB's new proposal on the U.S. economy, with its conclusion that "[r]ecognizing the fair value of employee stock options is unlikely to have a significant effect on the economy."

I applaud FASB for their continued hard work on this issue and for the release of their Exposure Document on March 31, 2004 and have included, in the submitted text of my opening statement, a letter I received from the Ohio Public Employees Retirement System (OPERS) expressing their strong support for FASB's proposal.

The Ohio Public Employees Retirement System is the 10th largest state pension fund in the United States, a $58.7 billion fund, serving three quarters of a million Ohioans. As their Executive Director, Laurie Hacking, states,

> Investor interests are best served when financial reporting provides useful information that is reliable and accurately depicts the underlying economics of events and transactions that have occurred. Achieving this reporting objective

> requires that FASB be neutral as it relates to the economic consequences of its accounting standards. Financial information should be reported in accordance with standards that assist investors in making rational decisions about capital allocation among various investment opportunities.

U.S. Financial markets remain the envy of the world due to the quality, timeliness and credibility of the financial information and disclosures provided by companies. The result is better allocation of resources and lower overall cost of capital. We here in Congress must ensure that this remains the case by allowing our standard-setter to operate independent of public and private special interests.

As we discuss FASB's proposal, I continue to encourage my colleagues to support the position that the role of FASB is to pursue transparency and accuracy in accounting standards, not to choose among competing public policies. We should not be setting accounting standards on a political basis.

Again, thank you Mr. Chairman for calling this hearing and I look forward to a thorough debate.

APR 1 4 2004

OPERS Ohio Public Employees Retirement System

277 East Town Street Columbus, Ohio 43215-4642 1-800-222-PERS (7377) www.opers.org

April 13, 2004

The Honorable Paul Gillmor
U.S. House of Representatives
1203 Longworth House Office Building
Washington, DC 20515-3505

Re: Financial Accounting Standards Board, Exposure Draft regarding Proposed Statement of Financial Accounting Standards (on stock option expensing) issued March 31, 2004, File Reference No. 1102-100

Dear Congressman Gillmor:

The Ohio Public Employees Retirement System (OPERS) is a $58.7 billion fund serving three quarters of a million Ohioans, making the system the 10th largest state pension fund in the U.S. On March 31, 2004, the Financial Accounting Standards Board (FASB) released its long anticipated Stock Option Expensing Exposure Draft that proposes companies deduct the cost of options from income, using a method based on fair value. We are writing to you to again express our views on H.R. 3574, "Stock Option Accounting Reform Act" and to urge Congress not to prevent the Financial Accounting Standards Board from doing its job of independently setting U.S. accounting standards. We believe that this pending legislation should be withdrawn and that the authority of FASB not be undermined by this legislation.

We strongly disagree with claims by opponents that there is no meaningful way to value employee stock options. First, FASB is only requiring that companies reflect the cost of employee compensation. FASB is not taking a position on whether or not companies should issue options. In fact, there is no rational reason not to treat options as an expense like other forms of compensation such as salaries, cash bonuses, restricted stock, and benefits. Second, the fair value of an option can be measured just as accurately as other items currently measured under the accrual accounting method.

Investor interests are best served when financial reporting provides useful information that is reliable and accurately depicts the underlying economics of events and transactions that have occurred. Achieving this reporting objective requires that FASB be neutral as it relates to the economic consequences of its accounting standards. Financial information should be reported in accordance with standards that assist investors in making rational decisions about capital allocation among various investment opportunities.

April 13, 2004
Page 2

We strongly support the FASB Expensing Stock Options Exposure Draft and urge you to act in the best interests of the capital markets, investors, the existing accounting standards setting process, and the public interest.

Thank you for providing us this opportunity to comment on this important and timely issue. Please feel free to contact Cynthia L. Richson, Corporate Governance Officer, at 614/222-0398, crichson@opers.org, or Jim Miller, legislative consultant, at james3558@earthlink.net should you need any additional information.

Sincerely,

Laurie Fiori Hacking

Laurie Hacking
Executive Director

OPENING REMARKS OF THE HONORABLE RUBEN HINOJOSA
HOUSE FINANCIAL SERVICES COMMITTEE
SUBCOMMITTEE ON CAPITAL MARKETS
THE FASB STOCK OPTIONS PROPOSAL: ITS EFFECT ON THE U.S. ECONOMY AND JOBS"
APRIL 21, 2004

Chairman Baker and Ranking Member Kanjorski,

I want to thank you for holding this very important and timely hearing.

Chairman Baker, I want to note, first and foremost, that I am a cosponsor of your legislation H.R. 3574, the "Stock Option Accounting Reform Act," and I remain an ardent supporter of this legislation despite FASB's March 31st proposed rulemaking that would require companies to report, as an expense, the value of stock topions they give to executives and rank-and-file employees.

In fact, FASB's recent proposed Rulemaking demonstrates how important it is that Congress pass your legislation, particularly Section 3 of your bill. Section 3 would prohibit the SEC from recognizing as "generally accepted" any accounting principle established by a "standard-setting-body" relating to the expensing of stock options pending the completion of an economic impact study by the Secretary of Commerce and the Secretary of Labor.

What everyone here needs to recognize is that stock options are an important tool to attract talent to new ventures and that mandatory expensing of stock options will stifle their issuance, reduce company profits, and deter innovation and economic growth. FASB's proposed rulemaking likely would result in the disappearance of stock options. The disappearance of stock options will inhibit a company's ability to attract and retain skilled employees.

If the FASB rule takes effect, many companies will stop issuing options to their rank-and-file employees. There is no reliable or accurate formula to properly value them, contrary to what FASB contends.

I want to include in my comments concerns that I see in global competition with large importing nations like China. Mr. Chairman, the Chinese government has incorporated stock options into its five-year economic plan to boost its technology industry.

As a Member of the House Manufacturing Caucus, I know all too well that many of America's manufacturing jobs have already been outsourced to China, thus negatively impacting the U.S. economy.

FASB's proposed rulemaking poses a similar risk in that venture capital companies and high-tech companies might relocate to China or other "stock-option-friendly-nations" if registered companies are required to expense their stock options.

Mr. Chairman, I want to work with you and the other cosponsors of your legislation to at least delay the implementation of FASB's proposed rulemaking, either by passing your legislation as a stand-alone measure, or working together to incorporate it into other legislation to ensure its passage.

Hopefully, we will succeed in this endeavor.

I yield back the balance of my time.

OPENING STATEMENT OF
RANKING DEMOCRATIC MEMBER PAUL E. KANJORSKI

SUBCOMMITTEE ON CAPITAL MARKETS, INSURANCE, AND GOVERNMENT SPONSORED ENTERPRISES

THE FASB STOCK OPTIONS PROPOSAL: ITS EFFECT ON THE U.S. ECONOMY AND JOBS

WEDNESDAY, APRIL 21, 2004

Mr. Chairman, we meet for the third time in the 108th Congress to study the accounting treatment of stock options. As I have noted at our past hearings, stock options have played an important role in the ongoing success of many American businesses and the creation of wealth for many American households. The accounting treatment of stock options, however, has also caused significant controversy for more than two decades.

At the end of March, the Financial Accounting Standards Board released its much-anticipated proposed rule on the accounting treatment of equity-based compensation. Among other things, this proposal includes a provision requiring most companies to begin recognizing the fair value of stock options as an expense at the time they are granted. This autonomous body, as I understand, now plans to hold a series of forums and meetings to solicit suggestions on ways to improve the proposal prior to the conclusion of the comment period at the end of June. It also hopes to finalize a new standard on stock options expensing by the year's end.

As we proceed today, I must caution my colleagues once again about the ongoing need to protect the independence of the Financial Accounting Standards Board. A decade ago, the Congress unfortunately strong-armed this private regulatory body into abandoning its efforts to adopt a rule requiring stock options expensing. We now know that this retreat contributed to the financial storm on Wall Street in 2001 and 2002.

In recent weeks, I have received a number of letters from some noteworthy parties concerning the desirability of maintaining the Financial Accounting Standards Board's independence. The American Institute of Certified Public Accountants, for example, asserts that setting accounting standards "must remain in the private sector" in order to protect investors. It further emphasizes that the Financial Accounting Standards Board should be allowed to complete its rulemaking process on stock options "without the intervention of Congress."

In another recent letter that I received from the chief executives of our Nation's four largest accounting firms, they urged us to "preserve the independence" of the Financial Accounting Standards Board. They also advised us to "avoid legislation that would have the effect of restricting" the organization's ability to determine accounting standards. Additional letters to me from Grant Thornton and BDO Seidman make similar points.

Mr. Chairman, I agree with the prudent observations of these leading accounting professionals. In my view, deciding what should be accounted for and how it should be accounted is the job of the Financial Accounting Standards Board, not the Congress.

Today's hearing focuses on the potential economic effects of the proposal to mandate the expensing of stock options. As we examine these matters, we are fortunate to have the head of the Congressional Budget Office with us. In a recent study, his agency determined that the proposed standard is "unlikely to have a significant effect on the economy" and that it could actually make it more productive. Many of our other witnesses, however, have reached a different conclusion about the economic effects of the expensing proposal.

Mr. Chairman, despite my strong reservations about interfering with the autonomy of the Financial Accounting Standards Board, I recognize that you may ultimately decide to mark up H.R. 3574, the Stock Option Accounting Reform Act. Before you make such a determination, it is my earnest hope that you will convene at least one more hearing on these matters so that we can learn directly the views of the Financial Accounting Standards Board and the Securities and Exchange Commission. Representatives from neither of these entities have appeared before our panel to testify since the issuance of the most recent stock options expensing proposal, and our analysis would be improved and fortified if we learned of their perspectives on these matters.

In closing, Mr. Chairman, to strengthen investor confidence we must allow the Financial Accounting Standards Board to proceed without political interference as it works to consider the issue of stock options expensing. I also look forward to hearing from our witnesses regarding these matters and yield back the balance of my time.

TESTIMONY OF ROBERT E. GRADY
MANAGING DIRECTOR, CARLYLE VENTURE PARTNERS, and
MEMBER OF THE BOARD OF DIRECTORS,
NATIONAL VENTURE CAPITAL ASSOCIATION ("NVCA")
BEFORE THE
SUBCOMMITTEE ON CAPITAL MARKETS, INSURANCE AND GOVERNMENT-SPONSORED ENTERPRISES
COMMITTEE ON FINANCIAL SERVICES
U.S. HOUSE OF REPRESENTATIVES
WASHINGTON, D.C.
APRIL 21, 2004

Good morning, Mr. Chairman and Members of the Subcommittee. My name is Robert Grady, and I am a Managing Director of the Carlyle Group, one of the world's largest private equity firms, and I am a member of the Board of Directors of the National Venture Capital Association ("NVCA"), which represents the majority of venture capital firms in the country. I have also served, for the last decade, on the faculty of the Stanford Graduate School of Business, where I am a Lecturer in Public Management. On behalf of the NVCA, thank you for the opportunity to appear before you this morning to discuss the Exposure Draft of the Financial Accounting Standards Board (the "FASB") regarding *Share-Based Payment,* which of course includes its proposal for the mandatory expensing of stock options.

The FASB has asked for comment on this exposure draft and our comment is simple. This proposal is inappropriate, incorrect as a matter of either financial or accounting theory, poorly thought out, and unworkable. In fact, it is surprising how little credence the FASB has given to either proper accounting treatment for options in the private company context, or the practical implementation issues that surround its proposal in the real world, where the use of broad-based employee stock option plans among by many thousands of private venture capital-backed companies in the Unties States is prevalent, and where the FASB has come up with no workable proposal to value those options or to address the increased uncertainty and unreliability that its proposal will introduce into income statement accounting. Instead, FASB has chosen to ignore the un-workability of its proposal so that it could respond in an entirely political fashion to what it perceives as a political issue. This is deeply disappointing, as it seems to be inconsistent with the mission of the FASB. Moreover, while the FASB's proposal may feel good in the short-term, in the long-term it is a disaster.

Before I comment directly on the Exposure Draft, please let me offer some statistics that make clear the typical real world use of stock options in our economy today. I am here today to speak on behalf of America's venture capitalists, firms that provide risk capital to job-creating companies, most of which do not have the resources or the history to borrow from banks or other debt providers or the size to raise capital in the public equity markets. The one thing they do have is the ability to create jobs as they seek to turn the innovative ideas of today into the big companies of tomorrow. The two funds I directly manage, established in 1997 and 2002 respectively, continue to have investments in 38 startup companies that today employ over 4,000 people. In the private companies on whose board I sit – Blackboard in Washington, DC; Panasas in Fremont, California; USBX in Los Angeles; Secure Elements in Herndon, Virginia; and Ingenio, in San Francisco, California – incentive stock options are granted to every employee, from the receptionist to the CEO.

This is typical in the venture capital world. According to a recent survey by our association, the NVCA, in over 70% of venture-backed companies, stock options were awarded to ALL employees.

The standard type of grant in venture-backed companies is a grant that is vested to encourage the employee to continue to work at the company over time. A very typical structure, that commonly in use most venture-backed companies today, calls for an option grant to vest over four years – with so-called "cliff vesting" of one quarter of the options granted vesting on the first anniversary of the grant, and then monthly vesting of the remaining three quarters of the grant on a straight-line basis over the next three years. This is important, because under the FASB's Exposure Draft, the normal grant of stock options, the one used by virtually every venture-backed company in America, would have to be valued 37 different times – per grant! Somehow, the FASB believes this will make financial statements more understandable.

Members of the Subcommittee might wonder if venture-backed companies are a tiny subset of American business, but they are not. According to study performed for the NVCA by Wharton Econometrics/Decision Resources ("DRI-WEFA"), in year 2000 venture-backed companies directly employed 12 million Americans, and directly or indirectly accounted for 27 million jobs. Venture-backed companies had sales of over $1.1 trillion, or about 11% of GDP. They had higher than average R&D expenditures as a percent of sales and patents generated per employee or per dollar of sales. They employed people in 49 of the 50 states. And all of these benefits occurred on far less than 11% of the capital invested in businesses in the United States – the companies have secured a number closer to 1% of the invested capital in the relevant time period. In short, Mr. Chairman, venture-backed companies are the job-creating machines of the American economy.

With that as background, let us now turn to the FASB's Exposure Draft and how its policies will work – or not work – if implemented.

First, I feel compelled to start with a fundamental conceptual point. Options are shares, or units of ownership. They are not claims of cash, or uses of the company's assets. They should be treated and disclosed as such: shares – in the denominator, if you will, of the Earnings Per Share (EPS) calculation. If the FASB were proposing in this Exposure Draft that when companies, public or private, report earnings per share, they be required to use a fully diluted share count, including all options outstanding, in the denominator, I believe that would be a fair and conceptually correct proposal.

This point is essential. At its heart, what this debate is all about is that many Americans (and people all over the world, for that matter), are willing to trade off cash compensation in favor of ownership. Our start-up companies are populated with people who are willing to work for "a piece of the rock". They are willing to earn less cash today, and thereby create less in terms of ongoing expenses by the company, so that over the long-term they can make the company worth more, because they are owners. They are thinking like owners. And this is a good thing for all those who choose to join them as shareholders along the way – because their interests are aligned as mutual owners of the securities of the company.

Even for those who believe that options are an expense, a rule which provided both formats – income statements with non-expensing, combined with pro forma footnote disclosure of the effect of expensing options, would allow such investors to see the effect and the magnitude of the purported expense.

Ironically, proponents of expensing say that requiring it will not have the dire effects on companies many predict because investors will merely strip out the effect of expensing to look at cash EPS. In other words, they will ignore GAAP, precisely because it will not be representative of the company's true expenses, and look to other measures. So the irony of the FASB's proposal is that it is likely to undermine confidence in and use of GAAP – which one presumes to be the exact opposite of the intended effect.

In the gymnastics the FASB has had to go through to get over this fundamental point – in trying to define units of ownership as expenses instead of shares – the FASB has tripped over numerous obstacles that simply underline why its proposal is flawed at the conceptual and accounting level.

The first obstacle is trying to define the appropriate measurement date at which to value the option. The FASB has suggested that the grant date is appropriate. The problem with this, of course, is that the value of the option at grant date is highly uncertain. It may never vest, because the employee may leave. It may never be exercised, because the stock may never be "in the money" in the appropriate time frame. This problem exists even for public companies.

For example, Intel has reported that it awarded options in 2000, 2001, and 2002, which, if option expensing had been required, would have required the taking of charges against income into the several billions of dollars, for options that remain underwater. An option remaining underwater is of course not exercised. The shares in question never exist – they are never issued. Yet FASB's proposal for expensing would require Intel to report these non-existent option shares in an identical fashion to what it would report if it spent billions of dollars of company cash. It is extremely difficult to understand how such a charge would make Intel's income statement more reliable. It is obvious that expensing would make income statements less reliable not more reliable.

Moving the measurement date to exercise date presents other difficulties. This would simply penalize the most successful companies – or those with the brightest prospects.

Consider the case of two companies, with identical revenues, an identical set of cash expenses, which have granted an identical number of options. The only difference between the two companies is that, because of good performance, one's stock price has grown substantially between grant date and exercise date and the other's has stagnated. The better performing company will have its income reduced sharply by nothing other than its superior stock performance. The poorly performing company will show higher "profits" because its stock has languished. The Subcommittee, and the FASB, may wish to consider the question of how this is in any way good for investors.

The second obstacle is in trying to determine what an option -- which is exactly that, an option to purchase stock -- which is most often granted at the fair market value of the stock, is worth at the date of grant. FASB has stated in its Exposure Draft that the market price of the option is the best indication of its fair value. But what about options which have never traded? The value of these must be modeled – and the choice of model and of methodology leads to radically different assessments of value.

The most common model currently in use today, of course, is the Black-Scholes model, named for the late Fisher Black and my former colleague on the Stanford Business School Faculty, Myron Scholes. Black-Scholes, of course, requires the use of several different inputs. Different inputs will yield different outcomes. So, once again, the use of models will decrease the reliability of income statements, not increase the reliability thereof.

This problem is especially difficult to overcome for private companies. So a third obstacle on which FASB has tripped is that its plan is totally inappropriate and unworkable for private companies. As a general matter, employee stock options in these companies have no trading history. Moreover, the underlying stocks of the companies have no trading history. In addition, in most cases, they are highly restricted. Even if there were a market in the options, many could not be traded. They are subject to vesting, as I have described, in an effort to retain employees. And most options granted to employees cannot be transferred, hedged, pledged or sold.

FASB implicitly argues in its Exposure Draft that no restrictions that exist during the vesting period – typically four years among startup companies – should be considered in valuing options. But this is utterly inconsistent with FASB's stated objective of recording options at fair value. Clearly an option subject to vesting restrictions is worth less than an option not subject to restrictions, yet FASB would have us record them at the same price.

A related fourth obstacle is that all of the methodologies for valuing options which have been traditionally used, on which the FASB's proposal is based, or on which it is seeking comment, rely on some estimate of volatility of the company's underlying stock price to determine the value of the option. In the case of private companies, the stock has of course never traded! So any estimate of volatility will be a guess. Moreover, the FASB Exposure Draft actually states that companies should be required to consider the extent to which "future experience is reasonably expected to differ from historical experience" in estimating volatility. It will be subject to manipulation and inaccuracy. Since the estimate of volatility will be subjective, so will the "expense" associated with the options. It would seem that the FASB should want more objective, not more subjective, income statement reporting.

Fifth, because of the problems outlined above in estimating the fair value of options, FASB's proposal would allow private companies to elect the use of the "intrinsic value" method for valuing options. Under this methodology, the value of the option is adjusted for each reporting period. This form of variable accounting would change the value of any given grant in every quarter, depending in stock price – or in the case of private companies, depending on an estimate of stock price. It would be massively confusing.

Finally, in seeking to identify the proper time period to which to attribute the expense that its Exposure Draft would require to be recorded, the FASB introduces and trips over new hurdles and obstacles. For example, options which vest on a graded schedule similar to the four year schedule I described earlier in my testimony – one quarter vesting after one year and one-forty-eighth vesting each month thereafter – would be viewed as 37 different option grants that a company would have to value and account for separately.

The Exposure Draft suggests that companies should group their employees for purposes of predicting exercise behavior. This would be a completely speculative exercise that would be almost preposterous in its unreliability.

In the end, Mr. Chairman, what is clear from the FASB's proposal is that it is responsive – not to the voluminous comment that has been provided by experts and actual companies, not to the obvious problems that have been pointed out both this morning and over the past two years in consultations that seem to have been ignored, but to the political process. At its heart, this is a political proposal.

It seems the FASB and Mr. Herz feel they must respond in a political fashion to the news reports of senior executives at companies like Tyco, Worldcom, or Adelphia looting their companies and overseeing the preparation of false accounting statements. And there should be a response to these atrocities – if found guilty, the individuals responsible should go to jail. But the fact that dishonest people have stolen money from their companies and their shareholders is not related to how companies, especially private companies, should account for units of ownership granted for purchase by employees because they believe in their company's mission and prospects.

In fact, just this week, the FASB Chairman Mr. Herz basically confirmed that he was embarked on an explicitly political course. On a conference call with press and investors on Monday, April 19th, he said, according to Dow Jones, that investors and analysts should make sure that "you make your views known to people in Washington."

Because the FASB has chosen an entirely political course, we at the NVCA believe that the political system should engage the debate and at least come forward with a proposal that is responsible from an accounting perspective, more accurate from a financial reporting perspective, and not likely to lead to mass confusion in the real world where investors and companies live.

In this regard, the NVCA believes that the legislation proposed by the Chairman of the Subcommittee, Representative Baker, H.R. 3574, represents a responsible approach that addresses some of the most obvious and egregious problems created by the FASB Exposure Draft. H.R. 3574 would exempt private companies from the requirement to expense employee stock options – which makes sense given the impossibility, as outlined above, of estimating the volatility of securities which have never, and may never, trade publicly, and therefore of accurately valuing options of privately held companies. It would also exempt companies from this requirement during their first three years as public companies, while a trading history is being established which makes an estimate of volatility more possible and less subject to manipulation or pure guesswork.

The NVCA has also previously endorsed the legislation which had been sponsored by Representatives Eshoo and Dreier, which would place a three-year moratorium on the requirement to expense stock options while more work is done to address the difficulties I have outlined above in accurately valuing options. In addition, both the Chairman's bill and the Dreier-Eshoo bill appropriately call for a study of the impacts of expensing on the U.S. economy. As I stated at the outset, startup companies that offer employees ownership have been some of the most job-creating enterprises in our entire economy, so it is appropriate to study the impact of disrupting this spectacularly successful system for before doing so for ill-thought-out political reasons.

Mr. Chairman, on behalf of the venture capital community and the start-up companies in which we invest, we appreciate the opportunity to appear before the Subcommittee this morning. We hope that the Congress will act now to take a more measured approach to this question and to address the multitude of problems associated with the FASB's ill-considered proposal.

Thank you.

# # #

Testimony Submitted

To

United States House of Representatives

Committee on Financial Services

April 21, 2004

Kevin A. Hassett*

AEI

* Kevin A. Hassett is Director of Economic Policy Studies at the American Enterprise Institute

Mr. Chairman, it is an honor to appear before you today to discuss the impact of options policy on publicly traded firms and the economy. I should say at the outset that my testimony will draw heavily on a recent publication that I coauthored with my colleague Peter Wallison.[1]

Overview

Since the Enron collapse in mid-2002, the Financial Accounting Standards Board (FASB) has been pressed to require that companies include the hypothetical expense of their employee stock options in their Generally Accepted Accounting Principles (GAAP) financial statements. Many lawmakers and commentators on financial matters have made public statements to the effect that employee stock options are a form of compensation, and the failure to show the cost of these instruments results in misleading financial reports.[2] In response, it appears that the FASB is set to require expensing despite significant disagreement among professionals on how to calculate that expense.

I will go into this case in more detail below, but it may be useful to wade through all of the technical jargon and give an example that highlights the state of affairs that is described in my testimony.

Suppose that a publicly traded publisher finished production of a book in December of 2003 and expected to release it in 2004. Some investors may read the book, become convinced that it might be a huge hit, and then buy the stock. Others might read it and think that it will be a bomb, and decide to sell the stock. The financial market---the most efficient "computer" on earth---will allow individuals on both sides to trade. If more money believes that the book will be a hit, the price of the company will likely rise. The accounting earnings in 2003, however, are only part of the calculus.

Now suppose that Washington policy makers decide that it is bad for investors that publishers have earnings that are so difficult to predict. FASB might require that firms construct a forecast of expected earnings for finished books carried into 2004 and include that in their top-line reported earnings for 2003. If there is no accepted model to forecast book success, then firms will have to struggle with their forecast. Which model should they choose?

Does this requirement help small investors? Putting the forecast into top line earnings will likely be counterproductive, making uninformed investors feel that the revenue forecast is more reliable than it is since the idea has been endorsed by FASB.

---

[1] Hassett, Kevin A. and Peter Wallison, "A Troubling Requirement," *Regulation Magazine,* Vol. 27, No. 1, pg. 52-58 (forthcoming 2004)

[2] Bodie, Kaplan and Merton (2002) provide a recent summary of the arguments in favor of expensing options.

When the forecasts turn out to be incorrect, as they invariably will, then the trial bar will use it as an excuse to sue. "Model A might have provided a better forecast *ex ante*," an accuser might say, "why did you chose Model B to forecast book revenues?" And the rule may have a real effect on activity, leading firms not to finish movies in one year if they hope to release it in the next.

Stock options play an important role in the financial structure of firms, especially start-up firms. These firms are required to release information concerning the options, and the efficient market digests that information and incorporates it into price. Exactly how the market finds the right price is a mystery, yet I am unaware of any data that suggests that the market misprices firms that rely on stock options. If we introduce into this picture the requirement that firms include an admittedly flawed estimate of options expense, it is hard to imagine how we are making things better. Indeed, there are reasons to believe that the requirement may discourage option use, taking away a valuable tool from our most entrepreneurial firms.

Some Background

Prior to the renewed interest in this question, the applicable rule—embodied in Statement of Financial Accounting Standard (SFAS) 123, issued in October 1995—required that the hypothetical compensation cost of employee stock options should be recorded at "fair value" as an expense in corporate income statements.

"Fair value" is a term of art in accounting that refers generally to the price at which a willing buyer and willing seller would trade an asset.[3] In recent years, accounting theorists have encouraged the use of fair value estimates for assets and liabilities, replacing valuations previously based on cost.[4] Fair value can be established with reference to a market price for an asset or a liability, or—in the absence of a market—through reference to markets for similar items or "option pricing models, matrix pricing, option-adjusted spread models, and fundamental analysis."

Because there is no reference market for employee stock options, SFAS 123 offered companies two ways of presenting their financial reports under Generally Accepted Accounting Principles (GAAP):

---

[3] In a Project Update of October 1, 2003, the FASB redefined "fair value" more precisely as "the amount at which an asset or liability could be exchanged in a current transaction between knowledgeable unrelated willing parties when neither is acting under compulsion." The Board also noted, "All estimates of fair value should maximize market inputs (observable market prices and market assumptions) for the item being measured...In general, the more market inputs the more reliable the estimate. Reliability encompasses representational faithfulness, neutrality, and verifiability."

[4] See, generally, discussion of fair value accounting in George J. Benston, "The Quality of Corporate Financial Statements and Their Auditors before and after Enron," Cato Institute, Policy Analysis No. 497, November 6, 2003.

- A company could use an option-pricing model—SFAS 123 specifically referred to Black-Scholes or a "binomial model"—for estimating the fair value of its options; in this case, the options' estimated value, as established by these models, was to be deducted as an expense in computing the company's earnings per share (EPS).

- Alternatively, a company could use the so-called "intrinsic value method" for estimating the fair value of its options. This method was simply the difference between the option strike price and the value of the underlying shares on the date of grant. Since in most cases the numbers were the same, the intrinsic value method resulted in no options expense in the computation of EPS. However, if a company chose the intrinsic value method, it was required by SFAS 123 to show, in a footnote to its financial statements, the hypothetical or pro forma effect on EPS of the issuance of the options, using Black-Scholes or the binomial option-pricing model.

Since 1995, most companies have chosen to use the intrinsic value method for establishing the fair value of their employee stock options, and have used the Black-Scholes options-pricing model for making the required pro forma disclosure in the footnotes to their financial reports. Accordingly, for the most part, the EPS of public companies in the United States have not reflected the hypothetical or fair value costs of their employee stock options. Instead, this has been disclosed in the footnotes to financial statements.[5]

---

[5] Reproduced below is the footnote disclosure of Morgan Stanley concerning the effect of applying SFAS 123 on its net income and EPS, as contained in its 10-K annual report for 2002:

Pro Forma Effect of SFAS No. 123. Had the Company elected to recognize compensation cost pursuant to SFAS No. 123 for its stock option plans and its employee stock purchase plan, net income would have been reduced by $250 million, $375 million and $488 million for fiscal 2002, fiscal 2001 and fiscal 2000, respectively, resulting in pro forma net income and earnings per share as follows:

	Fiscal 2002	Fiscal 2001	Fiscal 2000
	(dollars in millions, except per share data)		
Net income			
As reported	$ 2,988	$ 3,521	$ 5,456
Pro forma	2,738	3,146	4,968
Earnings per share			
As reported:			
Basic	$ 2.76	$ 3.21	$ 4.95
Diluted	2.69	3.11	4.73
Pro forma:			
Basic	$ 2.53	$ 2.87	$ 4.50
Diluted	2.45	2.76	4.29

The weighted average fair value at date of grant for stock options granted during fiscal 2002, fiscal 2001 and fiscal 2000 was $19.42, $26.43 and $30.48 per option, respectively. The fair value of stock options at

Responding to the calls for expensing stock options, the FASB readily and promptly agreed that stock options are a form of compensation and that SFAS 123 should be modified so that the value of these options would be included as an expense in computing a company's EPS. Initially, the FASB seemed to believe that this could be done rather easily through use of the Black-Scholes or binomial models, but as they have gathered more information on the accuracy and effectiveness of these models—particularly Black-Scholes—the FASB has appeared to back away from mandating the use of any particular model.[6] In a meeting on September 10, 2003, the Board reaffirmed its determination to require the expensing of options in financial reports issued in 2005, but removed the reference to Black-Scholes or the binomial method from SFAS 123. In doing so, the Board stated, "the use of any specific option-pricing model would not be precluded."

This suggests that FASB is prepared to require that employee stock options be expensed without actually designating the valuation method that should be used. In light of the uncertainties associated with all existing options-pricing models, one can see how FASB might adopt this approach. The Black-Scholes model, which the Board specified as one of the acceptable methods in 1995, has been shown to have significant deficiencies for valuing long-term instruments such as employee stock options. For example, one recent study concluded that Black-Scholes systematically overvalues options, while another found that, *ex ante*, Black Scholes numbers did a poor job of predicting *ex post* realized costs.[7] This is because Black-Scholes is unsuitable for valuing instruments—such as employee stock options—that are subject to a wide variety of contractual conditions and vesting arrangements, and have extremely long durations. Moreover, as described in Calomiris and Hubbard (2003) there is significant uncertainty about the proper formula or method for valuing employee stock options. Drawing on the discussion in Campbell, Lo and Mackinlay (1997) they document that uncertainty concerning the proper model of the underlying asset price is so high among financial economists, that ever more complicated and opaque methods---such as kernal density estimation and neural networks---have been utilized to provide a more accurate picture of the value of options. If financial economists are still uncertain how to value these options,

---

date of grant was estimated using the Black-Scholes option pricing model utilizing the following weighted average assumptions:

	Fiscal 2002	Fiscal 2001	Fiscal 2000
Risk-free interest rate	3.8%	4.7%	5.6%
Expected option life in years	6.2	6.1	5.3
Expected stock price volatility	50.7%	48.4%	43.4%
Expected dividend yield	1.9%	1.5%	1.1%

[6] Warren Buffet and Charles Munger recently put the Black Scholes critique quite succinctly in the Financial Times, saying, "The minute you get into longer-term options....its crazy to use Black Scholes." Bates, (1995) concludes that "substantial biases have been found in implicit volatilities from stock options" and speculates on the causes of the observed deviations between option prices and time series.

[7] See Financial Executive Research Foundation (2003), and Mollen, Harper and Burchman (2003)

FASB will undoubtedly have difficulty specifying a method. The essential difficulty is that there are many competing valuation candidates, each with pros and cons, which produce widely varying results depending on the specific circumstances of individual firms.

Although the debate over whether to expense employee stock options has thus far largely turned on the question of what would be the most useful financial disclosure for investors—and whether discouraging the use of stock options would be good economic or financial policy—the absence of any reliable or accepted method for establishing the value of employee stock options raises two significant issues that undercut the FASB's arguments for its position. First, the absence of any satisfactory method for estimating the value of employee stock options, when combined with a requirement that this uncertain and unascertainable value be included in computing EPS, appears to be inconsistent with the principles and objectives of accounting itself and could create considerable legal risks for companies. Second, and perhaps equally important, the absence of any reliable formula for ascertaining the value of employee stock options calls into question whether any fair value analysis is appropriate for use in this context.

By forcing companies to place values on their employee stock options, before deciding on a method for doing so, the FASB is making a serious error that will impair the quality of financial statements, violate basic principles of accounting, and lead to a rise in costly but meritless lawsuits. The more prudent and sensible course for the FASB, in our view, would be to focus its efforts on developing a satisfactory method of valuing these instruments. Only after this has been accomplished would it make sense to require that companies include the theoretical expense of employee stock options in their GAAP income statements.

Why Expense?

The conceptual roots of the drive to expense employee stock options can be found in the view that, by issuing stock options, companies are able to avoid the cash expense associated with other methods of employee compensation.[8] Thus, a company that might have to pay $500,000 in salary to attract an executive might be able to acquire his or her services for half that amount with an offer of stock options. From the employee's point of view the trade might be worth the difference in cash compensation because she believes that the company has good prospects for substantial share growth. The employee may also believe that she can enhance the likelihood or extent of that growth. In this example, the company has saved a hypothetical $250,000 by issuing stock options that do not appear—as would cash salary—as an expense on its income statement. The income statement, it is argued, thus understates the company's costs in producing its income and overstates the company's real earnings.

---

[8] Core and Guay (2001) find evidence that financially constrained firms rely more heavily on stock options. However, many large and highly profitable firms rely upon them as well. This likely reflects the fact that options can serve many different functions in addition to helping firms reduce the impact of liquidity contstraints, such as encouraging retention.

This is a fairly straightforward idea, and has been the basis of testimony to Congress by members of the FASB,[9] explaining why they believe the expensing of options is necessary. But as a concept this approach has significant flaws.

This is especially true if options are an effective compensation device for encouraging retention, which is often cited by managers as a key reason for their use. Employee turnover is costly to a firm in many ways, and an option may lower these expected future costs. In addition, firms with higher retention rates may be more attractive work places, lowering the required level of cash compensation that must be offered to lure desirable employees to a firm.

Since the theory is framed in terms of the value of the options in reducing the salary costs of the employer, it is not clear that some objective valuation for the options—their estimated fair value—is truly ascertainable. Fair value, by definition, is what a willing buyer and a willing seller would pay for the asset, and that is what was supposed to be measured by Black-Scholes or the binomial method, but that is not the value of the option *to the employee*. One reason for that of course is that he or she is in most cases not able to sell the option, so there is a liquidity discount that would be appropriate in valuing the option. But there are other reasons, too. A willing buyer and a willing seller would have to be considered diversified in their holdings of securities such as options. The employee is unlikely to be diversified, and thus the option represents a greater risk (the risk of non-diversification) to him than to the willing buyer—another reason for a discount from whatever value is established by Black-Scholes or some other model. On the other hand, as just mentioned, an employee may find a firm that relies more heavily on options to be a more attractive workplace.

Finally, and perhaps most significant, the employee is entering into an employment relationship with the company, and will have an opportunity to affect the value of the option that the hypothetical willing buyer in an arms length market transaction will not have. Thus, the employee may believe that her efforts on the part of the company will increase the value of the option and the underlying stock, and for this reason it is possible to argue that the option is worth more to her than it would be to a willing buyer.

All this suggests that using an option-pricing formula such as Black-Scholes—even assuming that it is capable of producing an accurate value for options with the characteristics of employee stock options—is not likely to establish a fair value for these instruments. If in fact the underlying accounting reason for expensing employee stock options is to capture the amount by which a company reduces its salary costs through use of options, that result cannot be achieved by determining the price at which a willing buyer and a willing seller would transact. In this sense, in light of the definition of fair

---

[9] See Statement of Robert H. Herz, Chairman, FASB, Roundtable on "Preserving Partnership Capitalism Through Stock Options for America's Workforce," United States Senate, May 8, 2003, pp.14-18.

value used in accounting texts, employee stock options are just not suitable for fair value treatment.

To be sure, the FASB takes the position—despite the anomaly discussed above—that the value they want companies to expense is not the value of the option to the employee, but the amount that the option would fetch if it could be sold to a willing buyer instead of awarded to the employee. Although this approach creates a somewhat more objective standard than the attempting to measure the value to the employee, it bears no real relationship to the theoretical basis for seeking to capture and expense the cash savings of the employer. At best, the price that a willing buyer would pay is a weak surrogate for what the option is worth to the employee. So we have in the end a requirement to use an inadequate option-pricing model in order to determine the value of what is in any event only a shadow of the actual thing we are trying to measure. It is hard to imagine a weaker case for the use of fair value accounting.

Nevertheless, it is still possible for accounting theorists to argue that an employee stock option has *some* value—i.e., its value is not zero—and good accounting practice should recognize a value of some kind, if only to vindicate the traditional accounting concept of conservatism.[10] But this would be correct only if it is consistent with other principles of accounting; however, it seems likely that a requirement for expensing options would call into question a number of other accounting concepts—particularly the requirements for reliability, comparability and consistency.

Reliability. The Statement of Financial Accounting Concepts No. 2, published by the FASB in 1980, defines reliability as "The quality of information that assures that information is reasonably free from error and bias and faithfully represents what it purports to represent." We have already noted above that the fair value of an employee stock option—i.e., its effect in reducing the cash compensation obligations of an employer—can never be measured by a formula that attempts to estimate the price that would be paid by a willing buyer to a willing seller. Thus, that estimate of value is not one that "faithfully represents what it purports to represent." In fact, it is at best a very rough theoretical measure of what it purports to represent, which is the amount by which a company's cash compensation obligations are reduced by the issuance of employee stock options.

Indeed, the FASB has received a large number of comments from business organizations to the effect that the Black-Scholes method of estimating the fair value of options overstates option values. The January 31, 2003 comment of the Business Roundtable is typical. The group noted that the fair value methodology under consideration by FASB does not recognize a number of characteristics of employee

---

[10] Conservatism as an accounting concept is defined in the Statement of Accounting Concepts No. 2 as "A prudent reaction to uncertainty to try to ensure that uncertainty and risks inherent in business situations are adequately considered." In this context, it would mean that employee stock options must have some value to the company and to the employee—a value that should be recognized in the interest of appropriately discounting earnings—even though the exact amount is not known.

options, "all of which reduce their value: (1) non-exercisability before vesting, (2) truncated term if employment terminates after vesting but before exercise, (3) inability of employees to hedge their option position or use their options as collateral, (4) ordinary income taxation of gains at exercise, and (5) for some companies grants, black-out periods, holding periods, ownership requirements, non-compete provisions and 'claw-back' provisions."

Acknowledging that the FASB believes that the standard of measurement should be the value of the option if it had been sold to a willing buyer—rather than its more subjective value to the employee—the Roundtable was still concerned that no model currently in existence could measure what an employee stock option would be worth in a hypothetical market. "Before deciding whether to propose changes to U.S. accounting standards for employee stock options," the Roundtable cautioned, "we believe the FASB should determine whether the 'fair value' of employee options, as measured by adjusted option-pricing models, reasonably estimates the foregone cash the company could have received from selling options *with the same terms* to the market." [emphasis in the original]

The Roundtable's comment makes clear that the accounting concept of reliability would be violated through use of any known options-pricing model, since none of them take adequate account of the many ways in which the value of employee stock options can be diminished by contractual terms that would affect the price at which a willing buyer and a willing seller would transact.

Quite apart from this deficiency, as noted in this testimony and in Calomiris and Hubbard (2003), even without the manifold contractual terms that alter the value of an employee stock option, there is no options-pricing model currently in existence that clearly gives the best possible assessment of the value of options across all firms. Because of these factors, whatever number is ultimately developed would have to be little more than a guess, and thus would not "faithfully represent what it purports to represent."

Reliability is also called into question by the FASB's failure to prescribe a model. This opens the possibility of management manipulation, also a factor in assessing reliability. In his Cato paper, Professor Benston notes that in order to be of value to investors financial statements must be based on "trustworthy" numbers. "Unfortunately," he writes, "a financial report based on fair values can rarely be achieved within the requirement that the numbers also be trustworthy. It is often said that that there is a trade-off between trustworthiness and relevance, but information is relevant and useful for decision-making to the degree that it is accurate and unbiased (where the bias is not known). Therefore, trustworthy numbers are more relevant than fair values that are much more subject to managerial manipulation than are historical costs."[11] Accordingly, at least with respect to the standard of reliability—or trustworthiness in Professor Benston's

---

[11] Benston, op. cit., p. 5.

terms—a fair value established for employee stock options through use of a faulty model, or one subject to management manipulation, would be less useful than no valuation at all.

It is also important to note that the FASB has itself pointed out that with respect to fair value estimates, "the more market inputs the more reliable the estimate," and that "reliability encompasses representational fairness, neutrality, and verifiability." [12] It is doubtful that a number derived from a wholly artificial model, which contains assumptions about an unknown future and is subject to management bias in the choice of the model utilized, meets any of these tests.

To be sure, defenders of the FASB's position have argued that employee stock options certainly have *some* value—"not zero," as some have noted—and failure to include this value in the computation of EPS is inherently misleading. But this is only a partial answer. The assets that Enron's management vastly overvalued probably also had *some* value. One of the arguments against fair value accounting is that it allows managements too much discretion in establishing the values of assets and liabilities. In principle, the FASB and the accounting profession should be resisting efforts to break down the standards for how fair value can be established, not requiring companies to include in their EPS numbers for which there is no adequate conceptual basis. It is not necessarily an improvement in financial reporting to substitute an arbitrary value when the actual value cannot be ascertained. Doing so impairs the credibility and trustworthiness of the financial statement, and certainly does not meet the accounting test of reliability—i.e., "faithfully representing what it purports to represent."

Consistency. The Statement of Financial Accounting Concepts No. 2 defines "consistency" as "conformity from period to period with unchanging policies and procedures." This concept would also be violated by a FASB requirement that companies estimate the fair value of their employee stock options before there is in place an agreed technology for doing so. In the minutes of a meeting on September 10, 2003, the FASB made clear that no preferred or accepted method for valuing employee stock options currently exists. The Board deleted the references to Black-Scholes and the binomial method from SFAS 123 and is recorded as deciding, "The use of any specific option-pricing model would not be precluded." The inability of the Board to specify a particular model has significant consequences that will be discussed below under "Comparability," but the absence of any accepted standard or method also has significant consequences for the concept of consistency.

Under the consistency concept in accounting, a company is supposed to report its results from period to period without changing its policies and procedures. This principle works where policies and procedures remain unchanged for extended periods, but is useless if there is a constant updating and modification required by changing accounting rules. The Board's September 10 discussion of company obligations reflects a view of at least some members of the Board that the technology of options-pricing would improve

---

[12] See note 2.

in the future. For example, according to the minutes, in a discussion of the consequences of permitting the use of models other than Black-Scholes, Board member Edward W. Trott noted that other models might be developed that would improve on Black-Scholes: "a more robust and dynamic valuation model could incorporate better information and allow for improvement of information and modeling techniques over time."

This view is likely to have been the basis for the Board's decision to reduce the focus on the Black-Scholes and the binomial model as the accepted option-pricing technologies. But leaving open the choice of models not only leaves open the possibility of management manipulation in the choice of model, it also creates the prospect that companies will be required to change modeling techniques as the technology improves over time, and this will clearly disrupt consistency of presentation.

More troubling is the position of the company that adopts one method for estimating the value of its employee stock options, but finds as it proceeds from year to year that the standard used by others—perhaps others in its industry—has changed. A new method may have been introduced that is deemed superior. Would the company be required to change the pricing model it has been using, and thus change its EPS computation? If it did this, would it be required to restate its net income and EPS for all the preceding years in which it had used the older and presumably inferior model? Later in this testimony, I discuss the legal implications of such a change, but for present purposes I note only that an evolving standard for what is the proper way to estimate the fair value of employee stock options is a serious threat to the accounting concept of consistency of presentation.

Comparability. The accounting concept of comparability is defined as "the quality of information that enables users to identify similarities in and differences between two sets of economic phenomena." For investors, adherence to the concept of comparability is essential to the process of comparing the financial results of two or more companies. Obviously, the entire conceptual structure of accounting in the United States, the collection of rules known as Generally Accepted Accounting Principles (GAAP), was developed in order to assure that companies prepare and publish their financial reports under the same set of rules. Without that, it would not be possible to compare one company with another, or even to compare a company's results in one year with those in a preceding or subsequent year.

The possibility that the FASB might require companies to estimate the value of their employee stock options without specifying a particular method for doing so presents a unique challenge to the concept of comparability. In order to compare the GAAP financial results of any two companies, investors will have to understand the options-pricing model the companies used as well as the inputs to that model. This would be a difficult process even if a particular model were specified, because investors would have to evaluate whether the values the company selected for inclusion in the model were appropriate, given the company's history and circumstances. The process would be even more difficult if the companies chose entirely different option-pricing models for this purpose.

For example, those companies that chose to use the intrinsic value method of estimating the fair value of their employee stock options have been required since the promulgation of SFAS 123 in 1995 to provide supplemental information in the footnotes to their financial statements about the assumptions they used as inputs to the model. Most have used the Black-Scholes model, and their inputs have included assumptions concerning the expected volatility of their stock, the risk-free interest rate at the date of grant, the expected option life in years, and the expected dividend yield on their stock. Several of these are obviously extremely difficult to estimate and involve unknowable future events. In reviewing various corporate financial reports it becomes clear that companies chose substantially different estimates of volatility and expected option life. Different choices for these two values can have a major impact on the expense that is attributable to employee stock options.

This example even assumes that the model chosen is correct. In practice, the underlying assumption that the share price follows a geometric Brownian motion has been demonstrated time and again to be a crude simplification (this literature dates back all the way to Mandelbrot, 1963. See Lo and Mackinlay, 1990, for a more recent contribution.) As discussed in Calomiris and Hubbard (2003), even relatively small errors in the modeling of the serial correlation of returns over time can lead Black-Scholes estimates to be off by a factor of two. Small errors are highly likely given the volatile nature of stocks, and option models have not held up particularly well when confronted with the empirical data. Bates (1995) reviews the empirical literature and concludes, "substantial biases have been found in implicit volatilities from stock and stock index options."[13] These problems suggest that reasonable and well-trained options practitioners might go about the valuation process in different ways, choose significantly different models, and arrive at significantly different values.

Under these circumstances, it would be important for investors to be able to assess the appropriateness and validity of the inputs selected by any two companies they wish to compare, but very difficult for them to do so. Assuming both companies use the Black-Scholes model, the investor might understand how the model works, but be unable to determine whether the input assumptions were reasonable. It would be a still harder task if the companies did not even use the same model—a possibility that is suggested by the FASB's recent decision that "the use of any specific option-pricing model would not be precluded."

Over time the profession may converge to a model of the data generating process and the option itself that does not vary so significantly across time and firms. While this is consistent with the idea that option-pricing technology will improve over time—a notion that seems to underlie the Board's determination to proceed—it creates a highly uncertain landscape for both companies and investors. With a wide variety of option-pricing models in use, investors will be unable to make effective comparisons of bottom line GAAP results.

---

[13] Bates (1995), p.60.

Legal risks. As discussed in many of the comments to the FASB, and in the balance of this testimony, neither of the two models that the Board initially seemed to endorse—the Black-Scholes and binomial models—has been found effective. Instead, the Board has apparently decided not to endorse a particular model, but to leave the choice up to companies and their auditors. This state of affairs creates a serious legal risk for both companies and auditors to which the Board seems oblivious. In the absence of a designated and approved method for valuing employee stock options, companies will have to make choices, not only about the model to be used but the various inputs that the model requires. These choices can have a substantial impact on the reported earnings of a company, and that in turn can leave companies open to class action lawsuits by disgruntled shareholders.

As an example, consider a company that chooses a model and makes input assumptions that reduce its reported earnings by 5 percent each year for a ten-year period. At the end of that period, looking back over the actual experience of the company, one of the following becomes clear: (i) the expense it charged to earnings was less than what its options-pricing model would have required if the inputs to the model had borne a closer resemblance to its actual experience; (ii) the options-pricing model it used was less accurate than other models that were available at the time it adopted its model; or (iii) the technology for options-pricing had evolved over the 10 year period, so that the company's model—at the state of the art when adopted—had been superseded by superior models. Any of these facts will expose the company to lawsuits based on the allegation that its earnings were overstated over many years. Shareholders who purchased shares during this period might have a cause of action based on the company's failure to correctly calculate its employee options costs.

While it is true that the securities laws require some demonstration of *scienter*—intent to mislead—before liability will attach, in the real world companies are constantly challenged with lawsuits on facts far flimsier than those recited above. And they are frequently driven to settle these suits because of the drain on management time, the adverse publicity these suits produce, or the fact that large corporations are generally unsympathetic defendants in jury trials.

Circumstances might be considerably different if the FASB were in a position to specify an options-pricing model that would be acceptable for all companies. In that case, the company would at least have the defense that it did not adopt a particular model in order to achieve favorable earnings results. However, it does not appear that the FASB is able to specify an options-pricing model, and will leave it to companies to select or develop their own models. In a sense, this is the worst of all possible worlds for public companies. They are required to estimate an important component of their EPS—the most sensitive element of their financial reports—and yet they are left without any sense of how to do it. This situation creates low hanging fruit, ripe for plucking by the class action bar.

In summary, it seems clear that the FASB has no idea how companies might be able to establish the fair value of employee stock options, but is nevertheless proceeding down the path toward requiring the expensing of options. In part, this may be the result of political pressure that originated with a misreading of the Enron and Worldcom debacles. The responsible course, consistent with the accounting concepts of reliability, consistency and comparability, would be for the Board to wait until it or some other entity has created a model for pricing employee stock options that is generally recognized as "faithfully representing what it purports to represent." To do less would open up a Pandora's box of potential lawsuits, and expose firms to vexing terrain that may adversely affect both the quality of their financial reports and the results of their operations.

In this light, it is worth noting that the current system of disclosure has much to recommend it. Given the uncertainty associated with estimating the fair value of employee stock options, it seems appropriate that disclosure occur in the footnotes to the financial statements rather than in the computation of net income. In this case, investors who are interested in what effect a company's employee stock options might have on its earnings per share can see an estimate in the footnotes, but because of the uncertainty associated with the estimate—most are now made using the inadequate Black-Scholes model—companies will not be distorting their EPS with a weakly derived number. Differences of opinion concerning the value of these options arise, and affect market prices, just as differences of opinion about other aspects of publicly traded company do. This circumstance is vastly superior to one where FASB endorses a practice it knows to be misleading in response to political pressures.

References

Bates, David S. "Testing Option Pricing Models," NBER working paper No. 5129, May 1995

Benston, George J. "The Quality of Corporate Financial Statements and Their Auditors before and after Enron," Cato Institute, Policy Analysis No. 497, November 6, 2003.

Bodie, Zvi, Kaplan, Robert S., and Merton, Robert C., "For the Last Time: Stock Options Are and Expense," Harvard Business Review, p. 3-11, March 2003

Bream, Judith, Jane Croft, and Andrew Hill, "Buffett Urges Rebellion Against Executive Greed," Financial Times, May 5, 2003

Calomiris, Charles, and Hubbard, R. Glenn, "Options Pricing Models and Accounting Practice." mimeo, Columbia University, December, 2003

Campbell, John Y. Lo, Andrew W., and Mackinlay, A. Craig, "The Econometrics of Financial Markets," Princeton University Press, 1997

Core, J.E. and W.R. Guay, "Stock Options for non-Executive Employees," Journal of Financial Economics, 61, 253-287, 2001

Financial Accounting Standards Board, "Statement of Financial Accounting Concepts No. 2: Qualitative Characteristics of Accounting Information," Norwalk, CT: FASB, 1980

———, "Statement of Financial Accounting Standard No. 123: Accounting for Stock-Based Compensation," Norwalk, CT: FASB, 1995

———, "Statement of Financial Accounting Standard No. 121: Accounting for the Impairment of Long-Lived Assets and for Long-Lived Assets to Be Disposed of," Norwalk, CT: FASB, 1995

———, "Equity Based Compensation (EBC): Valuation and Scope," Minutes, FASB Board Meeting, September 10, 2003

———, "Project Update: Fair Value Measurement Project," Norwalk, CT: FASB, 2003

Financial Executive Research Foundation, "Valuing Employee Stock Options: A Comparison of Alternative Models," Florham Park, NJ: FERF, 2003

Hassett, Kevin A. and Peter Wallison, "A Troubling Requirement," Regulation Magazine, Vol. 27, No. 1, pg. 52-58 (forthcoming 2004)

Herz, Robert H, "Preserving Partnership Capitalism Through Stock Options for America's Workforce," Statement, United States Senate, May 8, 2003, pp.14-18.

Lo, Andrew W., and Mackinlay, A. Craig, "When Are Contrarian Profits Due to Stock Market Overreaction?"Review of Financial Studies, 3, 175-208, 1990

Mandelbrot, B. "the Variation of Certain Speculative Prices," Journal of Business, 36, 394-419, 1963

Morgan Stanley Dean Witter and Co, "Annual Report," SEC Filing 001-11758, 2002

Mollen, Rodney, David Harper and Seymour Burchman, "Black-Scholes: A Failed Model for Executive Options," Perspectives, 9, issue 1 2000, http://www.imakenews.com/sibson/e_article000137189.cfm

Sanger, Stephen W., On Behalf of The Business Roundtable, "Response to FASB's Invitation to Comment on Stock Option Accounting," January 31, 2003, http://www.fasb.org/ocl/1102-001/14775.pdf

Kevin A. Hassett is Director of Economic Policy Studies and Resident Scholar at the American Enterprise Institute. Before joining AEI, Dr. Hassett was a senior economist at the Board of Governors of the Federal Reserve System and an associate professor of economics and finance at the Graduate School of Business of Columbia University. He was the chief economic advisor to John McCain during the 2000 primaries. He has also served as a policy consultant to the U.S. Department of the Treasury during both the former Bush and Clinton administrations. He holds a B.A. from Swarthmore College and a Ph.D. from the University of Pennsylvania.

Dr. Hassett is a member of the Joint Committee on Taxation's Dynamic Scoring Advisory Panel. He is the author, coauthor or editor of six books on economics and economic policy. He has published scholarly articles in the American Economic Review, the Economic Journal, the Quarterly Journal of Economics, the Review of Economics and Statistics, the Journal of Public Economics, and many other professional journals. His popular writings have been published in the Wall Street Journal, the Atlantic Monthly, USA Today, the Washington Post, and numerous other outlets. His economic commentaries are regularly aired on radio and television including recent appearances on the Today Show, the CBS Morning Show, Newshour with Jim Lehrer, Hardball, Moneyline and Power Lunch.

CONGRESS OF THE UNITED STATES
CONGRESSIONAL BUDGET OFFICE

A CBO PAPER

APRIL 2004

Accounting for Employee Stock Options

A CBO PAPER

Accounting for Employee Stock Options

April 2004

The Congress of the United States ■ Congressional Budget Office

Preface

In March 2003, the Financial Accounting Standards Board (FASB) began reconsidering the accounting standard for equity-based compensation. The accounting board released an exposure draft for a revised standard on March 31, 2004. That revised standard would require firms to recognize the fair value of employee stock options as an expense, as was first proposed by FASB more than 10 years ago.

This Congressional Budget Office (CBO) paper assesses whether, under the current accounting standard, firms that grant employee stock options without recognizing an expense overstate their reported income. The paper presents the relevant issues, describes the current standard for employee stock options, compares the intrinsic value and fair value methods of measurement, and weighs the potential economic effects of revising the current standard. The report was prepared at the request of Congressman Brad Sherman in his capacity as a member of the House Committee on Financial Services.

Judith S. Ruud of CBO's Microeconomic and Financial Studies Division prepared the paper under the direction of Roger Hitchner and Marvin Phaup. Early investigation of the subject was conducted by Douglas Gruener, a summer intern at CBO. George J. Benston of Emory University and Deborah Lucas of Northwestern University reviewed a draft of the paper and provided valuable suggestions. Wendy Kiska, Angelo Mascaro, David Torregrosa, Philip Webre, and Thomas Woodward, all of CBO, also provided helpful comments.

Christine Bogusz and Leah Mazade edited the paper, and John Skeen proofread it. Maureen Costantino prepared the paper for publication and designed the cover, and Annette Kalicki produced the electronic versions for CBO's Web site (www.cbo.gov).

Douglas Holtz-Eakin
Director

April 2004

CONTENTS

Tables

Boxes

Summary

Current accounting standards require firms to recognize as an expense (deduct from their income) the value of the compensation they provide in the form of employee stock options. For some types of employee stock options they grant, however, firms can choose how to measure that value. They can use the immediate-exercise value (intrinsic value), which is usually zero, or an estimate of the market value (fair value), which is almost always greater than zero. As a result, firms may assign a cost of zero to that portion of compensation made up of grants of employee stock options. That practice results in overstatement of reported net income.

In March 2003, the Financial Accounting Standards Board (FASB), the private-sector organization that sets standards for financial accounting and reporting in the United States, announced that it would reconsider the accounting standard for equity-based compensation. On March 31, 2004, FASB released an exposure draft that proposes revising the standard to require—not merely encourage—firms to recognize the fair value of all employee stock options as compensation expense for financial-reporting purposes. The prospect of that revision has generated considerable debate.

Some analysts argue that requiring firms to recognize as an expense the fair value of employee stock options is unnecessary or ill-advised. Underpinning those arguments are different assumptions about whether the information on fair value is currently transparent to users of financial reports.

Analysts who believe that information about fair value is adequately transparent consider it unnecessary to change the current standard. Although information about fair value is not reflected in net income, it is already available to investors in the notes to firms' annual financial reports. (In those notes, firms must disclose the fair value of the grants of employee stock options for which they recognized the intrinsic value.)

Other observers maintain that recognizing the fair value of employee stock options is ill-advised because that information is not now transparent and making it so could have negative consequences. Recognition might reveal new information to investors that could drive down the stock prices of firms that grant employee stock options. That result could in turn damage the economy, some analysts argue.

Still other analysts oppose the recognition of the fair value of employee stock options on more basic grounds. For example, they assert that the value of those options cannot be estimated reliably and that recognizing an estimate of the expense would reduce the accuracy of reported net income. Others oppose recognition because they do not view the granting of employee stock options as an expense to the firm at all but simply a redistribution of equity.

The Congressional Budget Office's (CBO's) analysis of this accounting issue comes to the following conclusions:

- If firms do not recognize as an expense the fair value of employee stock options, measured when the options are granted, the firms' reported net income will be overstated.

- Changes in the value of employee stock options after they have been granted as well as the exercising of those options are irrelevant to a firm's income statement because they affect shareholders directly, not the firm itself. Specifically, they transfer wealth from existing shareholders to holders of employee stock options.

- Although complicated to calculate, the fair value of employee stock options may be estimated as reliably as many other expenses.

- Recognizing the fair value of employee stock options is unlikely to have a significant effect on the economy (because the information has already been disclosed); however, it could make fair value information more transparent to less-sophisticated investors.

Accounting for Employee Stock Options

For more than 50 years, organizations that set accounting standards have espoused the principle of measuring the fair value of employee stock options provided as part of a compensation package and recognizing that value as an operating expense. Businesses that adhere to that principle subtract the options' fair value—the estimated amount for which the options could be bought or sold in a current transaction—from their revenue in determining their earnings, which are reflected on their income statements (see Box 1). The information provided by the income statements and by other financial reporting and disclosures is used by investors and others outside the firms who are seeking to assess their profitability.

Proposals to require firms to recognize the fair value of employee stock options as an expense—the current standard encourages but does not require that practice—have been put forward in the past, provoking significant controversy. The central concern driving such proposals was expressed as early as 1953 by the Committee on Accounting Procedures (the accounting standards board of that era):

> To the extent that such options and rights [that is, options to purchase or rights to subscribe for shares of a corporation's capital stock] involve a measurable amount of compensation, this cost of services received should be accounted for as such. The amount of compensation involved may be substantial and omission of such costs from the corporation's accounting may result in overstatement of net income to a significant degree.[1]

The issue of requiring firms to recognize the fair value of employee stock options was raised most recently in March 2003 when the Financial Accounting Standards Board (FASB)—the independent private-sector board that currently sets U.S. financial accounting standards—announced that it planned to reconsider the current standard for equity-based compensation. This Congressional Budget Office (CBO) paper describes the issues that surround the debate about changing that standard, analyzing the current accounting requirement, the arguments advanced for and against requiring fair value recognition, and how such a change might affect the economy. The report also compares the methods now being used to value employee stock options, presenting a detailed example to illustrate the general effects of those methods.

The Key Issue: Intrinsic Versus Fair Value

In 1993, FASB recommended a change in the accounting treatment of employee stock options. It proposed that firms recognize the fair value of the options (measured when the options are granted) as an expense on their income statements over the period in which employees perform the services for which the options serve as compensation. (That period usually corresponds to the vesting period—the waiting period most companies require before the option holder may exercise the option.) However, FASB's proposal encountered severe opposition, mostly from the managers of firms granting such options. Those managers preferred to continue to use the accounting treatment permitted under what was then the current standard—that is, to recognize the intrinsic (or immediate-exercise) value of employee stock options rather than the options' fair value.[2] Their preference derived at least in part from the fact that at the time options are granted, the intrinsic value is almost always less than the fair value and thus a smaller amount is subtracted from firms' earnings.

1. Committee on Accounting Procedures, ***Compensation Involved in Stock Option and Stock Purchase Plans***, Accounting Research Bulletin No. 43 (1953), Chapter 13B.

2. That treatment was established in 1972 by FASB's predecessor, the Accounting Principles Board, in its Opinion No. 25, ***Accounting for Stock Issued to Employees*** (referred to hereafter as Opinion 25).

Box 1.

The Accounting Framework

There are two basic accounting statements, the balance sheet and the income statement. Each provides information on a firm's financial condition to investors and others outside the firm (creditors, for example).

The balance sheet is a summary of the firm's net worth at a point in time. It shows what the firm owns (assets) and how the firm is financed (liabilities and shareholders' equity). The accounting identity of the balance sheet is that assets equal liabilities plus shareholders' equity (what shareholders would have after the firm had discharged all its obligations).

The income statement shows the firm's performance for a specified period, such as a quarter or a year, measured by its earnings. For the income statement, net income equals revenue minus expenses. In general, revenue is the economic benefit generated by the firm's activities, and expenses are the associated costs. Compensation and depreciation are examples of two types of expenses.

An accrual basis of accounting underlies most financial reporting. Under accrual accounting, revenue is recognized when it is earned and can be objectively measured. When possible, expenses are matched with revenue and are recognized in the same period. If an expense applies to multiple periods and cannot be definitively matched with revenue, it is apportioned in some manner over those periods. If the expense cannot be matched with revenue, it is recognized when it is incurred.

The intrinsic value of an employee stock option is the extent to which an option's strike price—the specified price at which the underlying stock may be purchased—is below the stock's current market price. For example, an option to buy one share of stock at a strike price of $30 per share on a stock whose current market price is $35 has an intrinsic value of $5. Employee stock options may be structured so that their intrinsic value is zero—in the previous example, by setting the option's strike price at $35 or more.

The opposition engendered by FASB's proposed change strengthened until intervention by the Congress appeared likely, so the accounting board amended its proposal to encourage—but not require—recognition of the fair value of employee stock options.[3] However, FASB did require that firms electing to use the intrinsic value method disclose the effects of fair value recognition on their income.

3. The Senate passed a resolution against the proposal. See amendment 1668 to the Consumer Reporting Reform Act, S. 783, 103rd Congress, 1st sess. (1993).

The Current Accounting Standard

The current standard, which is spelled out in FASB Statement No. 123 (FAS 123), effectively allows companies to choose between two methods of valuing compensatory stock options:[4] they can recognize as an expense either the options' fair value or their intrinsic value. If they elect to use the intrinsic value method, as most do, they must disclose the estimated fair value in the notes to their financial statements.[5] As mentioned earlier, FAS 123 encourages use of the fair value method—which recognizes

4. Employee stock options may be compensatory or noncompensatory. Compensatory stock options are granted to employees in exchange for their services. Noncompensatory plans, such as employee stock ownership plans, are intended to serve other goals, such as promoting employees' loyalty or raising capital without having to make a public offering of stock. FAS 123 applies only to compensatory stock options.

5. For example, when Cisco reported its quarterly earnings in November 2002, it disclosed that those earnings would have been 60 percent lower under "fair value" accounting. (Specifically, its earnings of $618 million would have been reduced to $250 million if the $368 million in options it had granted had been recognized as an expense.) See Scott Thurm, "Cisco Discloses Expense Data on Stock Options," *Wall Street Journal*, November 22, 2002, p. B6.

an option's estimated market value on the date the option is granted—but does not require it.[6] Firms estimate such values through the use of both analytic option-pricing methods and the options' prevailing market prices. If the market price of a stock is greater than zero, the fair value of an employee stock option will also be greater than zero.

Companies that use the intrinsic value method almost always grant fixed stock options with a strike price at or above their stock's prevailing market price. (If the strike price was set below the prevailing market price—so that the option had a positive intrinsic value, or was "in the money"—the company would be required to count that difference as an expense.) As noted earlier, an option with a strike price equal to or greater than the current market price of the underlying stock has an intrinsic value of zero.

The intrinsic value method understates the market value of employee stock options for at least two reasons. First, it assigns no value to the probability that the market price of the stock will rise above the strike price. Second, it does not account for the time value of the money that the option holder saves by being allowed to defer the purchase of the stock.[7] Yet an option has a positive fair value even if the strike price exceeds the market price of the stock when the option is granted because the time value of money and the chance that the stock's market price will exceed the option's strike price before expiration are always greater than zero. (Indeed, the longer the life of the option—the period during which it can be exercised—the greater the chance that the stock's price will exceed the strike price.)

The majority of companies that grant employee stock options have fixed stock option plans and until recently have chosen to use the intrinsic value method—that is, to merely disclose the fair value of the options that they grant rather than to recognize that amount as an expense. Until 2002, only two major firms (Boeing and Winn-Dixie Stores) had elected to use the fair value method in accounting for employee stock options. Since July 2002, however, nearly 500 U.S. firms have announced that they will voluntarily adopt that valuation method.[8]

FASB's Proposal

In March 2003, FASB announced plans to reconsider the current standard for equity-based compensation. Its stated objective was to cooperate with the International Accounting Standards Board (IASB) to establish a single international accounting standard for such compensation.[9] On March 31, 2004, FASB released its proposal to require firms to recognize the fair value of employee stock options—eliminating the alternative of recognizing the intrinsic value and merely disclosing the fair value in a note.[10] The prospect of that revision has prompted considerable controversy, with the managers of many firms that grant such options reiterating their opposition to the requirement. For many observers, the challenge of this issue is to understand the arguments being offered on both sides of the debate.

Why Firms Grant Stock Options

Firms grant employee stock options as compensation for any of a number of reasons: to minimize the firm's compensation costs, to conserve cash, and to avoid the limits on the tax deductibility of cash compensation. Employee

6. FAS 123 allows firms to account for employee stock options as prescribed by Opinion 25. Under the Opinion 25 standard, the measurement date for determining the compensation expense of employee stock options is the first date on which the number of shares that the employee is entitled to receive and the exercise price are known. For fixed stock options, those parameters are generally known at the time that the options are granted. (Fixed stock options, so called because the number of shares to which an employee is entitled is known at the time of the grant, are the most common form of stock compensation plan.) In contrast, the measurement date for determining the compensation expense of performance stock options (options for which vesting depends on both the employee's continued service to an employer and the achievement of performance goals, such as exceeding a sales target) may be later than the date on which they are granted. That is because the terms of the award (the number of shares that may be purchased and the strike price) depend on events that occur after the options are awarded.

7. The time value of money is the idea that a dollar now is worth more than a dollar in the future, even after adjusting for inflation, because a dollar in hand today could earn interest, for example, until the time that the dollar in the future was received.

8. See David Reilly, "Foreign Firms to Expense Options," *Wall Street Journal*, February 19, 2004, p. A2.

9. In February 2004, the IASB issued a rule to require the expensing of employee stock options. See Reilly, "Foreign Firms to Expense Options."

10. Financial Accounting Standards Board, *Proposed Statement of Financial Accounting Standards: Share-Based Payment* (No. 1102-100, an amendment of FASB Statements No. 123 and 95), March 31, 2004, available at www.fasb.org/draft/ed_intropg_share-based_payment.shtml.

stock option grants may also be desirable from the shareholders' standpoint because the options help align managers' incentives with shareholders' interests. Some critics argue, however, that the current accounting standard may contribute to an excessive use of such options—which may actually work against that alignment objective.

A firm creates value for its owners through its economic activity. In the case of a corporate firm, shareholders are the owners, contributing capital in return for owning shares of the business. Shareholders possess a so-called residual-ownership claim—that is, they bear the ultimate risk of loss and receive the benefits of profitability after all prior claims have been satisfied. Shareholders' risk of loss is limited to their investment; their gain is limited only by a firm's ability to create value.

Shareholders have what is known as a principal-agent relationship with the management of a firm. Managers are essentially agents of the owners, or principals. Left to their own devices, managers may act in their own best interest, which may not be the same as that of the shareholders—a phenomenon known as the agency problem. Shareholders can encourage managers to take actions that are consistent with their own interests by devising appropriate managerial incentives and then monitoring managers' performance.

Compensating managers with stock or with employee stock options may give those executives a stronger incentive to take actions that, for example, increase the price of the firm's stock. However, compensating managers with employee stock options does not completely solve the agency problem.

Another reason that firms grant employee stock options is to minimize their compensation expenses. Market forces determine the total compensation of workers. Employee stock options are often part of a package that includes wages, benefits, and working conditions. Firms try to structure such packages to appeal to workers and spur their efforts at the lowest cost to the firm.

For highly compensated employees, granting stock options can be less expensive for firms than other forms of compensation, such as cash salaries or outright grants of stock. For tax purposes, compensation (as well as other expenses) is normally deducted from a firm's gross income to arrive at its taxable income. But tax legislation enacted in 1993 disallows the deductibility of compensation paid to executives that exceeds $1 million—unless that compensation is "performance based." Fixed stock options are deemed performance-based compensation for tax purposes. Employee stock options therefore may reduce taxable income—and taxes—when cash compensation does not.

The current accounting treatment of employee stock options provides an additional incentive for firms to grant options as part of employees' compensation because it allows firms to recognize the expense of some employee stock options at less than their market value—in most cases, at a value of zero. That treatment helps accommodate the seemingly conflicting incentives firms face in reporting their income for financial-accounting and for tax purposes. For financial-reporting purposes, firms prefer to maximize their reported income, but for tax-reporting purposes, they are interested in minimizing it. Current standards effectively allow firms to do both to some extent: they may record a compensation expense of zero for employee stock option grants in their financial reports, but they may also deduct the actual exercise value of those options as compensation expense on their tax returns.

Potential Economic Effects of Fair Value Recognition

Recognizing the fair value of the employee stock options that firms grant would enable analysts and investors to more easily assess firms' compensation expenses and how those expenses affected firms' profits. That improved transparency would also aid corporate committees that approve managers' compensation packages. But some opponents of requiring firms to recognize the fair value of employee stock options contend that such a requirement might negatively affect the U.S. economy by lowering the price of firms' stock and hindering firms' access to capital.

Whether or not a requirement to recognize the fair value of employee stock options would reduce stock prices is an unsettled question. On the one hand, recognizing the options' fair value as an expense might drive down firms' stock prices if the current method of merely disclosing the fair value prevents investors from understanding the firms' actual profitability. Lower stock prices in turn might hurt the ability of those firms to raise capital, invest, and grow. (Lower stock prices could also lessen firms' propensity to grant employee stock options.) On the other hand, if equity markets are efficient at processing the disclosed information about the fair value of options, which is not recognized in income statements, then the options' effect is already incorporated in stock prices, and a change in accounting treatment will have no further impact.

Experience to date suggests that the accounting change proposed by FASB will not necessarily have an adverse effect on stock prices of all firms that grant compensatory options. Studies of companies that have announced within the past three years that they will voluntarily switch to the fair value method have found no significant change in stock prices as a result of that announcement.[11] Of course, those firms that voluntarily changed to the fair value method might be those that anticipated a favorable outcome or no effect from doing so. Nevertheless, the results indicate that firms' stock prices are unlikely to experience a uniform adverse impact from the proposed change.

Experience has also shown that it is unnecessary for firms to overstate their net income in order to raise capital. Investors that perceive opportunities for growth in a firm's revenue and earnings have shown themselves willing to invest despite a less-than-outstanding current income statement.[12] Furthermore, many companies in the start-up phase of their operations turn to venture capitalists and private equity firms for fund-raising. Those organizations are made up of skilled investors who will be able to look past the stock options' expense to see the firm's potential.

If stock prices and access to capital are little affected, recognizing the fair value of employee stock options rather than merely disclosing it is unlikely to hurt the overall economy. In fact, if recognition of that expense better informs investors about firms' profitability than disclosure does, capital will be allocated more efficiently, and the economy will be more productive. To the extent that grants of employee stock options are motivated by the discrepancy between the economic and accounting values of those options, recognizing their fair value may reduce the number of options that are granted, but it should not create an unwarranted bias against their use.

11. See Ashish Garg and William Wilson, "Expensing of Options: What Do the Markets Say?" *CrossCurrents* (Fall 2003), pp. 2-9; and "Option Expensing Announcement Has No Impact on Share Price, Towers Perrin Event Study Affirms," available at www.towersperrin.com/hrservices/global/default.htm.

12. Throughout the 1990s, for example, many firms with little or no revenue successfully sold shares. For a discussion, see Robert N. McCauley, Judith S. Ruud, and Frank Iacono, "Cheap Equity Capital for Young Firms," in *Dodging Bullets: Changing U.S. Corporate Capital Structure in the 1980s and 1990s* (Cambridge, Mass.: MIT Press, 1999), pp. 247-264.

Valuing and Recognizing Employee Stock Options

Because the value of an option changes with time and as a result of other factors, including fluctuations in the price of the underlying stock, a point must be chosen at which to measure that value. Under the fair value method of the current accounting standard, the value of employee stock options is measured when they are granted. However, the options' value might also be measured at the end of the vesting period or when they are exercised, and arguments for measuring value at those points have been made. An important additional question is whether the options' value can be reliably estimated, whatever point is eventually chosen.

An option's value at the end of the exercise period is almost always different from its value when it was granted. In general, and all other things being equal, the longer the exercise period of an option, the higher the option's value will be—because of the greater chance that the market price of the stock will rise above the strike price. If the market price of the stock fails to exceed the option's strike price, the option holder will not exercise the option.

The Difficulty of Measuring the Value of Employee Stock Options

Employee stock options are difficult to value precisely. Mathematical models have been developed to value exchange-traded options (including call options), but in order to use them for employee stock options, the models must be adjusted to account for the differences between the two kinds of options. (See Box 2, which describes how employee stock options differ from call options.) For example, exchange-traded options are transferable without restriction, whereas employee stock options have a significant vesting period and even then usually cannot be sold (only exercised). Employee stock options also have a longer exercise period than most exchange-traded options have. As a result, the actual value of employee stock options is likely to be different from the value predicted by models developed for exchange-traded options.

Box 2.

How Employee Stock Options Differ from Call Options

Employee stock options are sometimes described as call options because their fundamental function is the same. Both types of securities give the holder the right to buy a specified number of shares of a firm's stock at a specified price (the strike price, or exercise price) until a given date (the expiration date). However, employee stock options differ from call options in several respects. An important distinction is that employee stock options, unlike call options, are corporate securities (that is, issued by corporations).

In general, the two parties to an option contract are the creator or issuer of the option, also known as the seller or writer, and the purchaser of the option, also known as the buyer or holder. With employee stock options, the corporation is the writer and the employee recipient of the employee stock option is the holder. At the inception of the option contract, the writer receives the price paid for the option, referred to as the premium. (In the case of employee stock options, the premium is the forgone cash wages.) Call options and employee stock options both confer on the holder the right to gain from increases in the stock price, with the risk of loss limited to the price paid. A rise in the price of the underlying stock results in gains for the holder, equal to the excess of the market price over the exercise price. Gains to the holder are losses to the writer.

Unlike call options, employee stock options usually have a vesting period—a specified waiting period before they may be exercised—which typically ranges from two to four years. In addition, employee stock options are usually nontransferable, meaning that the employees may not sell them to others.

Another difference is that the exercise of employee stock options affects the corporation's holdings of cash and its number of shares outstanding. Because employee stock options are written by corporations rather than by individuals, the holder pays the strike price to the corporation when he or she exercises the options. As a result, the firm's cash increases, and the firm issues new shares. In contrast, the exercise of ordinary call options results in the transfer of existing shares from one shareholder to the option holder and affects neither the value of the firm's assets nor the number of shares outstanding.

Yet despite those difficulties, many market participants regard current valuation methods as reliable. Firms are already using current methods to calculate the fair value of all employee stock options as required for disclosure in the notes of their audited financial reports. Moreover, option-pricing models are used by traders and investors whose money is at risk to value options that are much more complex than employee stock options.

Another indication that the value of employee stock options may be estimated reliably is the fact that in some instances, firms that grant such options and the employees who receive them can enter into other financial transactions designed to protect against losses. Such transactions, known as hedging, are financial techniques that are structured so that the gain or loss on one holding is offset by the gain or loss on another. (For example, if an investor wanted to completely hedge the payoff of writing (selling) a call option, he or she could simultaneously buy a call option with the same terms.)[13]

13. However, there are also ways to hedge a financial instrument without buying or selling the same instrument, and there are ways to partially hedge, so that the risk of loss or gain is lessened but not eliminated. For an explanation of how firms hedge their exposure, see Gene Amromin and Nellie Liang, "Hedging Employee Stock Options, Corporate Taxes, and Debt," *National Tax Journal*, vol. 56, no. 3 (September 2003), pp. 513-533. For a discussion of ways that recipients may hedge, see, for example, J. Carr Bettis, John M. Bizjak, and Michael L. Lemmon, "Managerial Ownership, Incentive Contracting, and the Use of Zero-Cost Collars and Equity Swaps by Corporate Insiders," *Journal of Financial and Quantitative Analysis*, vol. 36, no. 3 (September 2001), pp. 345-370.

When Should the Value of Employee Stock Options Be Measured?

Because the estimated fair value of employee stock options changes continually from the granting date until the exercise date, *when* options are valued determines the amount that firms recognize on their income statements. The value of firm-written employee stock options may be measured at three different points: when they are granted, when the vesting period ends, or when they are exercised.

Valuing Options When They Are Granted. Most analysis supports valuing employee stock options when they are granted because their value at that point most closely corresponds to the cost to the firm of the compensation that they represent. According to that rationale, such options are given in lieu of cash compensation, and their value is approximated by their market value—that is, the firm incurs a cost when it grants employee stock options, a cost equal to the value for which the options could be sold. In theory, employees in competitive labor markets who receive options are subject to an equivalent reduction (in the amount of the options' value) in their cash compensation.[14]

Another factor that determines the compensation expense of the employee stock options that a firm grants is the number of options that are expected to vest. (If employees do not remain with the firm long enough to satisfy the options' vesting period, they forfeit the options granted to them.) Firms are permitted to estimate the value of the options that they expect will not be exercised and to factor in that amount when they calculate the compensation expense of the options that must be recognized. Under the current accounting standard—regardless of whether the firm is using the fair value or intrinsic value method—firms do not recognize any compensation expense for options that they expect will be forfeited by employees who fail to satisfy vesting requirements.

The fair value method of the current accounting standard requires firms to measure the value of employee stock options (that are expected to vest) when the options are granted. According to FASB, that value constitutes the entire amount of the compensation given to employees in the form of stock options. Any subsequent gain or loss in the options' value does not affect the value of the firm granting them but is instead a direct transfer of wealth from current shareholders to option holders (see the later discussion).

Valuing Options When They Vest. Because employees cannot exercise their options until the end of the vesting period, some analysts contend that the options' value should not be measured until then. An advantage of waiting is that by that time, the number of vested options is known and does not have to be estimated (as it does if the options' value is measured when the options are granted). But the firm, not the employee, is the relevant reporting entity whose finances are being disclosed under the various accounting standards. As such, the appropriate issues are the cost of the options to the firm and when the firm incurs that cost. The firm obligates itself as a writer of the options on the date that it grants them—options are binding contracts between the firm and the employee and must be fulfilled. Thus, the options' value at vesting is irrelevant to the options' cost to the firm; the firm already incurred that cost when the options were granted.

Valuing Options When They Are Exercised. Because the value of employee stock options is realized only when the options are exercised, some observers argue that that is the appropriate time to measure their value. Indeed, for tax purposes, the gain that employees realize when they exercise most compensatory stock options is the value that the firm may deduct as compensation expense from its gross income in determining its taxable income; it is also the measure of the compensation received by the individuals who exercise the options. But for financial-accounting purposes, the relevant issues are the options' cost to the firm and when the firm incurs that cost—that is, the value of the options when they are granted.

When employees exercise their stock options, they buy shares of stock from the firm for less than the stock's market value. However, changes in the value of employee stock options between the time they are granted and the time they are exercised do not represent an additional cost to the firm (and so are not recorded on the firm's income statement). Rather, they simply transfer wealth between existing shareholders and stock option holders.

That transfer of wealth represents a gain to the employees who are exercising the stock options—and a loss to existing shareholders—but it has no effect on the value of the firm. When employees exercise their stock options, the

14. If employee stock options were given in excess of competitive market compensation, that would imply that the boards of directors of firms were not fulfilling their fiduciary duties to shareholders.

firm experiences no outflow of resources. To fulfill the employee stock option contract that it wrote, the firm is required only to issue additional equity claims (shares of stock), which it can do at any time at no cost to itself—although such an issuance does reduce the value of the claims of existing equityholders.[15] The value of the firm is affected only when the options are granted—that is, when the firm incurred the cost of granting the options to employees as part of their compensation instead of selling the shares to investors.

When Should the Expense of Employee Stock Options Be Recognized?

Compensation is an operating expense, a cost of doing business. For the sake of accuracy, it should be treated like other operating expenses—matched with revenue and recognized in the same period. Thus, under the current accounting standard, the expense of employee stock options is measured when the options are granted and is recognized over the time (the vesting period) during which employees render services to the firm in exchange for the compensation that the options represent. The justification for recognizing the expense over the vesting period is that the employee earns the compensation (the stock options) only by continuing to work for the firm during that time.

Some observers, however, question whether employee stock options are indeed compensation. They claim that such options are "capital" income (income earned from investment ownership of a security) rather than labor compensation. But that argument fails to distinguish two separate events: the granting of an employee stock option, which conveys a specific amount of compensation, and subsequent gains or losses from changes in the option's value. The initial grant is compensation; subsequent gains and losses may be considered investment income for the option's holder.

In contrast to operating expenses, financing transactions, such as sales of stock, usually do not affect a firm's income statement. Rather, they affect its balance sheet by changing the firm's assets and the claims on those assets (in the form of liabilities and equity). Financing transactions do not directly affect the amount of income earned by the firm and thus do not augment the investment of existing shareholders. When stock is issued, for example, cash assets and shareholders' equity both increase (along with the number of shares outstanding), but no income results from that transaction.

The use of employee stock options effectively involves two types of transactions: the payment of compensation in the form of employee stock options (reflected on the income statement) and, when the options are exercised, a financing transaction (reflected on the balance sheet). That "hybrid" transaction requires recognizing the value of the options when they are granted as a cost on the income statement—but not any subsequent gains and losses in that value. As the following example shows, that treatment is consistent with the fair value method of accounting.

Comparing Accounting Alternatives: An Example

CBO prepared an example to show how a firm can account for some of the different forms of compensation that it grants to its employees. In this example, the firm has assets of $2,000, no debt, shareholders' equity of $2,000, annual revenue of $1,000, and fixed market-determined compensation expenses of $1,000 annually (the firm grants no dividends and pays no taxes). Before presenting the accounting for grants of employee stock options as compensation, the example shows the accounting for grants of stock and purchased call options in lieu of cash compensation.

Granting Cash, Stock, and Purchased Call Options as Compensation

The firm's financial statements will differ depending on whether it pays all compensation in cash or pays $200 worth of stock or purchased call options in lieu of cash compensation (see Table 1). Although net income is zero in all three cases (because total expenses are equal to revenues), granting stock for part of employees' pay will leave the firm with $200 more in cash assets.[16] Granting stock

15. Share price dilution results when the number of ownership claims on the firm increase, but the firm's market value does not rise proportionately. See the example in the last section for further discussion.

16. Under current accounting rules, if the firm grants stock in lieu of cash compensation, the value of that stock is recognized on the firm's income statement as compensation expense.

Table 1.

Comparison of Accounting Treatments for Selected Forms of Compensation: Cash, Stock, and Purchased Call Options

(Dollars)

	Firm Pays Compensation Entirely in Cash	Firm Grants Stock in Lieu of $200 of Cash Compensation	Firm Grants Purchased Call Options in Lieu of $200 of Cash Compensation
	Income Statement		
Revenues	1,000	1,000	1,000
Expenses			
Cash compensation	-1,000	-800	-800
Stock compensation	n.a.	-200	n.a.
Purchased call option compensation	n.a.	n.a.	-200
Net Income	**0**	**0**	**0**
	Balance Sheet[a]		
Assets			
Assets at the beginning of the year	2,000	2,000	2,000
Plus cash conserved by compensating with stock	n.a.	200	n.a.
Assets at the end of the year	2,000	2,200	2,000
Equity			
Owners' equity at the beginning of the year	2,000	2,000	2,000
Additional owners' equity	0	200	0
Owners' equity at the end of the year	2,000	2,200	2,000

Source: Congressional Budget Office.

Notes: n.a. = not applicable.

The year referred to in this table is the one in which the stock options are granted.

a. In this example, the firm has no liabilities. For a review of income statements and balance sheets, see Box 1.

causes owners' equity to be $200 higher, because employees have in effect contributed $200 to owners' equity by accepting stock instead of cash compensation. (It is as if employees were paid $1,000 in cash, and then the employees paid $200 of that cash to the firm in exchange for stock.) By granting compensation in the form of stock, the firm has more total owners' equity, but it also has more shares outstanding. Existing shareholders will suffer no loss in the value of their shares from the increase in shares if employees paid the fair market value for the new shares in forgone cash compensation.

If the firm pays a portion of employees' compensation with call options purchased from a third party, its financial statements will be similar to those under the cash-compensation scenario. (In this case, it is as if employees were paid $1,000 in cash and then the employees paid $200 of that cash to the third party in exchange for the call options.) The firm recognizes as an expense the fair value of the options it purchased. Because a third party wrote the options, the firm's existing shareholders will not face the prospect of any share price dilution (reduction in wealth) if the options are exercised. In contrast, with employee stock options that the firm writes itself, the fair value may not be recognized as an expense on the

Table 2.

Comparison of Accounting Treatments for Employee Stock Options

(Dollars)

	Firm Grants $200 Worth of At-the-Money Options in Lieu of Cash Compensation	
	Fair Value Method	Intrinsic Value Method
Income Statement		
Revenues	1,000	1,000
Expenses		
Cash compensation	-800	-800
Option compensation	-200	0
Net Income	**0**	**200**
Balance Sheet[a]		
Assets		
Assets at the beginning of the year	2,000	2,000
Plus cash conserved by compensating with options	200	200
Assets at the end of the year	2,200	2,200
Equity		
Owners' equity at the beginning of the year	2,000	2,000
Addition to owners' equity from net income	0	200
Option holders' equity	200	0
Owners' and option holders' equity at the end of the year	2,200	2,200

Source: Congressional Budget Office.

Notes: The year referred to in this table is the one in which the stock options are granted.

In this example, the fair value of the options is recognized (subtracted from income) when the options are granted. That accounting method is identical to the treatment of the grant of $200 in stock compensation noted in Table 1.

Under the intrinsic value method of accounting, the exercise value of the options is also recognized when they are granted. (In this case, that value is zero.) However, the current accounting standard is slightly more complicated and hence difficult to include in this table: valuation occurs at grant and recognition occurs over the vesting period. (In this example, the options vest immediately.)

An option is "at the money" if the share price of the underlying stock is equal to the strike price of the option.

a. In this example, the firm has no liabilities. For a review of income statements and balance sheets, see Box 1.

firm's income statement, and existing shareholders will experience share price dilution if the options are exercised.

Granting Employee Stock Options in Lieu of Equivalent Cash Compensation

If the firm grants employee stock options as compensation, the accounting treatment is more complex. In this scenario, the firm grants at-the-money options with a fair value of $200 in lieu of that amount of cash compensation (by assumption, the options vest immediately). Issuing employee stock options instead of cash permits the firm to retain cash equal to the value of the options and gives employees a contingent claim on the firm. By substituting employee stock options for $200 in cash compensation, the firm retains $200 more in cash. Whether the firm reports net income of zero or $200, however, depends on which method it uses to value the options (see Table 2).

With the fair value method, the firm recognizes as an expense the fair value of the options at grant ($200), so its net income is unchanged relative to paying all compensation in cash. (That accounting treatment is identical to that of the scenario in which the firm grants $200 in stock compensation.) The intrinsic value method recognizes the immediate-exercise value of the options (zero), rather than the fair value ($200), and thus reports net income of $200. Under both methods of valuation, cash assets are higher by $200.

If the employee stock options that the firm has granted subsequently change in value, that change will have no effect on the firm's income statement or balance sheet under either accounting method. (Similarly, a change in the market value of a stock will have no effect on a firm's financial accounting after the stock is granted as compensation.) If the options granted in this example increase in value by, say, $100, the firm's reported net income will still be zero.

Letting Options Expire or Exercising Them

At the end of the life of an option (its expiration), its holder will either exercise it at a gain or allow it to expire unexercised. At that point, the firm's income is unaffected under both fair value and intrinsic value accounting, whether the option is exercised or expires unexercised.

Options Expire Unexercised. If the employee stock options that were worth $200 when the firm granted them subsequently fall in value and are not in-the-money, then the holders will choose to let the options expire unexercised. The final balance sheet and income statement numbers in that scenario are identical under both the fair value and intrinsic value methods (see the first two columns of Table 3). Although the options have decreased in value, that decline will have no effect on the firm's income under either accounting method.

Options Are Exercised. If those options that were worth $200 when the firm granted them subsequently increase in value and are in the money, then the holders will choose to exercise them by paying the firm the strike price in exchange for the stock. Suppose that the employee stock options granted in this example were for 100 shares of stock, with a strike price of $10, and that the market price of the stock has risen to $13. In that case, option holders pay the firm $1,000 in cash (100 shares of stock times the strike price of $10 per share), which increases owners' equity by the same amount (see the last two columns of Table 3).

While the income statement and the ending value of the balance sheet are the same under both accounting methods when employee stock options are exercised, the balance sheet entries differ. Under the fair value method, the option holders' equity is transferred to owners' equity upon the exercise of the employee stock options, because exercising the options results in the option holders' receiving ownership shares. Under the intrinsic value method, there is no option holders' equity to transfer.

What the financial statements do not show, however, is the economic effect of the exercise of stock options on existing shareholders. When firm-written stock options are exercised, wealth is transferred from existing shareholders to those exercising the options. Such share price dilution is not a cost to the firm per se, but it is certainly relevant to existing shareholders, as shown below.[17]

If immediately before the exercise of the employee stock options, the firm had 500 shares of its stock outstanding, trading at $13 per share, then the market value of the firm was $6,500 ($13 times 500). Upon the exercise of the employee stock options for 100 shares, the option holders pay a total of $1,000 to the firm. That transaction simultaneously increases the market value of the firm to $7,500 and boosts the number of shares outstanding to 600. Thus, immediately after the exercise of the employee stock options, the market price of a share of the firm's stock falls to $12.50 ($7,500 divided by 600). Therefore, the exercise of the employee stock options caused existing shareholders to transfer 50 cents per share of the value of their shares to those exercising the options.

The Bottom Line: Reporting Differences Between the Two Accounting Methods

The fair value method and intrinsic value method of accounting for employee stock options result in different reported net income for the same firm. The firm in this example has no annual net income from operations. But by using the intrinsic value method of accounting, the firm reports $200 in net income in the year in which the employee stock options were granted, an overstatement equal to the value of the options on the granting date. No subsequent transaction reverses or offsets that overstatement.

---

17. If the firm had purchased call options from another entity to grant to employees rather than writing them itself, the exercise of those purchased call options would not result in share price dilution for existing shareholders.

Table 3.

Comparison of Accounting Treatments for Employee Stock Options at Expiration

(Dollars)

	Options Are Unexercised		100 Options Are Exercised at a Strike Price of $10	
	Fair Value Method	Intrinsic Value Method	Fair Value Method	Intrinsic Value Method
	Income Statement			
Revenues	1,000	1,000	1,000	1,000
Expenses—Cash Compensation	-1,000	-1,000	-1,000	-1,000
Net Income	**0**	**0**	**0**	**0**
	Balance Sheet[a]			
Assets				
Assets at the beginning of the year	2,200	2,200	2,200	2,200
Cash received (paid) from option exercise	n.a.	n.a.	1,000	1,000
Assets at the end of the year	2,200	2,200	3,200	3,200
Equity				
Option holders' equity at the beginning of the year	200	0	200	0
Transfer to owners' equity	-200	0	-200	0
Option holders' equity at the end of the year	0	0	0	0
Owners' equity at the beginning of the year	2,000	2,200	2,000	2,200
Transfer from option holders' equity	200	0	200	0
Change in owners' equity from option exercise	n.a.	n.a.	1,000	1,000
Owners' equity at the end of the year	2,200	2,200	3,200	3,200

Source: Congressional Budget Office.

Notes: n.a. = not applicable.

The year referred to in this table is the year in which the options expire.

a. In this example, the firm has no liabilities. For a review of income statements and balance sheets, see Box 1.

Testimony of Professor Douglas L. Kruse
School of Management and Labor Relations
Rutgers University
New Brunswick, New Jersey 08903

before the
U.S. House of Representatives
Committee on House Financial Services Subcommittee on Capital Markets,
Insurance and Government Sponsored Enterprises
2129 Rayburn House Office Building.

April 21, 2004

Chairman Baker, Ranking Member Kanjorski, and Members of the Subcommittee, thank you for the opportunity to testify. I am a professor at the School of Management and Labor Relations at Rutgers University, New Brunswick, New Jersey. I have specialized in the economic analysis of broad-based employee ownership, stock options, and profit sharing in the U.S. economy for thirty years. I have a Ph.D in Economics from Harvard University and serve as a Research Associate at the National Bureau of Economic Research (NBER) in Cambridge, Massachusetts. At the NBER I am co-principal investigator of a multi-year research project on shared capitalism with Harvard professor Richard Freeman and my Rutgers colleague Joseph Blasi, which is funded by the Russell Sage and Rockefeller Foundations. I am also co-author with Prof. Blasi and Aaron Bernstein of Business Week of the recent book, In The Company of Owners,[1] which contrasts the broad-based stock options of high technology companies to the concentrated options and ownership—mainly in the hands of top executives—in traditional corporations. I want to summarize my main points briefly and refer to material and charts which I am respectfully submitting to have added to the public record.

In 2000, together with the scholars who are part of the NBER project, I began a collaboration with the National Opinion Research Center at the University of Chicago to add questions on these important issues to the U.S. General Social Survey which is mainly funded by the National Science Foundation. This survey, completed in 2002, interviewed a random sample of the entire U.S. working population. The data are public property, and are the basis for my initial evidence.

This national survey found that the vast number of stock option holders are members of the middle and working class, have moderate incomes, and are non-managers. Stock options and Employee Stock Purchase Plans in our country are a broad-based phenomenon despite the fact that there has been so much attention paid to how some top executives have clearly abused them very badly. Fourteen million citizens or 13% of all private sector employees and 25% of all employees of joint stock corporations hold stock options. Twenty three million citizens own company stock, representing 21% of private sector employees and 39% of joint stock company employees. An estimated 15 million of them own stock through Employee Stock Purchase Plans

[1] Joseph Blasi, Douglas Kruse, and Aaron Bernstein. In The Company of Owners: The Truth About Stock Options and Why Every Employee Should Have Them (New York: Basic Books, 2003).

which are the most democratic form of U.S. shared capitalism.[2] I would like to call your attention to the chart in Appendix I of my testimony, showing the incomes of all holders of stock options in the United States. As you can see, 79% of all stock option holders make less than $75,000 per year. Tables 2-9 in Appendix II at the end of my testimony indicate how employees holding stock options are distributed in the U.S. population. They are

- Heavily concentrated in high tech but also very common -- representing about 20% of employees -- in other industries
- Mostly concentrated in the middle class and working class – only 6% are in the upper class
- Mostly held by non-managers
- Spread among different regions and political groups
- Equally accessible to union and non-union workplaces

Appendix III also indicates how workers owning company stock – many of them through Employee Stock Purchase Plans (ESPPs)– are broadly distributed among all categories of employees, and across the political and social spectrum.

I have strong reservations about expensing unless the interests of regular workers are addressed, because expensing could change the incentives for companies to include regular workers in options and ESPPs on which our nascent economic democratic system of shared capitalism is built. Policymakers and economists widely observe that behavior follows incentives. That is the basis of Congress' entire approach to employee benefits. The effect of expensing on net income will create an incentive for some companies to reduce the expense by decreasing both the size of the benefit and the number of employees participating in the plans.

One might argue that companies who believe in employee ownership will continue to do it anyway. However, this is not persuasive. As an example, companies believe in retirement savings but the system would clearly fall apart without government incentives. When companies were required to account for defined benefit plan obligations, post-retiree health benefits, and Employee Stock Ownership Plans (ESOPs), there were significant reductions in public companies offering these to regular workers (although other factors were also involved).

---

[2] See the Wall Street Journal, September 4, 2003, page D1

There is evidence that, in anticipation of expensing, companies have been cutting regular workers from stock option and ESPPs, and concentrating employee ownership in the hands of top executives. Four studies in 2003 that analyzed hundreds of corporations documented that the companies were already cutting back on the participation and size of benefits for middle and lower level managers and employees in broader stock option plans and ESPPs.[3] The companies intend further cutbacks and are largely protecting the access to options of top executives. One-third to one-half are making large cuts in stock option plans and half to two-thirds plan cuts in ESPPs. This may represent a substantial threat to broad-based employee ownership. I must tell the committee that I have personally attended corporate seminars on labor relations where I have heard company after company executive privately admit to doing just this.

In the last few days we attempted to independently confirm some of this evidence with a preliminary investigation. The first ten of the largest Fortune 20 public companies that recently filed their proxies for 2003 with the SEC were examined to see if there is any evidence of concentration of stock options in the hands of the top five executives between 2002 and 2003 when option expensing became widely anticipated. Six of the ten had said earlier that they will expense stock options.[4] Five of the six have already increased the percent of stock options going to their top five executives while reducing the portion of the pie going to other employees. All six of the expensing companies have increased the percent of the stock option pie going to their CEO from 2002 to 2003. Four of the six also increased the raw number of options going to the CEO, while two increased the raw number of options going to the top five executives.

Out of all ten companies, six increased the percent of the stock option pie going to top executives from 2002 to 2003, and the increase was 50% on average and 25% at the median. Seven out of the ten increased the percent of the stock option pie going to the CEO from 2002 to 2003 and the increase was 83% on average and 32% at the median. If this trend continues this will be deeply troubling. The public has been repeatedly told that executive excess and abuse of

---

[3] See Issue Brief: The Future of Broad-based Options, by Corey Rosen, January 2002, National Center for Employee Ownership, www.nceo.org The studies cited are by Sibson Consulting/WorldatWork, Mellon Financial, Mercer Human Resource Consulting, and Deloitte & Touche.

[4] The identification of who announced expensing or not was based on "More Companies Voluntarily Adopt Expensing Fair Value of Stock Options" by Bear Stearns from September 2003. We used Lexis-Nexis to attempt update the list where applicable. It is available at http://216.239.39.104/search?q=cache:x6l56xzDn1gJ:www.thecorporatelibrary.com/special/exp-options/ExpensingStockOptions09-4-03.pdf+list+of+companies+that+expense+stock+options&hl=en&ie=UTF-8

stock options was one motivation for expensing. If expensing results in a further concentration of stock options in the hands of top executives, and cutbacks of broad-based plans as an unintended consequence, it will be nothing short of "supposed executive comp reform on the backs of the working middle class."

If this is the result, it will also possibly involve bad news for shareholders. In chapters 1 and 2 of the book which I have entered into the record, we show how broad-based employee ownership contributed to building up some of the leading technology firms that have served investors well over the long-term. In Table 7, the General Social Survey demonstrates that 16% of work sites of publicly-traded companies actually granted stock options to a majority of employees in 2002. Appendix IV shows how this plays out in the biotechnology industry with most stock options and stock option profits going to non-executive employees, the exact same pattern the book documents in 100 High Tech companies. Chapter 7 of our book reviews twenty years of evidence on the improved productivity and total shareholder return of companies that use broad employee ownership and stock options and profit sharing effectively.[5]

Ironically, I have just completed a new study -- which I also request to be entered into the record --with my colleague Joseph Blasi that looks at the entire universe of data on the two thousand largest corporations in the country for the last 11 years, covering over 16,000 boards of directors decisions. This study shows that marginal increases in many forms of executive compensation, including various measures of stock option increases, do not predict future total

[5] Unlike the research on executive compensation, there is a growing record of evidence on broad-based options. See James Sesil, Maya Kroumova, and Douglas Kruse, and Joseph Blasi, "Broad-based Employee Stock Options in the U.S.: Company Performance and Characteristics," Academy of Management National Conference, Toronto, Canada, 2000.; James Sesil, Maya Kroumova, and Joseph Blasi, and Douglas Kruse, "Broad-based Employee Stock Options in U.S. New Economy Firms," British Journal of Industrial Relations, Volume 4, Number 2, June 2002, pps. 273-294; Joseph R. Blasi, Douglas Kruse, and James Sesil, Maya Kroumova, and Ed Carberry, Stock Options, Corporate Performance and Organizational Change (Oakland, Ca.: National Center for Employee Ownership, 2000) (The full research report is available at www.nceo.org/library/optionreport.html); Christopher Ittner, Richard Lambert, and David Larcker, "The Structure and Performance Consequences Of Equity Grants To Employees Of New Economy Companies," Philadelphia, Pa. : University of Pennsylvania, Wharton School of Business, January 2001. A recent related study by Richard Freeman, Douglas Kruse, and Joseph Blasi demonstrates using General Social Survey data that workers to got stock option grants in 2002 were more careful about monitoring the work behavior of co-workers. See "Monitoring Colleagues at Work: Profit Sharing, Employee Ownership, and Broad-Based Stock Options." Presented at the 2004 Association for Comparative Economic Studies conference, San Diego, CA. This paper is part of the National Bureau of Economic Research's Shared Capitalism. This will also be entered into the record.

shareholder return for 1, 3, and 5 years.[6] Why then does it make sense to adopt policies like expensing that appear to encourage concentration of stock options?

Here is my conclusion. If there is to be expensing of stock options and certain contributions from Employee Stock Purchase Plans, then I believe that it makes sense for Congress to make sure that the decent working Americans who did not abuse employee ownership or stock options do not pay the price while top executives continue to protect their privileges. One possibility is to have options expensed for the top five executives as a current Senate and House bill proposes. Another possibility is to create parallel tax credits at some level that would allow only companies with truly broad-based option programs to offset their option expense. Companies would have the choice of using this new incentive or using the old existing incentive that allows them to deduct option profits from corporate income before taxes when options are exercised. The result of both ideas would be the same: expensing would not weaken shared capitalism and end up being paid for by workers. The vast number of stock option holders are members of the middle and working class, have moderate incomes, and are non-managers. Finally, I would like to call your attention to a bill in the House to create a Presidential Commission on Employee Ownership which I think deserves your support in light of these questions. That would be the right thing for the President to do. Thank you.

[6] This article contains tables showing the entire descriptive statistical history of executive stock options for the last eleven years. See "Corporate Governance, Executive Compensation, and Strategic Human Resource Management From 1992-2002 A Portrait Of What Took Place," Joseph R. Blasi and Douglas L. Kruse, School of Management and Labor Relations, Rutgers University, New Brunswick, N.J., April 2004. Cited in the New York Times in "Option Pie: Overeating Is a Health Hazard," by Gretchen Morgenson, April 4, 2004.

APPENDICES

Appendix I. The Incomes of U.S. Employees Holding Stock Options.

79% of workers holding stock options have salaries less than $75,000 per year

	% of employees holding stock options with this salary
<$15,000.	6.7%
$15-30,000.	20.6%
$30-50,000.	29.0%
$50-75,000.	23.2%
>$75,000.	20.6%

Source: Analysis by Profs. Douglas Kruse and Joseph Blasi of Rutgers University and Prof. Richard Freeman of Harvard University of the General Social Survey for 2002 based on a random sample of all U.S. employees. The General Social Survey was conducted by the National Opinion Research Center at the University of Chicago, with support from the U.S. National Science Foundation. The data are public information and available for all researchers.

Appendix II. Tables on Broad Use of Stock Options.

Table 1. Americans Holding Stock Options

Total number of citizens holding stock options: 14 million

	% of workers
All private sector Company workers	13%
Only corporations with stock	25%

Source: Analysis by Profs. Douglas Kruse and Joseph Blasi of Rutgers University and Prof. Richard Freeman of Harvard University of the General Social Survey for 2002 based on a random sample of all U.S. employees.

Table 2. Percent of Workers Holding Stock Options in Different Industries.

	% of workers in this industry holding stock options
Computer Services	57%
Communications	43%
Finance	27%
Durable Manufacturing	23%
Non-durable Manufacturing	17%
Transportation	13%
Wholesale Services	11%
Retail Services	11%

Source: Analysis by Profs. Douglas Kruse and Joseph Blasi of Rutgers University and Prof. Richard Freeman of Harvard University of the General Social Survey for 2002 based on a random sample of all U.S. employees.

Table 3. Economic Class of Workers Holding Stock Options.

	% of workers with stock options in this class
Upper class	6%
Middle class	48%
Working class	45%
Lower class	2%

Source: Analysis by Profs. Douglas Kruse and Joseph Blasi of Rutgers University and Prof. Richard Freeman of Harvard University of the General Social Survey for 2002 based on a random sample of all U.S. employees. Workers reported their own economic class.

Table 4. Workers Holding Stock Options By Occupation.

	% of workers holding stock options in this occupation
Service workers	4%
Blue collar workers	10%
White collar workers	17%
Professional workers	17%
Management support^	23%
Management	15%

^Management support includes accountants, underwriters, financial and other analysts, HR staff, purchasing, buyers, business and promotion employees, construction inspectors, compliance officers and other inspectors.

Source: Analysis by Profs. Douglas Kruse and Joseph Blasi of Rutgers University and Prof. Richard Freeman of Harvard University of the General Social Survey for 2002 based on a random sample of all U.S. employees.

Table 5. Workers Holding Stock Options by Salary Category

Annual Salary	% of workers in each salary group holding stock options
<$15,000.	4%
$15-30,000.	10%
$30-50,000.	15%
$50-75,000.	24%
>$75,000.	41%

Source: Analysis by Profs. Douglas Kruse and Joseph Blasi of Rutgers University and Prof. Richard Freeman of Harvard University of the General Social Survey for 2002 based on a random sample of all U.S. employees.

Table 6. Stock Options: Union and Non-union Workers.

	% of workers holding stock options in each group
Union workers	15%
Non-union workers	14%

Source: Analysis by Profs. Douglas Kruse and Joseph Blasi of Rutgers University and Prof. Richard Freeman of Harvard University of the General Social Survey for 2002 based on a random sample of all U.S. employees.

Table 7. Company Locations That Grant Stock Options To Most Employees.

	% of company locations that granted stock options to more than half of their employees in 2002
All workplaces in the private sector	5%
All workplaces in closely-held companies*	4%
All workplaces in stock market companies	16%

*These include pre-IPO companies.

Note: This survey looked at a random sample of physical locations of companies around the entire nation. The results indicate what percent of workplaces visited at random would have broad-based stock options: 5 in 100 of all private sector workplaces, 4 in 100 of all potentially pre-IPO closely-held companies, and 16 in 100 of all workplaces connected to public stock market companies.

Source: Analysis by Profs. Douglas Kruse and Joseph Blasi of Rutgers University and Prof. Richard Freeman of Harvard University of the National Organizations Survey for 2002 based on a random sample of all U.S. employees.

Table 8. Small Businesses Granting Stock Options To Broad Groups of Workers.

Small business = a business with less than 100 workers in a single location

Percent of all small businesses in the U.S. which:	
Granted stock options in 2002 to half or more of the company's workers	3%
Granted stock options in 2002 to 10-49% of the company's workers	2%

Source: Analysis by Profs. Douglas Kruse and Joseph Blasi of Rutgers University and Prof. Richard Freeman of Harvard University of the National Organizations Survey for 2002 based on a random sample of all U.S. employees.

Table 9. Swing Voters Holding Stock Options And The Presidential Election.

Workers holding stock options and their concentration among swing voters who are Independents, who vote in Presidential elections, who consider themselves moderate or conservative, and who live in the South or the Midwest.

	Percent of Workers Holding Stock Options Who Are:
Democrats	33.5%
Independents	34.2%
Republicans	32.3%
Voted in the 2000 Presidential election	72%
Liberal	22%
Moderate	40%
Conservative	38%
Residing in the East	15%
Residing in the Midwest	24%
Residing in the South	41%
Residing in the West	20%

Source: Analysis by Profs. Douglas Kruse and Joseph Blasi of Rutgers University and Prof. Richard Freeman of Harvard University of the National Organizations Survey for 2002 based on a random sample of all U.S. employees.

*This information is based on a surveys taken of a national random sample of all working adults and all workplaces in the United States. The General Social Survey of individuals was conducted in 2002 by the National Opinion Research Center at the University of Chicago and receives major support from the National Science Foundation of the U.S. Government. The National Organizations Survey of individuals was conducted in 2003 by the National Opinion Research Center at the University of Chicago. Professors Joseph Blasi and Douglas Kruse of Rutgers University's School of Management and Labor Relations and Professor Richard Freeman of Harvard University's Department of Economics designed a segment of the surveys on employee ownership and profit sharing that was supported principally by the Rockefeller Foundation, the Russell Sage Foundation, the Beyster Institute of Entrepreneurial Employee Ownership, the Employee Ownership Foundation, the National Center for Employee Ownership and the Profit Sharing Council of America. Numbers have been rounded to the nearest percent.

Appendix III. Results of the General Social Survey on Shared Capitalism Programs in the U.S.

Note: Four tables follow in this section.

Table 10: Participation in Shared Capitalism Programs, by Job Characteristics

Figures represent percentages of all private-sector employees in category at left who are covered by program at top of column. Based on 2002 General Social Survey.

	Percent covered by:		Percent who hold:		Sample size
	Profit sharing	Gainsharing	Company stock	Stock options	
	(1)	(2)	(3)	(4)	(5)
Overall	33.5%	23.2%	21.2%	13.1%	1242
Industry					
Ag./mining/constr.	21.1%	13.7%	13.8%	5.3%	95
Durable mfg.	53.2%	39.4%	33.7%	23.4%	94
Non-durable mfg.	49.1%	26.8%	29.6%	16.7%	112
Transportation	33.3%	21.2%	29.2%	12.5%	66
Comms./utilities	46.8%	38.3%	55.3%	42.6%	47
Wholesale	32.7%	21.8%	23.2%	10.7%	55
Retail	27.9%	22.7%	15.8%	10.5%	229
Finance/insurance	51.1%	39.8%	39.8%	27.1%	88
Computer services	54.2%	37.5%	58.3%	56.5%	24
Other services	24.8%	15.3%	9.4%	4.8%	412
Occupation					
Management	49.2%	33.9%	28.8%	14.8%	124
Mgt.-related	60.4%	45.3%	39.6%	22.6%	53
Professional	30.0%	20.6%	21.6%	17.3%	160
Other white-collar	38.2%	27.5%	23.4%	16.7%	382
Service	12.5%	8.0%	7.4%	4.0%	176
Blue-collar	31.6%	20.5%	20.1%	10.0%	332
Hours of work					
Full-time	37.4%	26.4%	24.5%	15.3%	994
Part-time	16.9%	10.6%	5.8%	2.4%	207
Union member			^	^	
Yes	11.4%	6.8%	27.6%	14.9%	88
No	34.9%	22.9%	21.8%	13.6%	733
Employer tenure	^	^			
0-2 years	31.1%	23.1%	12.9%	7.8%	537
2-4 years	33.5%	22.7%	25.0%	16.7%	203
5-9 years	39.3%	23.1%	30.2%	21.0%	234
10+ years	33.5%	23.8%	27.5%	14.6%	260
Yearly work earnings					
<$15,000	18.3%	14.7%	5.5%	4.0%	251

$15-30,000	28.1%	18.4%	18.0%	9.7%	320
$30-50,000	37.5%	27.0%	28.4%	14.9%	293
$50-75,000	59.0%	36.8%	36.6%	24.3%	144
$75,000+	64.0%	45.3%	50.7%	41.3%	75
Size of establishment					
1-9 employees	21.3%	15.0%	10.3%	5.6%	253
10-49 employees	30.7%	20.4%	13.3%	6.2%	323
50-99 employees	39.5%	31.4%	21.4%	14.5%	172
100-400 employees	40.9%	26.4%	27.6%	20.2%	254
500-999 employees	44.3%	25.3%	30.8%	23.1%	79
1000-1999 employees	42.2%	37.5%	38.8%	16.9%	64
2000+ employees	34.2%	21.5%	46.8%	29.5%	79

Profit sharing is defined as eligibility for bonuses based on overall organizational performance.
Gainsharing is defined as eligibility for bonuses based on department or plant performance.
^ Differences among categories are not statistically significant at the 95% level for the union member variable in columns 3 and 4, and the tenure variable in columns 1 and 2. Differences among categories are statistically significant at the 99.9% level for all other breakdowns.

SOURCE: Analysis of the General Social Survey and the National Organizations Study by Douglas Kruse of Rutgers University, Joseph Blasi of Rutgers University and Richard Freeman of Harvard University, Decemb for the Shared Capitalism Project of the National Bureau of Economic Research in Cambridge, Massachusetts

Note: The General Social Survey was administered to a national random sample of working adults by the Nat Opinion Research Center of the University of Chicago in 2002. The National Organizations Study was administered by the same group to employers of respondents of the General Social Survey.

Table 11: Participation in Shared Capitalism Programs, from Survey of Individuals

Based on analysis of 2002 General Social Survey

		All private sector (1)	For-profit companies (2)	Not-for-profit orgs. (3)	Companies with stock (4)^^^
Percent of employees covered					
Profit sharing					
In profit-sharing plan		33.5%	34.8%	20.0%	40.1%
Received profit share last year		23.8%	24.7%	14.5%	27.4%
Gainsharing					
In gainsharing plan		23.2%	23.7%	17.3%	27.7%
Received gainsharing bonus last year		17.1%	17.5%	12.7%	19.8%
Own company stock		21.2%	23.3%	0.0%	39.3%
Hold stock options		13.1%	14.4%	0.0%	24.5%
Number of employees covered (millions)					
Total employees in economy^		108.8	99.0	9.8	58.7
Profit sharing					
In profit-sharing plan		36.5	34.5	2.0	23.5
Received profit share last year		25.9	24.5	1.4	16.1
Gainsharing					
In gainsharing plan		25.2	23.5	1.7	16.2
Received gainsharing bonus last year		18.6	17.3	1.2	11.6
Own company stock		23.0	23.0	0.0	23.0
Hold stock options^^		14.3	14.3	0.0	14.3
Size of financial stakes					
Bonus size if received profit sharing					
Dollar value	Mean	$7,135	$7,368	$2,751	$7,795
	Median	$1,500	$1,700	$1,000	$1,300
Percent of salary	Mean	8.5%	8.7%	4.1%	8.4%
	Median	4.5%	4.6%	2.1%	3.8%
Bonus size if received gainsharing					
Dollar value	Mean	$7,797	$8,160	$2,552	$9,363
	Median	$1,500	$1,500	$760	$1,500
Percent of salary	Mean	8.9%	9.3%	4.2%	10.0%
	Median	3.8%	4.0%	2.1%	3.5%
Company stock value if own stock					
Dollar value	Mean	$84,409	$84,409	---	$84,409

	Median	$10,000	$10,000	---	$10,000
Percent of salary	Mean	99.6%	99.6%	---	99.6%
	Median	21.2%	21.2%	---	21.2%
Sample size		1242	1130	112	670

Profit sharing is defined as eligibility for bonuses based on overall organizational performance.
Gainsharing is defined as eligibility for bonuses based on department or plant performance.

^ The figure for total private sector employees comes from Bureau of Labor Statistics establishment data for July 2002. The BLS does not provide employee counts for not-for-profit organizations and companies with stock, so columns 2-4 are estimates based on the distribution of respondents in the General Social Survey sample.

^^ The percent of employees reporting that they hold stock options could be slightly lower because employees have confused stock options with Employee Stock Purchase Plans, however the researchers made every effort avoid this confusion by careful wording of the questions and explanation of each question to the respondents. Data in Table 2 showing a substantial increase in employees who were granted stock options between 1999 an 2002 suggests that there has been a substantial increase in the number of employees holding stock options.

^^^ "Companies with stock" refers to companies whose employees reported that they had stock in the Genera Social Survey . It is possible that this underestimates the number of companies with stock.

Table 12: Political Views and Selected Other Characteristics of Shared Capitalism Employees

Figures are the percent of workers in each column heading (e.g. holding stock options) having the characteristic at the left of the table.

	Hold employer stock		Hold stock options		Profit sharing	
	Yes (5)	No (6)	Yes (7)	No (8)	Yes (3)	No (4)
Total	100.0%	100.0%	100.0%	100.0%	100.0%	100.0%
Political identification and participation						
Political party						
Democrat	31.3%	31.9%	33.5%	31.5%	34.3%	30.3%
Independent	36.6%	38.9%	34.2%	39.2%	32.6% *	41.5%
Republican	32.1%	29.3%	32.3%	29.3%	33.1%	28.2%
Strength of affiliation						
Strong Democrat	14.9%	12.2%	17.4%	12.3%	13.8%	12.4%
Not strong Democrat	16.4%	19.7%	16.2%	19.3%	20.5%	18.0%
Independent, near Democrat	11.5%	9.7%	11.8%	9.8%	8.5%	10.9%
Independent	14.9% *	22.9%	11.8% *	22.7%	17.6% *	23.1%
Independent, near Republican	10.3% *	6.3%	10.6%	6.6%	6.5%	7.4%
Not strong Republican	20.2%	16.8%	20.5%	16.8%	20.5% *	16.0%
Strong Republican	10.3%	11.3%	9.9%	11.3%	11.4%	10.9%
Voting						
Voted in 2000 election	68.8% *	58.2%	71.6% *	58.6%	66.1% *	57.4%
If voted in 2000, voted for Gore^	40.8%	42.0%	40.0%	42.2%	37.6%	44.0%
If voted in 1996, voted for Clinton^	61.3%	59.7%	65.1%	59.3%	56.8%	62.5%
Self-rated ideology						
Liberal	22.7%	27.0%	22.4%	26.7%	27.9%	25.4%
Moderate	40.2%	42.2%	40.0%	41.9%	37.0%	44.5%
Conservative	37.1%	30.8%	37.6%	31.4%	35.2%	30.1%
Group affiliations						
Attend religious svcs. 1/wk or more	24.1%	25.8%	17.3%	20.3%	17.2%	21.0%
Union member--self or spouse	17.2%	14.3%	13.3%	15.2%	7.5% *	19.1%
Region: East	15.2% *	22.8%	15.4%	22.2%	15.7% *	23.5%
Midwest	26.6%	23.5%	23.5%	24.3%	25.9%	23.8%

South	38.0%	34.8%	40.8%	34.6%	38.2%	34.2%
West	20.2%	18.9%	20.4%	18.8%	20.3%	18.5%
Social issues						
Favor gun permits	85.9%	82.1%	85.5%	82.4%	81.5%	83.8%
Have gun in home	34.1%	35.5%	34.6%	35.4%	40.7%	32.2%
Favor abortion if woman wants it for any reason	48.2%	45.2%	62.3% *	43.6%	54.7% *	39.5%
Homosexual relations not wrong at all	32.5%	34.4%	30.8%	34.3%	37.8%	32.3%
Economic issues						
Subjective class identification						
Lower class	1.1% *	3.7%	1.9%	3.4%	1.7%	3.7%
Working class	45.3% *	56.7%	45.1% *	55.7%	46.1% *	58.6%
Middle class	50.2% *	37.5%	47.5% *	39.0%	48.5% *	35.9%
Upper class	3.4%	2.2%	5.6% *	2.0%	3.6%	1.8%
Confidence in major companies						
A great deal	17.9%	16.9%	11.9%	17.7%	19.4%	16.2%
Only some	66.3%	65.9%	67.8%	66.0%	69.1%	64.7%
Hardly any	15.8%	17.2%	20.3%	16.3%	11.5% *	19.2%
Satisfaction w/financial situation						
Satisfied	34.6% *	25.0%	36.1% *	25.4%	34.4% *	23.1%
More or less	46.6%	46.3%	44.2%	46.8%	46.2%	46.2%
Not at all	18.8% *	28.7%	19.8%	27.8%	19.5% *	30.7%
Change in financial situation in past few years						
Getting better	67.7% *	47.4%	65.1% *	49.8%	61.5% *	46.6%
Getting worse	9.8% *	17.7%	14.0%	16.4%	10.0% *	19.4%
Stayed the same	22.6% *	34.9%	20.9% *	33.8%	28.5%	34.1%
Have good chance of improving std. of living						
Strongly agree	24.2%	21.8%	20.3%	22.7%	27.1%	19.9%
Agree	54.7%	52.7%	54.2%	52.7%	54.3%	53.5%
Neither	8.4%	12.2%	10.2%	11.5%	11.4%	10.0%
Disagree	11.6%	11.2%	15.3%	10.9%	6.4% *	14.0%
Strongly disagree	1.1%	2.2%	0.0%	2.2%	0.7%	2.6%

* Significant difference between "yes" and "no" columns at the 95% level.

Table 13: Participation in Shared Capitalism Programs, from Survey of Establishments or Workplaces.

Based on analysis of 2003 National Organizations Survey

	All private sector (1)	For-profit companies (2)	Not-for-profit orgs. (3)	Privately-held companies^ (4)	Publicly-held companies (5)
Percent of employees covered^^					
Profit sharing	38.4%	50.2%	22.5%	41.3%	69.8%
Gainsharing	13.2%	21.1%	1.8%	10.6%	26.7%
Own company stock	20.6%	37.9%	0.0%	33.4%	60.8%
Granted stock options in past year	2.5%	4.8%	0.0%	0.8%	10.2%
Percent of establishments that cover any employees*					
Profit sharing	61.9%	64.5%	41.2%	64.1%	82.3%
Gainsharing	35.0%	38.7%	9.1%	39.2%	46.8%
Own company stock	32.6%	37.8%	0.0%	45.8%	75.0%
Granted stock options in past year	14.1%	16.3%	0.0%	10.0%	52.7%
Percent of establishments that cover 50% or more of employees*					
Profit sharing	46.0%	47.9%	32.4%	45.3%	64.5%
Gainsharing	22.9%	25.3%	6.1%	26.4%	27.4%
Own company stock	16.1%	18.7%	0.0%	16.1%	51.9%
Granted stock options in past year	4.8%	5.6%	0.0%	4.2%	16.4%
Sample size	315	276	36	133	67

Profit sharing is defined as eligibility for bonuses based on overall organizational performance.
Gainsharing is defined as eligibility for bonuses based on department or plant performance.
^ Column 4 includes privately-held corporations and partnerships.
^^ Weighted by establishment size to reflect economy-wide percentage of employees covered.

SOURCE: Analysis of the General Social Survey and the National Organizations Study by Douglas Kruse of Rutgers University, Joseph Blasi of Rutgers University and Richard Freeman of Harvard University, December 2003, for the Shared Capitalism Project of the National Bureau of Economic Research in Cambridge, Massachusetts.

NOTE: For a downloadable copy of the full data tables in Word ort PDF on this survey of shared capitalism see:

http://www.rci.rutgers.edu/~blasi

Appendix IV. Employee Equity In The Biotechnology Industry's Top Ten Companies.

Non-executive employees

26,489	Total Employees in the ten companies
14%	Average total employee equity for non-exec employees
23%	Average total employee equity for all insiders*
61%	Share of average total employee equity non-exec hold
95%	Share of 2002 stock option profits going to non-exec employees
81%	Share of 2002 stock options granted to non-exec employees
77%	Share of all company stock options in hands on non-exec employees
$156. Billion	Total market value of the ten corporations at the end of 2002
$1.131 Billion	Total 2002 stock option profits of non-exec employees as a group
0.72%	Non-exec employees 2002 option profits as % of market value
36%	Portion of the Nasdaq Biotech Index represented by the 10 firms

Source: Analysis of SEC filings by Profs. Joseph Blasi and Douglas Kruse, Rutge University, March 2004. *includes board members as reported.
Note: The 14% total employee equity of non-executives is 12% from broad-based stock options and 2% from ESPPs and 401ks. Stock option holding are after exercise and dilution.

Top Five Executive employees

50	Total top five execs in the ten companies
9%	Average total employee equity for top 5 execs*
5%	Share of 2002 stock option profits going to top 5 exec employees
19%	Share of 2002 stock options granted to top 5 exec employees
23%	Share of all company stock options in hands on top 5 exec employees
$56. Million	Total 2002 stock option profits of top 5 exec employees as a group
0.04%	Exec 2002 option profits as a share of end of total market value
23%	Average employee equity for non-executive and executive employees
26%	Average institutional shareholder ownership of over 5% stakes
36%	Portion of the Nasdaq Biotech Index represented by the 10 firms

Source: Analysis of SEC filings. *includes board members as reported.

Note: The 14% total employee equity of non-executives is 12% from broad-based stock options and 2% from ESPPs and 401ks. Stock option holding are after exercise and dilution.

Testimony of George Scalise
President, Semiconductor Industry Association

Before the Committee on Financial Services
Subcommittee on Capital Markets, Insurance and Government Sponsored Enterprises

April 21, 2004

Mr. Chairman, members of the subcommittee, thank you for inviting me to appear before you today to discuss the very important issue of employee stock options. My name is George Scalise and I am the president of the Semiconductor Industry Association. SIA supports HR 3574, the Stock Option Accounting Reform Act, and we commend your leadership, Chairman Baker, and the leadership of more than 30 members of the Financial Services Committee who are now co-sponsors of the legislation.

Since 1977 SIA has been the leading voice for the U.S. semiconductor industry. Today, SIA member companies comprise more than 85 percent of the U.S. semiconductor industry. Collectively, the chip industry employs a domestic workforce of 255,000 people across the country. The U.S. semiconductor industry is **the** most competitive in the world, and the mission of the SIA – and all of the policy objectives we support -- is to retain that lead.

I will comment on the problems I see with the accounting for employee stock options (ESO), but I also want to leave you with a very clear picture of the implications this issue has for U.S. competitiveness. In addition, I want to leave no doubt that we are talking about **employee** stock options – SIA members give 80-95+ percent of options to employees who are outside the executive offices. Expensing the top five will help address concerns you may have about executive compensation – I trust no one on the panel has concerns about providing an equity stake to non-executive employees. Because options are granted to such a wide cross section of our employees, any requirement to expense all employee stock options, as FASB as proposed, will be material to our members' earnings – thus it is vital that the accounting be right. I believe the current FASB proposal raises more questions than it answers about our ability to value options accurately.

The U.S. High Tech Ecosystem

Just as major industry sectors such as automobiles and steel drove U.S. economic growth in the 20th century, information technology industries, especially semiconductors, are a critical growth engine for the U.S. economy today. The inter-connected web of entities that comprise information technology have helped deliver higher productivity, lower inflation, jobs, better health care, unprecedented prosperity and standards of living, military superiority and increased national security. Semiconductors are, in effect, the brains and nerve center for almost all electronic products today and are thus at the heart of the entire IT sector, enabling everything from advanced computers to medical equipment to weapons systems and contributing **$75 billion annually** to U.S. GDP, more than another other single manufacturing technology.

While semiconductors are at the base of the competitive U.S. information technology sector, the IT sector as a whole is in fact part of a complex and dynamic innovation ecosystem. The interplay between our world class research universities, leading edge industrial R&D, advanced manufacturing, and venture capital is what keeps the U.S. competitive. Superior science and engineering talent is the key to holding this ecosystem together. Our members are engaged in constant global competition for the best and brightest engineers from around the world and contrary to common belief U.S. companies do not always win that fight.

Semiconductor companies, particularly in Taiwan and China, use stock options as a key recruitment tool – given that those regions do not tax employee options, it is already difficult for U.S. companies to win head-to-head competitions for specific employees. In fact, all you have to do to really understand this dynamic is to go to the Pudong area of Shanghai where you will find numerous expatriate engineers who were hired away from some large U.S. semiconductor companies – lured in large part by huge option grants. The same can be said for Taiwan where 5000 US trained engineers have moved there to work in the information technology industry.

In our industry, stock options are routinely given not only to executives, but also to those well below the executive level – in fact, 80-95 percent of options are granted by our members to those below the senior executive level. We must offer our employees the potential to share in the success they help generate through an equity stake – requiring expensing would severely limit our ability to compete for and retain talent. Jeff Thomas who is here with me today from Altera Corporation is a perfect example – I think you will find what he has to say very compelling. Because options are granted to a very broad cross section of our employee base, any requirement to expense broad based plans would have a material impact on earnings.

Getting the Accounting Right

SIA and its members believe providing the investing public with transparent, accurate and comparable information is of paramount importance and any changes to the rules must bolster this goal. Getting the accounting right is a formidable challenge.

Accountants in academia, the private sector and the public sector do not all agree that employee stock options are a corporate expense to be deducted from earnings. Some would have you believe that that fundamental threshold question is not debatable. Quite to the contrary – there is anything but a consensus view that employee stock options are a corporate expense.

Similarly, there is absolutely no consensus among experts on how to value employee stock options accurately, reliably and consistently if they were to be expensed. No one has yet found an appropriate method to value employee stock options. That is why, despite years of study by not just FASB but also by some of the smartest mathematicians and economists in the world, FASB still can't suggest a single, precise option pricing model. Let me reiterate that point. Despite working on this for more than a decade, despite convening an "Option Valuation Group," hand-picked by FASB to come up with a new model, despite all kinds of research by others – FASB is still left with a hypothetical model designed for something entirely different – freely tradable options. The just released exposure draft proposes the same two models – binomial and Black-Scholes – that it identified 10 years ago when it adopted the current standard. The valuation ball has moved not one inch. And I believe that you can't expense what you can't accurately value.

Why are employee stock options not a corporate expense? [1]. Briefly put, an employee stock option is an incentive compensation instrument designed to attract and retain the best available employees, and to provide an equity stake in order to increase the employee's productivity to a level in excess of that which could be achieved by cash or fringe compensation alone. Accordingly, the express

---

[1] This section relies in large part on *Stock Option Expensing: Getting the Accounting Right*, Kip Hagopian, March 29, 2004, as found at www.sia-online.org.

purpose of an ESO is not to raise new equity capital but to increase the value of the issuer's existing equity. The granting of employee stock options does not result in the creation of a quantifiable liability and leaves the employee with no claim on the assets of the firm – instead, they represent a means of allowing employees to reap the rewards of ownership. As a result, the granting of employee stock options does not meet the accounting definition of an expense. Instead, options represent dilution of ownership.

Beyond this core accounting issue, it also must be emphasized that employee stock options truly are unique financial instruments – significantly different than the type of options for which the Black Scholes model was designed -- which is why valuation remains an intractable challenge.

- Whereas tradable options are sold on the open market, ESOs may only be granted to employees. In other words, employees are the only market for ESOs. In its draft, FASB notes that the most accurate determination of fair value requires a willing buyer and a willing seller – however, by definition, such an arrangement cannot exist for ESOs, which are highly restricted.
- ESOs are not actually stock options until they vest, which may occur on periodic fixed dates or on a single fixed date several years out in the future.
- ESOs are not transferable to anyone at any time, even to another employee of the issuer. This means that neither the ESO agreement nor the option itself can be sold either before or after it vests. As a result, the only way that an employee can benefit financially from an ESO is to stay with the employer until the option vests, then exercise it and sell the underlying stock.

The broad and deep dispersion of options to all levels of employees within SIA member companies makes potential inaccuracies in valuation more troubling. Companies that issue only a small number of employee stock options – typically to top executives – will be less sensitive to inaccurate valuations being included in their financial statements because those numbers may be so small as to be immaterial. This situation appears to characterize many of the companies that recently chose to expense their employee stock options. SIA members, though, grant options to a large segment of their workforce and so fear the inclusion of a large, inaccurate expense. With the same number of options outstanding, companies could experience wild fluctuations in their reported earnings – these fluctuations would have no relation to the financial well-being or performance of the company.

Tax Treatment

Tax treatment for ESOs is fairly straight forward. When an ESO is exercised, the difference between the exercise price and the fair market value on the date of exercise is a taxable gain to the option holder and a tax-deductible expense to the company that granted it. The IRS prohibits the expensing of an ESO for tax purposes until it is exercised, mainly because the IRS does not believe that ESOs have a "readily ascertainable market value" at grant date. In the absence of such, the IRS has opted to wait until a value has been clearly determined. The FASB draft assumes that expensing would take place on the grant date, although they have solicited comments on this question.

Employee Stock Purchase Plans (ESPPs)

A major fatality of stock option expensing would also be the Employee Stock Purchase Plans (ESPP) which the majority of SIA member companies offer to their employees. ESPP plans allow all eligible employees throughout the world to buy company stock at a discount via payroll deduction several times a year. Usually the amount of the discount is 15% -- yet proposed changes would require expensing of any options granted with more than a 5% discount. It is very **<u>likely that many companies will not bother with a 5% discount and these</u> plans will cease to be offered**. These plans are open to 100% of our workforce, in companies that have such a program and employees actively participate in these plans. It is a very real way for employees to benefit as the value of a company increases, thus improving productivity. And when productivity improves, shareholder value goes up. In this way, all of the investors in a company benefit from ESPP plans. Yet FASB's exposure draft may kill ESPPs in one fell swoop.

Summary

SIA members believe that current accounting rules rightly require detailed disclosure on option grants, including their potential dilutive effects. In addition, market share prices directly reflect diluted earnings per share, therefore the cost of stock options is already reflected in the market price of stock. Impact on earnings per share and dilution caused by option grants, therefore, is information that should be made available in a consistent manner to shareholders. If an additional expense was added – in addition to calculating dilution – the effect of options grants would essentially be counted twice. Companies report diluted earnings per share already, which make this impact clear.

Part of the rationale for seeking expensing of ESOs is the quest for international convergence. The International Accounting Standards Board (IASB) – based in Europe – is seeking expensing as well. Adoption of the draft standard they put forward is very much up in the air. It must first go through a vigorous review process within the European Community – the outcome of that review is not at all a sure thing. It is not clear to SIA members why the actions or proposals of the IASB should govern the timetable for accounting changes in the United States.

In our industry, stock options are routinely given not only to executives, but also to those well below the executive level – as already noted, 80-95+ percent of options are granted by our members to those below the senior executive level. Options allow us to insure that our employees are able to fully share in the success they have helped make possible. In addition, they are a key means by which we attract and retain our best employees. It is also the best opportunity our employees have to build an equity position for their family. Our members are engaged in constant global competition for the best and brightest engineers from around the world and we must offer those employees the potential to enjoy the success they help generate through an equity stake – requiring expensing would severely limit our ability to compete for talent through such equity participation. I would urge you to pay very close attention to this fact as you seek to reach a position on this important legislation.

I would be happy to answer any questions you might have regarding our position.

STATEMENT OF PHILLIPS W. SMITH

Before the

SUBCOMMITTEE ON CAPITAL MARKETS, INSURANCE & GOVERNMENT SPONSORED ENTITIES

COMMITTEE ON FINANCIAL SERVICES

April 21, 2004

Thank you for allowing TASER International, AeA, and me personally to testify on the enormous impact stock options have on U.S. business development and job growth. I would like to commend the committee and you, in particular, Mr. Chairman, for your leadership on the Stock Option Accounting Reform Act. I support the legislation and urge the committee to act promptly to pass this important measure.

As an individual involved with five high technology start-ups as a CEO and Chairman of the Board, I have substantial experience in this area. Of the five companies I have helped launch, one was created in Denver without options in the early 1970's, one was built quite successfully in the Silicon Valley with options, and three additional companies have been started in Phoenix all with options. The most successful of those companies is the one I chair today, TASER International, Inc. In addition, I have a Ph.D. in Business Administration with a focus in the area of finance so I well understand the theoretical arguments being presented as to the expensing of all options, but I do not plan to take any of your time today discussing that as the topic has been covered by other people in far more depth.

TASER International, Inc., was founded in the 1990s with all the funding provided by myself and one other investor. We struggled through seven tough years prior to going public in 2001. Throughout the company's infancy, we used stock options for our office employees as a way to attract the best and brightest from larger companies. These people built the company to what it is today and I have a chart (see below) to show what the stock has done over the last year.

TASR Liquidity Characteristics

Common Stock Data

	TASR
Price:	$98.04
Shares Outstanding:	12,675,000
Market Capitalization:	$1,242,857,000
6-Month Average Daily Volume:	4,115,729
1% of Shares Outstanding:	126,750
Average Weekly Volume (past 4 weeks):	40,300,000
Dividend Yield:	0.00% ($0.00 annual)
52-Week High:	$98.04 (7-Apr-2004)
52-Week Low:	$1.50 (8-Apr-2003)
Short Interest:	3,770,290
Float:	8,850,000
Call Open Interest: Apr-04 $90.00:	3,236 contracts
Total:	51,140 contracts
Put Open Interest: Apr-04 $90.00:	278 contracts
Total:	56,785 contracts
Stock Loan:	50,000 shares at -9% rate available
Major Index:	Nasdaq Composite

Source: Bloomberg
Data as of 7-April-2004

Normalized Price Performance

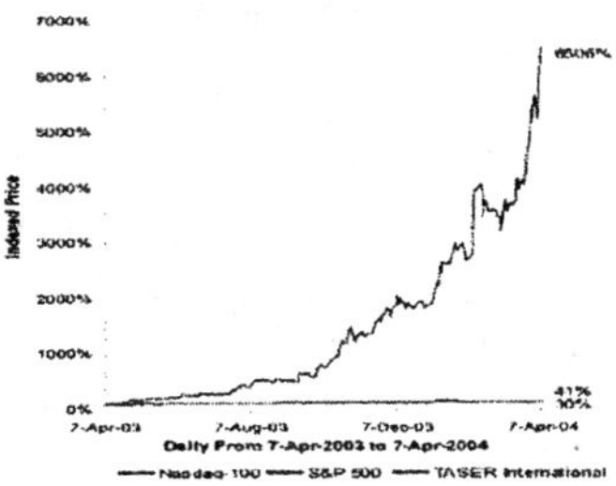

Just to put this in perspective, we have forty-two office employees that received early stock options. Our production employees are also now receiving stock options. Of the 42 employees plus four board members who received early options, 20 are now able to live their dreams because they have all achieved greater than $1 million of net worth from those options. The pending proposal from FASB would have kept 38 of those people from receiving options because the financial exposure to a young company like TASER International would have been so high we could not afford to offer stock options to workers below the top five senior executives. The current FASB proposal would do nothing but take away the potential for non-executives to live their dreams.

I am not really here to give any theoretical concepts, as you have probably seen and heard enough of the accounting theory. But I am here to give a realistic appraisal of what this FASB proposal would do to a young company like ours. The impacts would be profound on job growth, economic development, corporate governance, and workers' lives.

JOB GROWTH AND ECONOMIC DEVELOPMENT

First, on the stock options that were used to attract people to our company back in the early days. I have listed below a table of employment of our company and other suppliers in the Phoenix area.

Year	Number of Employees	% of Growth	Phoenix Area Supplier
2000	33		
2001	57	72	25 – 50
2002	73	28	50 – 100
2003	151	107	300 – 400

By looking at this table, you can see that we are one of the young growth "gazelle" companies that are big job creators for this country. And you can see that not only did we create new jobs for our own company, but there is a dramatic impact in the local marketplace because as we grow, it requires our suppliers to grow their employment base as well. Companies like TASER fuel the economic growth of our communities and the U.S. industrial base. We are the heart of our nation's economic recovery.

CORPORATE GOVERNANCE

The next area where options have been particularly critical has been in TASER's ability to attract really top quality board members to help guide the company strategically through a period of high growth. Let me describe our board members' backgrounds:

The first individual we recruited after going public was Bernie Kerik. Bernie was the New York Police Commissioner under Mayor Guiliani during the 9/11 crisis. He later went to Iraq to serve as the Minister of the Interior. To get a man of that caliber on the board of a young company like TASER, a company that just went public with lots of potential liability, we had to offer something above and beyond our incentive package of $1,000 per meeting. Options were the only incentive we could provide. They turned out to be lucrative, but at the time Commissioner Kerik joined us he took a chance and accepted the potential liability hoping it would work out.

Our second Board member is Dr. Mark Kroll. He is the chief technology officer for St. Jude Medical, a very large, well recognized and highly respected medical device company. Dr. Kroll is the chief technology officer for St. Jude Medical's heart and rhythm division. He is also a world-renowned expert in pace-makers and implantable cardiac defibrillators. How do you get a world-class scientist with 156 personal patents in his own portfolio to join a board like ours and effectively be our chief science advisor? The way we did it was to offer him options.

The third member of TASER's board is Dr. Matt McBrady, a Finance Professor at the Darden School of Business at the University of Virginia. Dr. McBrady is our financial expert and advises in complying with the Sarbanes-Oxley requirements. To get Dr. McBrady on our board, again we provided options.

Our fourth outside director is TASER's other original investor with me, Mr. Bruce Culver. Mr. Culver has founded two companies that are currently listed on the NASDAQ. He is a very well known entrepreneur and came on the board because he had a lot of stock in the company, but also because he got options to take the risk of being a board member.

So you can see simply by looking at these four individuals how essential it is that young companies have stock options to attract the management talent they need for direction and advice, particularly through the early high growth days of their development.

WORKERS' LIVES

Finally, returning to TASER's employees, we are incredibly proud of the pay-off our workforce has enjoyed through TASER's success. The options we used to attract high-level talent and the sacrifices our employees made throughout our early years have created 20 new millionaires living the American dream. Our strategy for growth and continued use of options will allow others to follow in their footsteps and achieve that same level of success.

The reality is that options serve a variety of purposes. The legislation you have proposed, Mr. Chairman, as I understand it, will basically address the egregious compensation concerns some Members of Congress have with the top five corporate officers, without affecting rank and file employees. If changes must be made, I believe your approach strikes a balance in targeting abuse while giving companies the ability to attract the individuals they need to succeed. Under your approach, companies like TASER could continue to grow.

I can tell you from a personal standpoint, having done five high technology start-ups myself, that if all stock options are expensed as recommended by the current FASB proposal, all that will be accomplished is to take away opportunity from the workers who really make these companies successful It will close the door on people who spend their lives fostering these start-up companies and helping them grow.

We at TASER International provided stock options to our employees not only to attract their talent, but also because we believe it is right for people who put their shoulder to the wheel to personally share in the financial success of our company.

There seems to be a lot of pressure to make us (the USA) like everybody else. Yet as we developed the greatest growth engines in the world, starting in the Silicon Valley through the beltway outside of Washington, we did it by using stock options. I can't tell you today that options were the only reason for that great growth, but I can tell you this, we all know that jobs are being exported. We know that we need to get people back to work and to create new jobs. It's young companies like TASER that are creating those jobs. Options are not the only reason companies get started or are successful, but they are one of the tools that help create growth. By tampering with that very successful model for growth and disassembling parts of it, by taking away options and forcing the expensing of these options, FASB is tampering with a model that has worked very well. The system is not broken. There is no need to change the way options have been treated

Finally, I'd like to raise one additional point for the committee's consideration. It is that this FASB proposal would disproportionately hurt smaller companies in relation to big companies.

I had to chuckle when Coca-Cola said they said were going to expense options. If you look how few people in Coca-Cola even get options and secondly, the way the valuation for stock options is computed, big companies enjoy a large advantage in expensing options in their profit and loss statements. The FASB valuation formula hurts young companies. Our stock is very volatile. I showed you the chart earlier. That chart reflects a lot of volatility in TASER's stock. Forcing us to expense stock options would provide us a double whammy. Because the stock of small companies is most volatile, expensing it under the FASB formula is a much bigger accounting hit to a small company, especially where the small company gives options to all employees. I urge the committee to consider the disparate impact of the FASB valuation formula as it moves forward in the coming months.

In conclusion, I do not think this is the intent of the Congress or its agents to penalize the engines of growth that are the biggest job creators. Yet, recognizing the pressure behind this options expensing movement, it is my hope that we can get the Stock Option Accounting Reform Act to the President before year-end. Bringing certainty, closure, and responsible reform to the options controversy would permit us to keep this excellent recruiting and motivating tool available to all people within our companies and not just the top five Executives.

Thank you for the opportunity to be here today.

Testimony of Jeff Thomas
Field Applications Engineer, Altera Corp.

Before the Committee on Financial Services
Subcommittee on Capital Markets, Insurance and Government Sponsored Enterprises

April 21, 2004

Introduction

Chairman Baker and members of the subcommittee: good afternoon and thank you for hearing my testimony today.

My name is Jeff Thomas. I am a Field Applications Engineer, or FAE, for Altera Corporation in San Jose, CA. Altera Corporation designs and sells programmable logic devices which are semiconductor chips that are used in a broad range of applications. In my role as an FAE, I provide on-site technical support to one of our largest customers, a major telecommunication company.

My responsibilities include training engineers on how to use our chips, helping our customers debug their systems, and ensuring that our chips work properly. In an average day, I will give a presentation on our latest technology, work in our customer's lab to help them debug a circuit, and write some code to help our customer implement their design.

I volunteered to participate in this hearing because stock options played a large role in my decision to pursue a career in a high tech field.

Personal History

I graduated from Carnegie Mellon University in 2000 with a bachelor's degree in Electrical and Computer Engineering. I had job offers from a broad range of companies. During my time at CMU, I had two summer internships at Fortune 500 companies. Both companies offered me a job upon graduation, but neither offered broad-based stock option plans.

I also interviewed with a number of high tech firms. All of my job offers from high tech firms included some type of employee stock option program. I decided that I wanted to work for a company where I had a stake in the success of the company. I liked the idea of being able to profit not only from my salary, but also from the growth of the company.

In retrospect, I can definitely say that I have seen difference in the behavior and performance of employees at high tech firms who have a vested interest in their company's success versus the people I worked with at companies that do not offer broad-based stock option plans.

Personal Experience

My first day at Altera, I was granted stock options that would vest over the next four years. Each year, 25% of my options vest, which means that if I have stayed with the company and the stock price has gone up, I can buy and sell the options and realize a profit.

Also, each year at my annual review, I am granted a new batch of options, based on my performance, that follow a similar vesting schedule. This ensures that I am motivated to stay with the company and work to increase the company's value.

Altera Perspective

Stock options are a great incentive for employees. People work hard, not only to advance their personal careers, but also to grow the company as a whole. They allow all employees to share in the success of the company. As the sales and profits of the company increase, employees benefit through appreciation of the stock price. This fosters an environment where employees will go out of their way and beyond their job description to grow the company.

Stock options are also a strong motivation to stay with a company. Because of the vesting schedule, employees are incentivized to stay with a good company to continue to increase their ownership stake. Since I believe in Altera's long term vision, I want to stay with the company and continue to build my share in the company through the stock option program. Because everyone at Altera has a stake in the company, they are committed to making the company successful in the long term.

Industry Perspective

This behavior is not unique to Altera. I see the same type of dedication and work ethic at other companies in Silicon Valley. All of my friends, whether they work at big telecom companies or small start-ups, share the same desire to see their company succeed because of their ownership stake. Engineers in the Valley often work long hours and weekends to ensure that their company succeeds. Each person has a personal stake in the company beyond their paycheck.

Already in my career, I have seen the effect of broad based stock option plans in action. I have been able to compare this to the atmosphere at companies that do not offer such a program. I can definitely say that employees who have stock options show a much stronger dedication to their company. Throughout my career, I want to continue working for a company that offers stock options to all employees because it means that everyone at the company is working toward the shared goal of increasing the company's value.

Conclusion

I believe that anything that would make it more difficult for a company to grant stock options to a broad base of employees will reduce the company's overall performance. The success of Silicon Valley is based on the work ethic and dedication of its employees. This work ethic is a direct result of the fact that employees know that they will share in the success of their company.

If a company is unable to grant it's employees an ownership stake, those employees will become much less concerned with the overall success of the company. I sincerely hope you will consider the positive impacts of stock options while you are determining the fate of this bill.

Thank you again Mr. Chairman and members of the subcommittee for hearing my testimony today. I would be happy to answer any questions you might have at this time.

THE WALL STREET JOURNAL. ONLINE

April 19, 2004 4:04 p.m. EDT

FASB Chairman Calls For Investors To Speak Up On Options

By LINGLING WEI
April 19, 2004 4:04 p.m.

Of DOW JONES NEWSWIRES

NEW YORK -- Financial Accounting Standards Board Chairman Robert Herz, acknowledging as "very well organized" the high-tech lobby against expensing stock options, called for investors to "make your views known."

During an investor conference call Monday hosted by Glass Lewis & Co., a San Francisco-based institutional investor advisory firm, Herz said "there definitely are risks" that the board's efforts to require stock-option expensing could be thwarted by congressional intervention.

"While we believe we will go through, I know one thing I can't control is Congress," Herz said, a remark reminiscent of FASB's failure a decade ago to require companies to treat employee options as a business expense. In the face of congressional pressure as well as strong opposition from corporations, the board compromised on the current rule that encourages expensing but doesn't require it. Companies do have to disclose the options expense in their financial footnotes.

Under the new standard FASB proposed at the end of March, companies will have to count the value of options against earnings, starting next year. The proposal is open to public comment until the end of June; FASB expects to put a final rule in place by year-end.

However, amid the heavy tech lobbying, two bills associated with stock options have been introduced in Congress. One would deter FASB from making the accounting change for three years, while the other would limit the expensing requirement to a company's five highest-paid executives.

"All we can do is to continue to march along with our (standard-setting) due process," Herz said. In the meantime, he said, investors and analysts, the very beneficiaries of the proposed rule change, should also make sure that "you make your views known to people in Washington."

A recent survey conducted by Broadgate Consultants found that the vast majority of the 302 portfolio managers and analysts polled support the FASB expensing proposal, saying the rule change will improve financial transparency and corporate governance.

There has also been a growing movement among shareholders of tech companies to demand stock-option expensing. Among them: Texas Instruments Inc. (TXN), PeopleSoft Inc. (PSFT),

Hewlett-Packard Co. (HPQ) and Apple Computer Inc. (AAPL).

Among those who participated in Monday's discussion with investors were Sir David Tweedie, chairman of the International Accounting Standards Board, the European counterpart to the FASB, and Lynn E. Turner, former chief accountant of the Securities and Exchange Commission and now managing director of research at Glass Lewis.

IASB already has passed a rule on stock-option expensing. The two boards have been working together since 2002, with the ultimate goal of having a single set of high-quality accounting standards worldwide. "We would be horrified" if Congress stepped in and blocked FASB's reform efforts on stock options, Tweedie said.

The chairmen of both boards have acknowledged that the biggest challenge for them to achieve convergence has so far come from heavy business lobbying for politicians' intervention in accounting standards. On the IASB part, the European Commission has threatened to reject its two standards on financial instruments, thanks to heavy lobbying by European banks and insurers.

During the call, in addition to calling for more involvement from investors in the standard-setting process, both chairmen also went through some details about how exactly to account for the compensation expense.

They noted that currently there is a slight difference between the IASB rule and the FASB proposal on how to account for the income-tax benefits derived from stock options. Tweedie, noting the willingness from both sides to solve the difference, said "hopefully next year, we both will have exactly the same standard."

-By Lingling Wei, Dow Jones Newswires; 201-938-2089; Lingling.Wei@dowjones.com

URL for this article:
http://online.wsj.com/article/0,,BT_CO_20040419_006291,00.html

PHILIP ANGELIDES
Treasurer
State of California

April 9, 2004

The Honorable Anna Eshoo
U.S. House of Representatives
205 Cannon Office Building
Washington, DC 20515

Dear ~~Congressmember Eshoo~~: Anna

I am writing to express my support for your legislation, *The Stock Option Accounting Reform Act* (H.R. 3574). This bipartisan bill will address growing concern regarding excessive executive compensation, while protecting broad-based stock option plans that provide long-term benefits to employees and stockholders.

H.R. 3574 calls for the expensing of options by only the top five executives of a company. Limiting expensing to the top five is consistent with existing U.S. Securities and Exchange Commission (SEC) requirements that apply generally to the top five officers of a company. In addition, H.R. 3574 calls for a study to determine a more accurate way to assess the value of stock options while preserving broad-based employee stock option plans – programs that grant stock options to 50 percent or more of full-time employees.

Particularly in light of the Financial Accounting Standards Board's (FASB's) recent proposal to require mandatory stock option expensing for all employees of a company, I believe H.R. 3574 is necessary to preserve the broad-based employee stock option plans that benefit middle class workers, spur innovation, and contribute to our nation's global technological leadership. Stock options offer millions of employees the opportunity to enjoy equity ownership, reap financial rewards and share in their company's success. Over the past 20 years, broad-based stock option plans have helped build some of the nation's most innovative companies while providing non-managers at these companies with financial opportunities that might otherwise be unattainable.

In April of 2003, in the wake of widespread revelations of excessive executive compensation, I called for new Equity Compensation Standards for the 1,000 largest companies in which the California Public Employees' Retirement System (CalPERS) and California State Teachers' Retirement System (CalSTRS) – the nation's first and third largest public pension funds – invest. These new standards mean that CalPERS and CalSTRS will vote their proxies in favor of only those equity compensation plans that, among other things, limit the award of stock options to the top five executives at publicly

915 CAPITOL MALL, ROOM 110, SACRAMENTO, CA 95814 • (916) 653-2995 • FAX (916) 653-3125

traded corporations to no more than 5 percent of a company's total stock options. Importantly, these standards will help curb abuses and excesses, while encouraging the adoption of broad-based employee stock option plans. In the summer of 2003, CalPERS and CalSTRS adopted these Equity Compensation Standards – the toughest such standards in the country, and the newest industry standard for this proxy season.

In contrast, FASB's proposal will not ensure good corporate governance. Ironically, it will increase a company's incentives to grant options to a select few executives without the involvement of other employees. This is the wrong approach for our economy, and I believe that Congress must take necessary action to ensure that workers and shareholders are protected from such executive compensation abuses.

I applaud your efforts in authoring this important piece of legislation. If I can be of any assistance on this matter, please do not hesitate to contact me, or have your staff contact my Deputy Treasurer, Ted Eliopoulos, at (916) 653-2995.

Sincerely,

Phil Angelides
State Treasurer

cc: Honorable Members, House Subcommittee on Capital Markets, Insurance, and Government Sponsored Enterprise
Honorable Members, House Committee on Financial Services
Honorable Members, California Congressional Delegation

APPENDIX

May 4, 2004

NEWS FROM:

U.S. Rep. Ed Royce

California's 40th district representative, 2202 Rayburn Building, Washington, D.C. www.royce.house.gov

For Immediate Release Contact: Julianne Lignelli
May 4, 2004 202-225-4111

Royce Statement at Capital Markets Subcommittee Hearing on Stock Options

"The FASB Stock Options Proposal: Its Effect on the U.S. Economy and Jobs"

WASHINGTON, D.C. - - U.S. Rep. Ed Royce (R-CA-40) chaired today's Subcommittee on Capital Markets, Insurance and Government Sponsored Enterprises hearing entitled "The FASB Stock Options Proposal: Its Effect on the U.S. Economy and Jobs." The following is his opening statement:

"This afternoon we are convened for the purpose of reviewing the pending Financial Accounting Standards Board employee stock option expensing proposal and the potential effect its adoption may have on job creation and the U.S. economy.

"In previous hearings on this subject I have expressed deep concerns about the potential economic consequences of FASB's proposal to require the mandatory expensing of employee stock options. Like other supporters of Chairman Baker's legislation, H.R. 3574, I believe that broad-based stock options have played an important and positive role in our economy.

"Stock options enable emerging companies, which often do not have a tremendous amount of excess cash or cash flow, to attract talented employees that would otherwise not work for such firms. Some people claim that issuing such options represent an expense to a firm; however, stock options do not represent a cost to an entity. No cash is ever dispersed from the company's treasury. Existing shareholders may see their ownership diminish through dilution, but current accounting standards already require potential dilution to be fully disclosed.

"In the not-so-certain case that employee options are actually exercised the employing company receives cash. Employees who accept options are taking a well-known risk. There are no guarantees a firm will succeed and its stock price will rise. We hear about the successes in business, but let's not forget there are far more failures.

"The specific purpose of today's hearing is to explore the economic impact of FASB's proposal. Economic behavior has already changed because of this proposal. Many technology firms have already announced that they will no longer issue employee options. As a result, many firms have not been able to attract needed employees. Whether an individual is risk averse, risk taking, or risk loving, he or she is not likely to leave their job with a large mature firm to go to a start-up for a compensation package containing less cash and no stock options.

Statement of Representative Ed Royce
"The FASB Stock Options Proposal: Its Effect on the U.S. Economy and Jobs"
Page 2 of 2

"If one accepts the premise that FASB's proposal will end broad-based stock option plans, as we know them today, then we should think about the potential long-term, negative consequences for our economy. Firms like Intel, Microsoft, Cisco, and Yahoo all used stock options at their early stages to attract employees. Would these firms have reached their amazing levels of success had stock options not been an available tool for recruitment? Will this proposal inhibit the development of the next Intel or Cisco? Established firms will survive and prosper under any new rule issued by FASB, but I am concerned new that new firms may not develop as a result. I believe that it is important for Congress to raise these concerns.

"We are very fortunate to have Mr. Herz and Mr. Batavick here today to help deal with these issues. I hope that in your opening remarks you will address questions such as:

- Has FASB field-tested valuation models;
- Has FASB considered the economic consequences of mandatory expensing;
- Has FASB considered that mandatory expensing could give foreign-based firms a competitive advantage in attracting employees;
- Is FASB concerned that its proposal could make financial comparability between firms more difficult; and lastly,
- Is FASB still open to considering other, non-binomial models?

"I look forward to hearing answers to these and many other questions."

###

May 4, 2004

Opening Statement by Congressman Paul E. Gillmor
House Financial Services Committee
Subcommittee on Capital Markets, Insurance, and Government Sponsored Enterprises
Hearing entitled, "The FASB Stock Options Proposal: Its Effect on the U.S. Economy and Jobs" Day 2

Thank you, Mr. Chairman, for holding this important hearing and allowing our Committee an opportunity to hear from the Financial Accounting Standards Board (FASB) on their recently released Exposure Draft regarding requiring firms to recognize the fair value of employee stock options as an expense.

I would like to remind my colleagues today of the Congressional Budget Office (CBO) Paper released on April 4, 2004 entitled, "Accounting for Employee Stock Options," and its important findings:

> If firms do not recognize as an expense the fair value of employee stock options, measured when the options are granted, the firms' reported net income will be overstated... Although complicated to calculate, the fair value of employee stock options may be estimated as reliably as many other expenses.

The Paper goes on to conclude, that "[r]ecognizing the fair value of employee stock options is unlikely to have a significant effect on the economy." I applaud FASB for their continued hard work on this issue and for the release of their Exposure Document.

U.S. Financial markets remain the envy of the world due to the quality, timeliness and credibility of the financial information and disclosures provided by companies. The result is better allocation of resources and lower overall cost of capital. We here in Congress must ensure that this remains the case by allowing our standard-setter to operate independent of public and private special interests.

As we discuss FASB's proposal this afternoon, I continue to encourage my colleagues to support the position that the role of FASB is to pursue transparency and accuracy in accounting standards, not to choose among competing public policies. We should not be setting accounting standards on a political basis.

Again, thank you Mr. Chairman for calling this hearing and I look forward to an informative session.

Testimony of

Robert H. Herz

Chairman

and

George J. Batavick

Board Member

Financial Accounting Standards Board

before the

Capital Markets, Insurance and Government Sponsored Enterprises

Subcommittee of the Committee on Financial Services

May 4, 2004

Testimony of
Robert H. Herz
Chairman
and
George J. Batavick
Board Member
Financial Accounting Standards Board
before the
Capital Markets, Insurance and Government Sponsored Enterprises Subcommittee of the Committee on Financial Services
May 4, 2004

Table of Contents

TABLE OF CONTENTS

Testimony of
Robert H. Herz
Chairman
and
George J. Batavick
Board Member
Financial Accounting Standards Board
before the
Capital Markets, Insurance and Government Sponsored Enterprises Subcommittee of the Committee on Financial Services

Prepared Statement

Robert H. Herz
Chairman
and
George J. Batavick
Board Member
Financial Accounting Standards Board

Chairman Baker, Ranking Member Kanjorski, and Members of the Subcommittee:

Good afternoon. I am Robert Herz, chairman of the Financial Accounting Standards Board ("FASB" or "Board"). With me is one of my fellow Board members, George Batavick. George is heading up the FASB's recently established Small Business Advisory Committee.

We are pleased to appear before you today on behalf of the FASB. We want to thank you for inviting us to participate in this very important and timely hearing, particularly since H.R. 3574, or any similar legislation, if enacted, would preempt and override our thorough, objective, and public due process to improve the accounting and financial reporting for equity-based compensation.

George and I have brief prepared remarks, and we would respectfully request that the full text of our testimony and all supporting materials be entered into the public record.

The FASB is an independent private-sector organization. Our ability to conduct our work in a systematic, thorough, and unbiased manner is fundamental to achieving our mission—to establish and improve general-purpose standards of financial accounting and reporting for both public and private enterprises. Those standards are essential to the growth and stability of the United States ("US") economy because creditors, investors, and other consumers of financial reports rely heavily on credible, transparent, comparable, and unbiased financial information to make rational resource allocation decisions.

Because the actions of the FASB affect so many organizations, our decision-making process must be open, thorough, and as objective as possible. Our Rules of Procedure require an extensive and public due process. That process involves public meetings, public hearings or roundtables, field visits or field tests, liaison meetings with interested parties, consultation with our advisory councils, and exposure of our proposed standards to external scrutiny and public comment.

Following the comment period, the Board actively redeliberates the issues. Those redeliberations often result in significant changes and improvements to the proposals we issue. Throughout the life of a project, the FASB members and staff also regularly meet informally with a wide range of interested parties to obtain their input and to better our understanding of their views.

The Board makes final decisions only after carefully considering and analyzing the input of interested parties. We do our best to balance the often conflicting perspectives of various parties and make independent, objective decisions guided by the fundamental concepts and key qualitative characteristics of sound, fair, and transparent financial reporting, including relevance, reliability, comparability, operationality, and cost effectiveness.

In March 2003, at a public meeting, the Board decided by unanimous vote to add a project to our agenda to address issues relating to improving the accounting for equity-based compensation. The project was in response to the high level of public concern expressed by many individual and institutional investors, financial analysts, creditors, the major accounting firms, study groups such as the Conference Board Commission on Public Trust and Private Enterprise, and many other parties, including a number of Members of Congress, about the need to improve the accounting for equity-based compensation. More specifically, many expressed support for eliminating the exception from expense recognition that presently exists only for so-called fixed plan employee stock options.

Many believe that the existing reporting for equity-based compensation results in significant distortions in the reporting of earnings, operating results, and operating cash flows of an enterprise—distortions that cannot be remedied solely by improvements in disclosures. The ultimate goal of the project is to develop a standard that results in reporting that more faithfully reflects the underlying economic effects of equity-based compensation arrangements and that brings about greater comparability of reporting in this important area. The project also provides an opportunity to achieve greater international convergence of accounting standards, an objective we have been encouraged to pursue by the Sarbanes-Oxley Act, the US Securities and Exchange Commission, and many other parties.

On March 31st of this year, the Board issued, by unanimous vote, a proposal for public comment to improve the accounting for a wide range of equity-based compensation arrangements. That proposal is the result of an extensive public due process that began in November 2002 before the project was added to the Board's agenda. That process included the issuance of a preliminary document for public comment, the review of over 300 comment letters and over 130 unsolicited letters, the review of relevant research studies, consultation with our advisory councils and valuation and compensation experts, field visits, public and private discussions with hundreds of individuals, including users, auditors, and preparers of the financial reports of small businesses, and active deliberations at 38 public Board meetings at which the provisions of the proposal were carefully developed with consideration given to the ongoing input received from interested parties.

Based on our extensive public due process to-date, the Board believes that the proposal would significantly improve the financial reporting for equity-based compensation arrangements. By creating greater transparency, completeness, and a more level playing field in the accounting for different forms of equity-based compensation, we believe that the proposal would enhance the comparability of reported results between enterprises that choose to compensate their employees in different ways. The proposal would achieve that through a number of provisions, including by eliminating the existing exception for fixed plan employee stock options, which, as indicated earlier, are the only form of equity-based compensation that is not currently required to be reported as an expense in the financial statements. The proposal also includes provisions that we believe would improve the transparency of the effects of equity-based compensation on reported cash flows.

The proposal reflects the view that all forms of equity-based compensation should be properly accounted for as such and that the existing exception for fixed plan employee stock options results in reporting that not only ignores the economic substance of those transactions but also distorts reported earnings, profitability, and other key financial metrics. Thus, under the current standards, the greater the use of fixed plan employee stock options, the greater the distortion of reported results. I would note that, in contrast, this distortion does not occur when enterprises use stock options, or similar instruments such as stock purchase warrants, for purposes other than compensating employees, for example, in acquiring goods or services or in financing or merger and acquisition transactions. In those cases, current accounting standards do require that stock options or warrants be valued and accounted for in the financial statements.

In the public company arena, the proposal would bring about greater comparability between the over 575 companies that have voluntarily opted to account for the cost of employee stock options and many others that have elected not to do so. It also would be responsive to the growing number of companies, including major technology companies, whose shareholders by a majority vote have approved nonbinding proxy resolutions mandating expensing of all employee stock options. Management of a number of those companies have indicated that they are awaiting completion of our project in order to respond to the demands of their shareholders.

The proposal also would result in substantial convergence in the accounting for equity-based compensation between our standards and international accounting standards that will, beginning next year, be followed by enterprises, including many small and nonpublic enterprises, in over 90 countries around the world. I also would note that our neighbor to the north, Canada, who often has followed the lead of the US in improving accounting standards, felt that it could not wait on this topic, and decided to mandate expensing of employee stock options beginning in January of this year. I understand that implementation of their new standard has to-date gone very smoothly.

Finally, I also would note, as indicated earlier, that improvements in accounting standards have economic consequences. More credible, comparable, and transparent financial information can enhance the efficiency of capital allocation in our markets. Most agree that efficient allocation of capital is essential to the growth and stability of the US economy.

With regard to potential economic consequences of our proposal, many economic experts that have reviewed the issue of the accounting for employee stock options, including Federal Reserve Chairman Alan Greenspan, former Federal Reserve Chairman Paul A. Volcker, Nobel Prize winning economists Robert C. Merton and Joseph E. Stiglitz, and groups like the Financial Economist Roundtable, the Republican Staff of the Joint Economic Committee of the US Congress, the Conference Board Commission on Public Trust and Private Enterprise (co-chaired by Peter G. Petersen and Secretary John W. Snow), major investment banks, and the Congressional Budget Office, all have indicated support for the mandatory expensing of all employee stock options. Indeed many of those experts have also indicated that mandatory expensing could have positive economic consequences because of the improvements in capital allocation that would result from eliminating the exception from expense recognition for fixed plan employee stock options, and, thus, having more credible, comparable, and transparent financial information.

I also would note that some of those experts and many compensation experts have indicated that the expensing of all employee stock options would result in a more accurate and meaningful assessment by employers of the true costs and benefits of the many available forms of equity-based compensation, thereby leading to sounder and more creative compensation approaches.

I would now like to hand over to George who will discuss the several special provisions contained in our proposal relating to small businesses, as well as other matters relating to our continuing work and due process on this important topic.

Thank you, Bob—and good afternoon everyone.

Before I outline the special small business provisions contained in our proposal to improve the accounting for equity-based compensation, I would first like to provide some brief background on small businesses and financial accounting and reporting standards.

First, there is no federal law requiring nonpublic enterprises to use FASB standards. Thus, for most small businesses, the use of our standards is primarily a private choice. For some small businesses, that choice may be influenced by whether they have plans to become a public enterprise.

For other small businesses, the decision to follow FASB standards may be influenced or controlled by their current or potential lenders, suppliers, other contracting parties, or State regulators. To the extent that one of those parties requires that the financial reports of a small business comply with our standards, that requirement presumably reflects that party's opinion that our standards result in better, more transparent, information for their respective purposes.

Second, it is also important to note that the FASB has long recognized as part of our public due process procedures that the costs of complying with our standards can fall disproportionately on small businesses. In recognition of that fact, the Board actively solicits and carefully considers requests from users, auditors, and preparers of the financial reports of small businesses to provide for special provisions to alleviate the costs of implementing our standards. Those requests come from our continuous and ongoing due process and deliberations throughout the life of a project.

In following our project on equity-based compensation, all interested parties, including large and small businesses, can take advantage of our free weekly Action Alert e-mail subscription, which discusses current agenda items and past Board decisions. Interested parties also can attend our open Board meetings, call in, or listen to our free web cast of our meetings on the day of the meeting, with replays of our meetings available for one week thereafter. Our meetings get extensive news coverage by the top news agencies, and our free website includes an up-to-date summary of all equity-based compensation issues discussed and our tentative decisions.

We actively seek input from various State CPA societies whose membership, in turn, briefs their clients, in many cases small businesses, on the status of this and other Board activities. In addition, liaison meetings with various groups having small business representation, and Board member and staff speaking engagements provide additional means of receiving valuable input from the small business community.

With respect to this proposal, it is our understanding that although the use of employee stock options is prevalent at some small businesses, particularly start-ups and venture capital backed enterprises that plan to become public enterprises, the vast majority of small businesses in the US do not grant employee stock options. As indicated earlier, however, for those small businesses that are affected by our proposal, the proposal includes several special provisions intended to alleviate the costs of implementing the proposed requirements.

First, the proposal includes a special provision that would permit most small businesses (including all that are nonpublic enterprises) to measure compensation cost using a simpler, less costly "intrinsic value method," rather than the fair-value-based method that would be required for most public enterprises. Under the intrinsic value method, the amount of compensation expense required to be reported would generally be equivalent to the amount of the income tax deduction for stock options.

Second, the proposal includes a special provision that provides that most small businesses that are nonpublic enterprises would have a simpler, less costly "prospective" transition to the proposed new requirements.

Finally, the proposal includes a special provision that provides that the effective date of the proposed standard for nonpublic enterprises would be delayed for one year until 2006.

I also would like to note that the proposal includes a Notice for Recipients ("Notice") that highlights and describes these special provisions. The Notice requests that respondents to the proposal indicate what other special provisions for small businesses might be appropriate and whether any or all such special provisions should also be extended to public enterprises that are small business issuers under the federal securities laws. The Notice also highlights and describes 19 other key aspects of the proposal, including the proposed mandatory recognition of compensation cost, valuation methods and guidance, measurement attribute and measurement date, employee stock purchase plans, attribution of compensation cost, modifications and settlements, disclosures, transition, cash flows, and the overall understandability of the proposal.

The Board currently plans to discuss the proposal's special provisions and other issues about the proposal with representatives of small businesses at the inaugural public meeting of our Small Business Advisory Committee on May 11. Our request for agenda items for this meeting showed interest in the proposal. We also plan to hold public roundtable meetings with valuation and compensation experts, and users, auditors, and preparers of financial reports in June to discuss a broad range of issues about the proposal.

Following the end of the proposal's comment period in June, the Board plans to redeliberate, at public meetings, issues raised in response to the proposal. Those redeliberations will include careful consideration of the ongoing input received from all parties, including ongoing input from the members of the Small Business Advisory Committee.

Only after carefully evaluating the input at public meetings will the Board consider whether to issue a final standard. The Board's current plans are to complete its redeliberations and be in a position to issue a final standard in the fourth quarter of this year.

On behalf of myself and Bob, I would again like to express our appreciation for inviting us to participate in this hearing. All of the information we obtain in connection with this hearing will be carefully considered.

In conclusion, let me assure you that you, and the users, auditors, and preparers of financial reports, including small business financial reports, can have confidence that the Board will continue to actively reach out and solicit input in response to our proposal. That input will be carefully considered in an open, thorough, and objective manner. Our ultimate goal is to develop an accounting standard that will faithfully report the underlying economic effects of equity-based compensation transactions and, thus, significantly improve the transparency and integrity of financial reporting in the US.

Thank you again, Chairman Baker. Bob and I would welcome the opportunity to respond to any questions.

Testimony of
Robert H. Herz
Chairman
and
George J. Batavick
Board Member
Financial Accounting Standards Board
before the
Capital Markets, Insurance and Government Sponsored Enterprises Subcommittee of the Committee on Financial Services
May 4, 2004

Full Text of Testimony

Chairman Baker, Ranking Member Kanjorski, and Members of the Subcommittee:

I am Robert Herz, chairman of the Financial Accounting Standards Board ("FASB" or "Board"). With me is one of my fellow Board members, George Batavick. George is heading up the FASB's recently established Small Business Advisory Committee ("SBAC").

We are pleased to appear before you today on behalf of the FASB. We want to thank you for inviting us to participate in this very important and timely hearing.

Our testimony includes a brief overview of (1) the FASB, including the importance of the Board's independence and the ability to conduct its work in a systematic, thorough, and objective manner, (2) the process the FASB follows in developing accounting standards, (3) the background and basis for the Board's unanimous decision to issue a proposal to improve the accounting for equity-based compensation, (4) the key provisions of the proposal, (5) the special provisions of the proposal applicable to small business, (6) how the proposal would improve financial reporting, (7) the current status of, and the FASB's plans relating to, the proposal, (8) some observations about some of the more common arguments offered by some opponents of the proposal, and (9) some observations about H.R. 3574.[1]

The FASB

The FASB is an independent private-sector organization.[2] We are not part of the federal government. Our independence from enterprises, auditors, and the federal government is fundamental to achieving our mission—to establish and improve standards of financial accounting and reporting for both public and private enterprises, including small businesses.[3] Those standards are essential to the efficient functioning of the capital markets and the United States ("US") economy because investors, creditors, and other consumers of financial reports rely heavily on credible, transparent, comparable, and unbiased financial information to make rational resource allocation decisions.

The FASB's independence, the importance of which was recently reaffirmed by the Sarbanes-Oxley Act of 2002 ("Act"),[4] is fundamental to our mission because our work is technical in nature, designed to provide preparers with the guidance necessary to report information about their economic activities. Our standards are

---

[1] H.R. 3574, 108th Congress, 1st Session (November 21, 2004).

[2] See Attachment 1 for information about the Financial Accounting Standards Board ("FASB" or "Board").

[3] See Attachment 2 for excerpts from recent materials about the importance of the FASB's independence and concerns about proposed legislation.

[4] Sarbanes-Oxley Act of 2002, Public Law Number 107-204, Sections 108-109.

the basis to measure and report on the underlying economic transactions of business enterprises. Like investors and creditors, Congress and other policy makers need an independent FASB to maintain the integrity of the standards in order to obtain the financial information necessary to properly assess and implement the public policies they favor. While bending the standards to favor a particular outcome may seem attractive to some in the short run, in the long run a biased accounting standard is harmful to investors, creditors, the capital markets, and the US economy.

The FASB's authority with respect to public enterprises comes from the US Securities and Exchange Commission ("SEC"). The SEC has the statutory authority to establish financial accounting and reporting standards for publicly held enterprises. For 30 years, the SEC has looked to the FASB for leadership in establishing and improving those standards. The SEC recently issued a Policy Statement reaffirming this longstanding relationship.[5]

The Policy Statement, consistent with the language and intent of the Act, also reemphasizes the importance of the FASB's independence described earlier.[6] It states:

> By virtue of today's Commission determination, the FASB will continue its role as the preeminent accounting standard setter in the private sector. In performing this role, the FASB must use independent judgment in setting standards and should not be constrained in its exploration and discussion of issues. This is necessary to ensure that the standards developed are free from bias and have the maximum credibility in the business and investing communities.[7]

The SEC, together with the private-sector Financial Accounting Foundation ("FAF"),[8] maintains active oversight of the FASB's activities.

What Process Does the FASB Follow in Developing Accounting Standards?

Because the actions of the FASB affect so many organizations, its decision-making process must be open, thorough, and as objective as possible. The FASB

[5] "Policy Statement: Reaffirming the Status of the FASB as a Designated Private-Sector Standard Setter," Exchange Act Release Nos. 33-8221; 34-47743; IC-26028; FR-70 (April 28, 2003).

[6] Sarbanes-Oxley Act of 2002, Sections 108-109; the legislative history of the Sarbanes-Oxley Act of 2002 ("Act") is clear that the provisions of the Act relating to the FASB were intended to "strengthen the independence of the FASB . . . from . . . companies whose financial statements must conform to FASB's rules." Senate Report 107-205, 107th Congress, 2d Session (July 3, 2002), page 13.

[7] Policy Statement, Page 5 of 8.

[8] See Attachment 1 for information about the Financial Accounting Foundation.

carefully considers the views of all interested parties, including users, auditors, and preparers of financial reports of both public and private enterprises, including small businesses.

Our Rules of Procedure require an extensive and thorough public due process.[9] That process involves public meetings, public hearings or roundtables, field visits or field tests, liaison meetings with interested parties, and exposure of our proposed standards to external scrutiny and public comment. The FASB members and staff also regularly meet informally with a wide range of interested parties to obtain their input and to better our understanding of their views. As discussed further below, many of our due process activities include active outreach to, and participation by, users, auditors, or preparers of the financial reports of small businesses. The Board makes final decisions only after carefully considering and analyzing the input of all interested parties.

While our process is similar to the Administrative Procedure Act process used for federal agency rule making, it provides for far more public deliberations of the relevant issues and far greater opportunities for interaction with the Board by all interested parties. It also is focused on making technical, rather than policy or legal, judgments. The FASB's Mission Statement and Rules of Procedure require that in making those judgments the Board must balance the often conflicting perspectives of various interested parties and make independent, objective decisions guided by the fundamental concepts and key qualitative characteristics of financial reporting set forth in our conceptual framework.

The FASB and the FAF, in consultation with interested parties, periodically review the FASB's due process procedures to ensure that the process is working efficiently and effectively for users, auditors, and preparers of financial reports.[10] Over the past two years, the FASB and the FAF have undertaken a significant number of actions to improve the Board's due process procedures. Some of those actions were intended to increase the quality and breadth of input to our process, including increasing the input from users, auditors, and preparers of small businesses. Those particular actions include the following:

- Establishing a SBAC in order to increase involvement by the small business community in developing accounting standards. The SBAC, whose members represent diverse perspectives and experiences, comprises lenders, investors and analysts, preparers of financial statements from a broad range of businesses, including controllers and chief financial officers, and auditors from the small business community.

[9] See Attachment 1 for information about the FASB's due process.

[10] The Securities and Exchange Commission ("SEC") also recently reviewed the FASB's due process and concluded that "the FASB has the capacity . . . and is capable of improving both the accuracy and effectiveness of financial reporting . . ." Policy Statement, page 5 of 8.

- Establishing a User Advisory Council ("UAC") in order to obtain more active user involvement in our process. The UAC comprises representatives of individual and institutional investors, investment and commercial banks, rating agencies, and other groups that represent investors and key users. Several of the members of the UAC are primarily users of financial reports of small businesses.

- Making our public Board meeting announcements available to interested parties more broadly through an email subscription service.

- Making our public Board meetings available to interested parties for monitoring via the telephone and via web cast on our website free of charge.

- Making all of our proposals for public comment, all of the comments received, and the full text of all our standards publicly available on our website.

What Are the Background and Basis for the Board's Unanimous Decision to Issue a Proposal to Improve the Accounting for Equity-Based Compensation?

A Brief History of the Accounting for Equity-Based Compensation

APB Opinion 25

US accountants and accounting standard setters have long debated the issue of the best way to report employee stock options. In 1972, the Accounting Principles Board ("APB"), the predecessor of the FASB, issued APB Opinion No. 25, *Accounting for Stock Issued to Employees.* Partly because techniques to estimate the value of stock options did not yet exist, the drafters of Opinion 25 created an exception to the normal financial reporting model.[11] That model encompasses the general principle that all of an enterprise's costs should be included in the enterprise's financial statements; otherwise, the enterprise's income is overstated.

Under the Opinion 25 exception, only stock options granted to employees that meet certain specified criteria (so-called fixed plan employee stock options) are not reported as an expense. All other options and all other forms of equity-based

[11] Opinion 25 measures stock issued to employees using the "intrinsic value based method." Under that method, compensation cost is the excess, if any, of the quoted market price of the stock at grant date or other measurement date over the amount an employee must pay to acquire the stock. Opinion 25, paragraph 10. The consequence of using the intrinsic value based method is that stock options are frequently issued with the quoted market price of the stock at grant date equal to the amount an employee must pay to acquire the stock and, thus, no expense is reported in the financial statements.

transactions result in expenses to be included in the financial statements consistent with the general principle.

Statement 123

Many parties agreed that the Opinion 25 exception was not the best approach to transparent financial reporting for employee stock options, and, in 1984, the FASB undertook a project to reconsider the issue. In 1993, after several delays in the project, the FASB issued an Exposure Draft, *Accounting for Stock-based Compensation,* for public comment. The Exposure Draft proposed to replace Opinion 25 and require recognition of compensation cost for all awards that eventually vest, based on their fair value at the grant date. For nonpublic enterprises, the Board decided to permit those enterprises to omit expected volatility from the fair value determination (so-called minimum value method) because "estimating expected volatility for the stock of a newly formed entity that is rarely traded, even privately, is not feasible."[12]

In 1995, however, when the FASB issued Statement No. 123, *Accounting for Stock-Based Compensation,* it permitted companies to continue to apply Opinion 25, while also requiring annual footnote disclosures of the fair values (or minimum value for nonpublic enterprises) of fixed plan employee stock options otherwise omitted from the financial statements. The following paragraphs of Statement 123 summarize the basis for the Board's decision to only *encourage,* rather than *require,* that all stock-based compensation be measured at fair value at date of grant and reported as an expense in determining an enterprise's net income:

> The Board continues to believe that financial statements would be more relevant and representationally faithful if the estimated fair value of employee stock options was included in determining an entity's net income, just as all other forms of compensation are included. To do so would be consistent with accounting for the cost of all other goods and services received as consideration for equity instruments. . . . However, in December 1994, the Board decided that the extent of improvement in financial reporting that was envisioned when this project was added to its technical agenda . . . was not attainable because the deliberate, logical consideration of issues that usually leads to improvement in financial

[12] Statement of Financial Accounting Standards No. 123, *Accounting for Stock-Based Compensation* (October 1995), paragraph 174.

> reporting was no longer present. Therefore, the Board decided to specify as preferable and to encourage but not to require recognition of compensation cost for all stock-based employee compensation, with required disclosure of the pro forma effects of such recognition by entities that continue to apply Opinion 25.
>
> The Board believes that disclosure of the pro forma effects of recognizing compensation cost according to the fair value based method will provide relevant new information that will be of value to the capital markets and thus will achieve some but not all of the original objectives of the project. However, the Board also continues to believe that disclosure is not an adequate substitute for recognition of assets, liabilities, equity, revenues, and expenses in financial statements. . . . *The Board chose a disclosure-based solution for stock-based employee compensation to bring closure to the divisive debate on this issue—not because it believes that solution is the best way to improve financial accounting and reporting.*[13]

In 2002, in Congressional testimony before the Committee on Banking, Housing and Urban Affairs, Dennis R. Beresford, who was the FASB chairman at the time Statement 123 was issued, shared his views about that Statement and the reasons for the Board's decision:

> As many of you may recall, the FASB had proposed that companies account for the expense represented by the fair value of stock options granted to officers and employees. The business community and accounting firms strongly opposed this proposal and a number of corporations engaged in a lobbying effort to stymie the FASB's initiative.
>
> Certain members of Congress were sufficiently influenced by the appeals from corporate executives that they were persuaded to introduce legislation to counter the FASB's proposal. The legislation would have prohibited public companies from following any final FASB rule on this matter. More importantly, the legislation would have imposed requirements that the SEC repeat the FASB's process on any new

[13] Statement 123, paragraphs 61 and 62 (emphasis added).

accounting proposals, thus effectively eviscerating the FASB. Faced with the strong possibility that its purpose would have been eliminated by this legislation, the FASB made a strategic decision to require companies to disclose the effect of stock options in a footnote to the financial statements but not record the expense in the income statement.[14]

Pertinent Events Following the Issuance of Statement 123

For many years following the issuance of Statement 123, only a handful of companies elected to adopt the fair value method of reporting employee stock options as an expense in the income statement. In addition, few investors and other users of financial statements expressed significant concerns with that practice.

Beginning in 2001, however, following the highly publicized bankruptcies of several major enterprises including Enron Corp., Global Crossing Ltd., and WorldCom, Inc., many investors and other users of financial statements began questioning enterprises' accounting and reporting for employee stock options. Moreover, many enterprises began considering whether to voluntarily expense all equity-based compensation consistent with the requirements of Statement 123. As of March 2003, when the Board added the project on equity-based compensation to its agenda, 179 public companies had adopted or announced their intention to adopt the fair-value-based accounting method in Statement 123.[15]

In 2001, the FASB's international counterpart, the International Accounting Standards Board ("IASB") took up the subject of the accounting for stock options. It needed to do so, not only because of the growing use of employee stock options around the world, but also because there was no existing literature in the international standards on this topic.

In November 2002, it proposed, as the FASB decided almost 10 years ago in developing Statement 123, that the appropriate accounting for employee stock options is to measure compensation for the fair value of the options at the date granted and to recognize the cost over the period the option vests.[16] And, also as the Board decided in developing Statement 123, the IASB proposed that the best

[14] Prepared statement at a hearing on Accounting and Investor Protection Issues Raised by Enron and Other Public Companies: Oversight of the Accounting Profession, Audit Quality and Independence, and Formulation of Accounting Principles (February 26, 2002), page 5 (emphasis added).
[15] FASB Proposed Statement of Financial Accounting Standards, *Share-Based Payment* (March 31, 2004), paragraph C5.
[16] IASB Proposed IFRS, *Share-based Payment* (November 2002); FASB Exposure Draft, *Accounting for Stock-based Compensation* (June 1993).

way to measure the fair value at grant date is to use established option-pricing models and then make certain adjustments for the unique features of employee stock options. However, the IASB's particular set of adjustments and allocation methods were somewhat different from those under the fair value method developed by the FASB in Statement 123. There also were some other important differences between the IASB's proposal and the Statement 123 approach. Nevertheless, the fundamental conclusions were the same.

As the IASB released its exposure draft, the FASB issued an Invitation to Comment that explained in detail the similarities of and differences between the IASB proposal and the existing US standards and that solicited comments on those differences.[17] The purpose of the Invitation to Comment was twofold: (1) to solicit comments on certain issues that the Board would discuss when, in accordance with its objectives of improving US financial accounting and reporting standards and promoting international convergence of high-quality accounting standards, it considered whether it should propose any further improvements to the US accounting standards on equity-based compensation and (2) to assist constituents that were planning to respond to the IASB's proposal.

The FASB received 302 comment letters in response to the Invitation to Comment. Most commentators from industry that made general observations about the accounting for equity-based compensation, many of whom were from the high-technology industry, were generally against mandatory expense recognition of all equity-based compensation. Those commentators raised a number of issues including (1) whether mandated expensing of fixed plan employee stock options has a clear or widely accepted rationale; (2) whether existing option pricing models, including Black-Scholes and binomial models, even when adjusted, produce inaccurate and misleading information; and (3) whether mandated expensing of fixed plan employee stock options will discourage broad-based compensation plans.

In contrast, most commentators that were users of financial statements, including creditors, individual investors, pension funds, mutual funds, and financial analysts, were generally supportive of mandatory expense recognition of all employee stock options. Some representative examples include the following:

> Stock options have become a disgrace insofar as accurate reporting of expenses is concerned for corporation[s].

---

[17] FASB Invitation to Comment, *Accounting for Stock-Based Compensation: A Comparison of FASB Statement No. 123,* Accounting for Stock-Based Compensation, *and Its Related Interpretations, and IASB Proposed IFRS,* Share-based Payment (November 2002).

I strongly recommend that there be a requirement for stock options to be expensed.

Benham M. Black, Partner, Black, Noland & Read, PLC, and Director, Virginia Financial Group, Inc. (an independent bank holding company with total assets of $1.04 billion), 1/31/03

[A]s a fiduciary, I continue to be infuriated with the tech industry . . . and their blatantly self-serving position on stock options. Options have contributed mightily to the current crisis of confidence that we have in the stock market, and I view the expensing of options as a long-overdue and necessary step towards restoring both confidence and rationality in the market. . . . The tech industry has been masterful at marshalling their shareholders own capital against them, given their vociferous lobbying against the proper accounting treatment of options, but the time has come to treat options for what they are—compensation—and force them to be treated on par with all other forms of compensation.

Kenneth F. Broad, CFA, Portfolio Manager, Transamerica Investment Management, LLC (a registered investment adviser managing $12.5 billion in equity and fixed-income assets for mutual funds, funds for funds, separately managed accounts, retirement plans and various for-profit and nonprofit enterprises), 1/31/03

CPF . . . supports the view that stock options are compensation, have a cost, and that those costs should be included on reported income statements.

Michael R. Fanning, Chief Executive Officer, Central Pension Fund of the International Union of Operating Engineers and Participating Employers (on behalf of over 150,000 participants of the CPF), 1/23/03

Investors support the core conclusions by the IASB and the FASB that stock based compensation should be recognized as an expense and that the amount of compensation expense should be based on the fair value of stock-based awards at grant date.

James E. Heard, Chief Executive Officer, Institutional Shareholder Services (serving more than 950 institutional investors and corporate clients worldwide), 1/31/03

The Institute urges the Board to move forward with a reconsideration of Statement No. 123 as soon as practicable. We continue to believe that accounting standards should (1) require the issuers to treat the fair value of stock options granted to employees to be recognized as expense in the income statement and (2) ensure uniformity in how stock options are valued for this purpose.

Gregory M. Smith, Director – Operations/Compliance & Fund Accounting, Investment Company Institute (a national association including 8,938 mutual funds, 535 closed-end investment companies and 6 sponsors of unit investment trusts; its mutual fund members have assets of about $6.539 trillion, accounting for approximately 95% of total industry assets, and 90.2 million individual shareholders), 1/31/03

The Council supports the principles outlined in the IASB's exposure draft, and we urge the Financial Accounting Standards Board to propose and approve similar rules. The IASB proposal is in line with the Council policy on the issue, which states that since stock options granted to employees, directors and non-employees are compensation and have a cost, companies should include these costs as an expense on their reported income statements and disclose their valuation assumptions.

Sarah A. B. Teslik, Executive Director, Council of Institutional Investors (an association of more than 130 corporate, public and union pension funds with more than $3 trillion in pension assets), 1/21/03

In addition, the Board received many letters and emails from individual investors and other members of the general public from around the country urging the Board to mandate expense recognition for all equity-based compensation. Representative examples include the following:

> I strongly recommend that employee stock options be mandated as an expense on corporate financial statements. As long as these options can be passed out like funny money, thereby encouraging those on the receiving end to manipulate the financial records to their advantage – people like me will stay away from the market.
>
> *John S. Clauss, Jr., Glendale, California, 2/10/03*

> We encourage you to . . . require employee stock options to be counted as an expense. If you don't take this action who do you think will make these greed-monger's start accounting for their massive profits? Do the RIGHT THING, Damn it! . . .
>
> *David and Nancy Gabrielsen, Beavercreek, Oregon, 2/11/03*

> Companies are not required to expense options, which means they can give out as many as they want.
>
> I urge the FASB to require employee stock options to be counted as an expense. . . .
>
> *Rob Rocco, Avon Lake, Ohio, 2/12/03*

FASB's Current Project to Improve the Accounting for Equity-Based Compensation

In March 2003, at a public meeting, the Board decided to add a project to its agenda to address issues relating to equity-based compensation. That decision was based largely on three reasons.

The first reason was the high level of public concern expressed by creditors, individual and institutional investors, pension funds, mutual funds, financial analysts, and other users of financial statements about the need to improve the financial accounting and reporting for equity-based compensation, in particular the need to eliminate the exception from expense recognition that presently exists *only* for fixed plan employee stock options. Those users of financial statements that have been urging the FASB to eliminate the exception for fixed plan employee stock options include:

- The Council of Institutional Investors (an association of more than 130 corporate, public, and union pension funds with more than $3 trillion in pension assets)

- Institutional Shareholder Services (serving more than 950 institutional investors and corporate clients worldwide)

- The Office of the State Comptroller of New York (an investor, shareholder, and sole trustee of the nation's second largest pension fund at approximately $100 billion in assets)

- Moody's Investor Services

- The Central Pension Fund of the International Union of Operating Engineers and Participating Employers (on behalf of more than 150,000 participants of the CPF)

- The Teachers Insurance and Annuity Association College Retirement Equities Fund (a financial services company with approximately $262 billion in assets under management, serving nearly 3 million education and research employees at 15,000 institutions)

- The Investment Company Institute (a national association including 8,938 mutual funds, 535 closed-end investment companies, and 6 sponsors of unit investment trusts; its mutual fund members have assets of about $6.539 trillion, accounting for approximately 95 percent of total industry assets, and 90.2 million individual shareholders)

- The Association for Investment Management and Research (a nonprofit professional organization of 61,600 financial analysts, portfolio managers, and other investment professionals)[18]

- The American Federation of Labor and Congress of Industrial Organizations (representing 13 million of America's workers in 65 member unions)

---

[18] A 2001 survey conducted by the Association for Investment Management and Research found that more than 80 percent of financial analysts and portfolio managers responding to the survey believed that stock options granted to employees are compensation and should be recognized as an expense in the income statements of the enterprises that grant them. AIMR, "Analysts, Portfolio Managers Want Employee Stock Options Expensed on Income Statements, Global AIMR Survey Shows" (November 19, 2001).

- The Conference Board Commission on Public Trust and Private Enterprise (co-chaired by Peter G. Peterson, chairman of the Blackstone Group, former Secretary of Commerce and chairman of the Federal Reserve Bank of New York, and John W. Snow, (former) chairman, CSX Corporation and former chairman, Business Roundtable).

As indicated above, fixed plan employee stock options are the *only* form of employee stock options that *are not* required to be reported as an expense in the income statements of the enterprises that grant them. All other forms of employee compensation, including cash salaries, bonuses, fringe benefits, restricted stock, stock warrants, performance-based stock options, indexed-based stock options, employee stock ownership plans, are (and have long been) required to be reported as an expense. Moreover, when equity-based grants of any form are issued to nonemployees for goods or services, they also are (and have long been) required to be reported as an expense. The exception for fixed plan employee stock options is clearly an anomaly in today's financial accounting and reporting.

Also as indicated above, creditors, investors, and other users of financial reports have urged the Board to address the exception for fixed plan employee stock options. Many have pointed to the negative impact that exception has had on promoting excessive awards of such options, particularly to corporate executives, and the negative behavioral aspects that it has had on corporate responsibility.[19] Clearly, many creditors, investors, and other users of financial reports want this issue addressed and resolved in the near term.[20]

In 2002, President Bush announced a ten-point plan to improve corporate responsibility.[21] That plan including the following statement: "The authors of accounting standards must be responsive to the needs of investors."[22] There is no other issue on the Board's agenda on which investors have been clearer about the need for an improvement in the existing accounting standards.

The second reason the Board decided to add a project to its agenda to address issues relating to equity-based compensation was because of the complexity and noncomparability and, thus, potential lack of transparency created by the

---

[19] The Conference Board, "Commission on Public Trust and Private Enterprise, Findings and Recommendations, Part 1: Executive Compensation" (September 17, 2002), page 10.
[20] The major US accounting firms also are generally supportive of expensing of all employee stock options. Letter from Jack A. Weisbaum to the Honorable Richard H. Baker and the Honorable Paul E. Kanjorski (March 19, 2004); Letter from Dennis M. Nally, Eugene O'Kelly, James H. Quigley, and James S. Turley to the Honorable Richard H. Baker and the Honorable Paul E. Kanjorski (March 17, 2004); Letter from Edward Nusbaum to the Honorable Richard H. Baker (March 17, 2004); "Big Four Shift View on Expensing Options," *Financial Executive's News* (May 1, 2003).
[21] Ten-Point Plan to Improve Corporate Responsibility and Protect America's Shareholders (March 7, 2002).
[22] *Id.*

alternative accounting treatments presently available for reporting equity-based compensation. That lack of transparency has been magnified by the recent trend noted above of enterprises adopting the voluntary fair value provisions of Statement 123. Some of those enterprises, including Citigroup Inc. and J.P. Morgan Chase & Co., have requested that the Board mandate the expensing of all employee stock options. It is also interesting to note some of those enterprises, including Wal-Mart Stores, Inc., Netflix Inc., and Home Depot, Inc., have historically offered broad-based stock option plans to many nonexecutive employees and have indicated that adopting fair value expensing for all employee stock options will not result in a curtailment of those programs.[23]

The third reason the Board decided to add a project to its agenda to address issues relating to equity-based compensation was the opportunity to achieve convergence to a common, high-quality international accounting standard in this area. As noted earlier, the IASB issued a proposal in November 2002 that would require that all stock options be expensed at their fair value at grant date. To maximize the opportunity for international convergence, the FASB concluded that it needed to consider the US accounting requirements for equity-based compensation concurrently with IASB's consideration of its proposal.

The FASB has long been committed to actively working with the IASB and other national accounting standard setters to promote international convergence of accounting standards concurrent with improving the quality of financial reporting.[24] Both the Act[25] and the Policy Statement[26] indicate the support of the US Congress and the SEC, respectively, for the FASB's convergence efforts.

Since March 2003, the Board has held 38 public meetings to discuss the project. Preparations for those meetings included thousands of hours of research on issues relating to the project, including the review of the results of many research studies on the topic.

In addition, the Board and staff have participated in public and private discussions about the project with hundreds of individuals, including members of the Financial Accounting Standards Advisory Council, the UAC, the Option Valuation Group,[27] and other groups and organizations representing preparers, auditors, and users of financial reports. The Board also has conducted field visits with a variety of

---

[23] News from Carl Levin, U.S. Senator, Michigan, "Stock Option Roundtable Dismissed as One-Sided" (May 8, 2003), page 2; Reed Hastings, "Expense It!" *The Wall Street Journal* (April 5, 2004).
[24] FASB, *Rules of Procedure* (December 1, 2002, as amended), page 2.
[25] Act, Section 108(a)(2).
[26] Policy Statement, page 4 of 8.
[27] The Board established the Option Valuation Group to provide information and advice on how to improve the guidance in Statement 123 on measuring the fair value of stock options. Proposed Statement of Financial Accounting Standards, *Share-Based Payment*, paragraph C37.

enterprises of various sizes, including small businesses, covering a range of industries to discuss issues relating to the project.

In February 2004, at a public meeting, the Board unanimously agreed to the issuance of a proposal for public comment. That proposal was issued on March 31, 2004.[28]

What Are the Key Provisions of the Proposal?

Scope

The scope of the proposal is very broad addressing the accounting for transactions in which an enterprise exchanges its valuable equity instruments for employee services, including employee stock purchase plans. It also addresses transactions in which an enterprise incurs liabilities that are based on the fair value of the enterprise's equity instruments or that may be settled by the issuance of those equity instruments in exchange for employee services. The proposal does not change the accounting for similar transactions involving parties other than employees or the accounting for employee stock ownership plans. The Board intends to reconsider the accounting for those transactions and plans in a later phase of its project on equity-based compensation.

Recognition

For public enterprises, the proposal would require that the cost of employee services received in exchange for equity instruments be measured based on the grant-date fair value of those instruments (with limited exceptions). That cost would be recognized over the requisite service period (often the vesting period). Generally, no compensation cost would be recognized for equity instruments that do not vest.

Measurement

The proposal would require that the grant-date fair value of employee stock options and similar instruments be estimated using existing option-pricing models adjusted for the unique characteristics of those options and instruments.

Disclosures

The proposal would require that the footnotes to financial statements of both public and nonpublic enterprises disclose the information that users of financial information need to understand the nature of the equity-based compensation transactions and the effects of those transactions on the financial statements.

[28] See Attachment 4 for a summary of the proposal.

Transition and Effective Date

The proposal would be applied to public enterprises prospectively for fiscal years beginning after December 15, 2004, as if all equity-based compensation awards granted, modified, or settled after December 15, 1994, had been accounted for using the fair-value-based method of accounting.

What Are the Special Provisions of the Proposal Applicable to Small Business?

Consistent with the requirements of its mission and due process, when the Board developed the proposal it evaluated whether the proposal would fill a significant need and whether the costs imposed to apply the provisions of the proposal, as compared to other alternatives, would be justified in relation to the overall benefits of the resulting information. As part of that evaluation, the Board carefully considered the impact of the proposal on nonpublic enterprises (most small businesses are nonpublic enterprises).

The Board noted that the available statistical data about small businesses and employee stock options appears to indicate that very few small businesses operate stock option plans and, therefore, are unlikely, to be affected by the proposal.[29] For those small businesses, however, that do operate such plans the Board concluded that the proposal should include special provisions that mitigate the incremental costs those enterprises would incur in complying with the proposal's provisions.

Those special provisions include permitting most small businesses to (1) use a simpler, less costly method to measure compensation cost; (2) use a simpler, less costly method to transition to the new requirements; and (3) have a delayed effective date.

Simpler, Less Costly Measurement Approach

Most nonpublic enterprises would be permitted (and public enterprises, in the limited circumstances in which it is not possible to reasonably estimate the fair value of an equity instrument at the grant date, would be required) to measure

[29] Andrew Pendleton, Joseph Blasi, Douglas Kruse, Erika Poutsma, and James Sesil, "Theoretical Study on Stock Options in Small and Medium Enterprises," Final Report to the Enterprise-Directorate General, Commission of the European Communities (October 2002), page 45 (indicating that the incidence of any form of share scheme among small and medium size businesses is very low); Douglas Kruse and Joseph Blasi, Rutgers University, and Richard Freeman, Harvard University, "Analysis of the National Organizations Survey of 2002" (2004), Table 8 (Indicating that 5 percent of small businesses in the U.S. granted options to 10 percent or more of employees in 2002); Beth Levin Crimmel and Jeffrey L. Schildkraut, "Stock Option Plans Surveyed by NCS," *Compensation and Working Conditions* (Spring 2001), Table 3, page 11 (referencing 1999 survey indicating that 2.1 percent of enterprises with 100 employees or fewer offered stock options to employees).

compensation cost using a simpler "intrinsic value method," rather then the fair-value-based method that would be required for other enterprises.[30]

Under the intrinsic value method, the compensation cost for any reporting period would be measured based on the difference between any excess of the fair value of the enterprises' stock and the exercise price of the employee stock options granted, with final measurement of compensation cost at settlement date. The total amount of compensation expense reported under the intrinsic value method would generally be equivalent to the total amount of income tax deduction for option grants presently reported by those enterprises.

The Board believes that applying the intrinsic value method described above lessens incremental costs that nonpublic enterprises may incur in applying the proposed requirements. The Board noted that nonpublic enterprises must currently calculate the intrinsic value method whenever employee stock options are granted (for financial reporting purposes) and whenever employee stock options are exercised (for income tax deduction purposes). The Board also noted that most nonpublic enterprises only prepare audited financial reports once a year. Finally, to the extent that a nonpublic enterprise is funded by a venture capital firm, the Board noted that those firms are required to determine the fair value of their investments for financial reporting purposes.

After considering the input from users, auditors, and preparers of nonpublic enterprises' financial reports, the Board concluded that the intrinsic value method provided more meaningful information than other alternatives, including the minimum value method alternative permitted in Statement 123.[31] In rejecting the minimum value method alternative, the Board noted that that method ignores a key element of what makes options valuable, that is the ability of the holder for a potentially lengthy period of time to capture the appreciation in the value of the underlying stock.[32] As such, it results in a measurement that is not representationally faithful to the underlying economics of the transaction. It also was noted that the minimum value method could be easily manipulated to result in zero compensation expense being recognized.[33]

---

[30] The International Accounting Standards Board's International Financial Reporting Standard (IFRS) 2, *Share-based Payment* (February 2004), paragraph 24, does not permit the use of the intrinsic value method for nonpublic or public enterprises, but does require that that method be used by nonpublic or public enterprises in the rare circumstance that the fair value of the equity instrument cannot be estimated reliably.

[31] Proposed Statement of Financial Accounting Standards, *Share-Based Payment*, paragraphs C68-C72.

[32] *Id.* paragraph C72.

[33] Mark Rubinstein, "On the Accounting Valuation of Employee Stock Options," *Journal of Derivatives* (Fall 1995), page 21.

Simpler, Less Costly Transition Approach

All nonpublic enterprises would apply the proposed standard prospectively and not be required (as other enterprises) to apply the requirements to any nonvested portion of awards that were granted before the date of adoption of the proposed standard.

Delayed Effective Date

The effective date of the proposed standard for most nonpublic enterprises would be delayed for one year (fiscal years after December 15, 2005), as compared with the proposed effective date for other enterprises (fiscal years after December 15, 2004).

Solicitation of Comments on Special Provisions

The Board specifically highlighted the special provisions applicable to small businesses in the following issues contained in the proposal's Notice for Recipients ("Notice") to encourage respondents to provide further input on those issues:

> *Issue 14(a):* This proposed Statement would permit nonpublic entities to elect to use an intrinsic value method of accounting (with final measurement of compensation cost at the settlement date) rather than the fair-value-based method, which is preferable. Do you agree with the Board's conclusion to allow an intrinsic value method for nonpublic entities? If not, why not?
>
> *Issue 14(b):* Consistent with its mission, when the Board developed this proposed Statement it evaluated whether it would fill a significant need and whether the costs imposed to apply this proposed Statement, as compared to other alternatives, would be justified in relation to the overall benefits of the resulting information. As part of that evaluation, the Board carefully considered the impact of this proposed Statement on nonpublic entities and made several decisions to mitigate the incremental costs those entities would incur in complying with its provisions. For example, the Board decided to permit those entities to elect to use either the fair-value-based method or the intrinsic value method (with final

> measurement of compensation cost at settlement date) of accounting for share-based compensation arrangements. Additionally, the Board selected transition provisions that it believes will minimize costs of transition (most nonpublic entities would use a prospective method of transition rather than the modified prospective method required for public entities). Moreover, the Board decided to extend the effective date of this proposed Statement for nonpublic entities to provide them additional time to study its requirements and plan for transition. Do you believe those decisions are appropriate? If not, why not? Should other modifications of this proposed Statement's provisions be made for those entities?
>
> *Issue 15:* Some argue that the cost-benefit considerations that led the Board to propose certain accounting alternatives for nonpublic entities should apply equally to small business issuers, as defined by the Securities Act of 1993 and the Securities Exchange Act of 1934. Do you believe that some or all of those alternatives should be extended to those public entities?[34]

Also as noted above, the Board plans to discuss the views of individuals representing small and medium-sized businesses regarding the above issues and other aspects of the proposal at the inaugural meeting of the SBAC.

The Board will carefully consider during its public redeliberations of the proposal the input received from users, auditors, and preparers of small business financial reports and carefully consider whether the proposed requirements are cost effective and meet the demands of those parties and the marketplace.

How Would the Proposal Improve Financial Reporting?

The proposal would improve financial reporting by requiring for the first time the recognition of all compensation cost incurred as a result of receiving services in exchange for valuable equity instruments issued by the employer. Recognizing all compensation cost relating to equity-based compensation in the financial statements improves the relevance and reliability of that financial information, helping users of financial information to understand better the economic transactions affecting an enterprise and to make better resource allocation

[34] Proposed Statement of Financial Accounting Standards, *Share-Based Payment*, pages v and vi; see Attachment 4 for the complete Notice for Recipients.

decisions. Such information specifically will help users of financial reports understand the impact that equity-based compensation arrangements have on an enterprise's financial condition and operations. That Board view was confirmed in a recent survey of 302 buy-side portfolio managers and research professionals, who by a four-to-one margin indicated that they believe the proposal will improve transparency in financial reporting.[35] That same survey found that "an overwhelming majority--90%--of respondents said they are opposed to any exemptions from the options expensing rule for 'start-ups' or technology companies."[36]

In addition, a recent survey of 30 institutional technology investors found that more than 90 percent support the Board's effort to require enterprises to report employee stock option expense in their income statements.[37] That same survey also found that nearly 70 percent of technology investors opposed exceptions from the proposal for "newly public companies."[38]

Both surveys are consistent with a 2001 survey of more than 18,000 analyst and portfolio managers in which 83 percent of respondents agreed that employee stock options are compensation and should be recognized as an expense in the income statements of the enterprises that grant them.[39]

Also of note, during the 2003 and current proxy season, shareholders at over 30 enterprises have voted in favor of nonbinding resolutions mandating expensing of all employee stock options at the date of grant.[40] Some of those enterprises, including Apple Computer, Inc., IBM, MBNA Corp., Texas Instruments Inc., and Wells Fargo have indicated they will comply with their shareholders' request only after the FASB's new standard becomes effective.[41]

---

[35] Broadgate Consultants, Inc., "Institutional Investors Support FASB Options Expensing Proposal" (April 7, 2004).
[36] *Id.;* see Attachment 5 for additional excerpts from materials about the proposal.
[37] Steven Milunovich and Richard Farmer, "Tech Stock Options—The Invisible Cash Flow Drain," Merrill Lynch Comment (February 3, 2004), page 7.
[38] *Id.* page 11 (emphasis added).
[39] AIMR, "Analysts, Portfolio Managers Want Employee Stock Options Expensed on Income Statements, Global AIMR Survey Shows."
[40] Statement for the Record of Damon A. Silvers, Associate General Counsel, American Federation of Labor and Congress of Industrial Organizations Before the Committee on Governmental Affairs Subcommittee on Financial Management, the Budget, and International Security, United States Senate (April 20, 2004); Louis Lavelle, "Shareholders United to Expense Options," *BusinessWeek* Online (May 27, 2003).
[41] "Apple Won't Expense Options Before Rule Change," *Reuters* (May 13, 2003); Brian Bergstein, "IBM Shareholders Vote to Expense Options," *The Associated Press* (April 27, 2004); Jonathan D. Epstein, "MBNA Listens, Will Deduct Stock Options from Earnings," *The News Journal* (May 7, 2003); Crayton Harrison, "Shareholders for Texas Instruments Vote to Expense Stock Options," *The Dallas Morning News Knight Ridder/Tribune News* (April 16, 2004); Mark Calvey, "Wells Shareholders Call on Bank to Expense Options," *San Francisco Business Times* (April 28, 2004).

The proposal also would improve comparability by eliminating one of the two different methods of accounting for equity-based compensation transactions that were available to most enterprises (the Opinion 25 method) and would also thereby simplify existing US generally accepted accounting principles ("GAAP"). The existing accounting for equity-based compensation had been specifically identified by many parties, including the SEC, as an example of a "rules-based standard" that has "fueled the demand for increased guidance" and that has led to further complex, detailed, and form-driven rules.[42] Eliminating different methods of accounting for the same transaction leads to improved comparability of financial statements because similar economic transactions are accounted for similarly. That should, in turn, result in accounting information that is more decision useful to creditors and investors.

The proposal also results in greater international comparability in the accounting for equity-based compensation. In February 2004, the IASB issued International Financial Reporting Standard (IFRS) 2, *Share-based Payment.*[43] Converging to a common set of high-quality financial accounting standards on an international basis for equity-based compensation improves the comparability of financial information around the world and simplifies the accounting for enterprises that report financial statements under both US GAAP and international accounting standards. As indicated above, both the Act and the Policy Statement indicate support of the US Congress and the SEC, respectively, for the FASB's convergence efforts.

What Is the Current Status of, and the FASB's Plans Relating to, the Proposal?

As indicated above, the Board issued the proposal for public comment on March 31, 2004. Also as indicated above, the proposal includes a Notice that highlights and describes twenty-two specific issues (three of which are related to small businesses) that respondents might wish to consider in developing their comments.[44] The comment period ends on June 30, 2004.

The Board plans to hold public roundtable meetings with interested users, auditors, preparers, and compensation and valuation experts to discuss the issues related to the proposal. Those roundtable meetings are scheduled to take place on

---

[42] Staff of the US SEC, "Study Pursuant to Section 108(d) of the Sarbanes-Oxley Act of 2002 on the Adoption by the United States Financial Reporting System of a Principles-Based Accounting System" (July 25, 2003), pages 24 and 25.

[43] Of note, in September 2003, the Accounting Standards Board ("AcSB") of Canada issued *Stock-Based Compensation and Other Stock-Based Payments,* Section 3870. Section 3870, consistent with IFRS 2 and the FASB proposal, requires the expensing of all equity-based compensation. Significant concerns in Canada about the inadequacies of the existing accounting for equity-based compensation led the AcSB to take the unusual action of requiring that Section 3870 become effective in 2004, prior to completion of the related FASB project and prior to the effective date of IFRS 2.

[44] See Attachment 4 for the Notice for Recipients.

June 24, 2004, in Palo Alto, California, and June 29, 2004 in Norwalk, Connecticut. The Board plans to seek participants for each meeting that represent a wide variety of users, preparers, and auditors of financial reports, and compensation and valuation experts. The Board also plans to discuss the views of interested parties representing small and medium-sized businesses regarding the proposal at the inaugural meeting of the SBAC to be held on May 11, 2004, in Norwalk, Connecticut.

Following the end of the comment period, the Board will redeliberate at public meetings the issues raised by the proposal. Those public redeliberations will be thorough and objective.

The redeliberations, consistent with the FASB's Rules of Procedure, will address the key conceptual, measurement, disclosure, and cost-benefit issues raised by the proposal and will include careful consideration of the input received by all parties. The redeliberations also will benefit from the FASB staff and Board's ongoing discussion of the key issues with interested parties from a broad range of perspectives, including valuation and compensation experts that the FASB has been consulting with and will continue to consult with throughout the entire process. As with virtually all FASB projects, the redeliberations will likely result in a number of changes that improve the proposal.

Only after carefully evaluating all of the key issues and carefully considering the input received in response to the proposal will the Board consider whether to issue a final standard. No final standard may be issued without approval by a majority vote of the Board.

The Board's current plans are to issue a final standard in the fourth quarter of this year. As with all of the FASB's activities, the FAF and the SEC will closely monitor and oversee the Board's due process on this important project.

Some Observations about Some of the More Common Arguments Offered by Some Opponents of the Proposal

Four of the more common arguments made by some of the opponents of the Board's proposal to improve the financial accounting and reporting for equity-based compensation are (1) employee stock options do not represent a cost and, therefore, should not be required to be expensed, (2) the cost of employee stock options cannot be reliably estimated, (3) mandatory expensing of employee stock options will eliminate broad-based stock option plans, and (4) mandatory expensing of fixed plan employee stock options will have negative economic consequences, including harmful implications to US technology leadership and job creation. The following presents some observations about each of those arguments.

Employee Stock Options Do Not Represent a Cost

In connection with the development of the proposal, the Board, after public deliberations, decided by a unanimous vote that goods and services received from any party in exchange for equity-based compensation should result in a cost that is recognized in the financial statements. That decision led to the proposed elimination of the existing exception that permits fixed plan employee stock options to avoid expense recognition.

The basis for the Board's proposed decision is that the Board agreed that all employee stock options, including fixed plan stock options, have value and those valuable financial instruments given to employees give rise to compensation cost that is properly included in measuring an enterprise's net income. Employee stock options provide an employee a valuable right to buy an enterprise's stock for a fixed price during a fixed time period. Similar rights are bought and sold in organized markets by speculators and other parties.

Furthermore, companies issue similar options and warrants to outside parties to acquire goods and services and in connection with acquisitions and financing transactions (and the fair value of those exchanges are always reported on the face of the financial statements without exception). If such rights were not valuable, employees, speculators, and other parties would not purchase them. Because employees purchase those rights with services, those consumed services represent an expense that is properly included in measuring an enterprise's net income.

The Board also discussed and disagreed with the related argument made by some parties that equity-based compensation should not be reported as a cost and deducted from earnings, but instead should only be reflected in diluted earnings per share when the options are exercised. The Board noted that the argument ignores the fact that all equity-based compensation, other than fixed plan employee stock options, is currently reported as a cost and deducted from earnings.

The Board believes that information about dilution from stock and stock option issuances is relevant information for investors. Diluted earnings per share, however, do not reflect all of the effects of equity-based compensation transactions.[45]

In addition to potential dilution, equity-based compensation transactions also affect the amount of the enterprise's employee compensation costs. As noted earlier, under existing accounting standards, all forms of equity-based

[45] Of note, the diluted earnings per share calculation takes into account only those stock options that are in-the-money and ignores the potential dilutive impact of options that are either at- or out-of-the-money. FASB Statement No. 128, *Earnings per Share* (February 1997), paragraphs 20-23.

compensation, except for fixed plan employee stock options, are reported as part of an enterprise's employee compensation costs.

The Board believes that all compensation costs, including fixed plan employee stock options costs, must be reported as an expense and deducted from earnings in order to provide investors with sound, fair, and credible information about an enterprise's net income. As the Congressional Budget Office recently concluded in its paper analyzing the accounting for employee stock options, "[i]f firms do not recognize as an expense the fair value of employee stock options, measured when the options are granted, the firms' reported net income will be overstated."[46] More recently, in expressing support for the proposal in testimony before the Joint Economic Committee, Federal Reserve System Chairman Alan Greenspan stated:

> "With respect to stock options, I think it would be a bad mistake for the Congress to impede FASB in this regard." . . .
>
> "The whole point of accounting is to tell somebody whether a specific strategy is working or not." . . .
>
> "[Not expensing employee stock options results in] 'a distorted view as to what the profitability of a particular operation is and you will get a distortion in the allocation of capital." . . .
>
> "But the point of issue is not whether it is more or less profitable, but are the figures right? And in this regard, as best I can judge the FASB changes in recommendations with respect to accounting procedures strike me as correct, and it's not clear to me what purpose the Congress is in this particular procedure." . . .
>
> "I think the Congress would err in going forward and endeavoring to impede FASB in its particular activities."[47]

---

[46] Congressional Budget Office, "Accounting for Employee Stock Options" (April 2003), Summary, Section 2 of 3, pages 1 and 2 (emphasis added).
[47] Dear colleague letter from The Honorable Pete Stark, Joint Economic Committee, Congress of the United States, "Greenspan Says Congress Impeding FASB Stock Options Rules Would be a 'Bad Mistake'" (April 27, 2004).

The Cost of Employee Stock Options Cannot Be Reliably Estimated

In its public deliberations leading to the development of the proposal, the Board did not find persuasive the argument that the estimated fair value of employee stock options based on currently available valuation techniques would be so unreliable as to impair the credibility and comparability of financial statements. To the contrary, the Board believes that use of the Opinion 25 intrinsic value method has and would continue to impair not only the relevance and reliability, but also the credibility, of financial statements by omitting a potentially significant component of the total cost of employee services.

The Board notes that thousands of public enterprises have been estimating the fair value of employee stock options, generally consistent with the approach contained in the proposal, and have been reporting those amounts in their audited financial statement footnotes for eight years. Moreover, 576 enterprises, 116 of which represent 41 percent of the S&P 500 index based on market capitalization, have estimated and reported or will soon estimate and report all of their employee stock options as an expense in their audited and certified financial statements generally consistent with the proposal's approach.[48]

In addition, many valuation experts and many other parties, including the Congressional Budget Office, agree that employee stock options can be reliably valued.[49] It is widely acknowledged that far more complicated financial instruments, including long-dated and complex derivatives, and convertible bonds containing embedded long-dated options, are valued in the marketplace daily and that value is routinely reported by enterprises.[50]

Uncertainties inherent in estimates of the fair value of equity-based payment arrangements are generally no more significant than the uncertainties inherent in measurements of, for example, loan loss reserves, valuation allowances for deferred tax assets, and pensions and other postretirement benefit obligations.[51] For those items, as well for many other items in accounting involving the use of estimates, enterprises are required to use appropriate measurement techniques, relevant data, and management judgment in the preparation of financial

---

[48] Pat McConnell, Janet Pegg, Chris Senyek, and Dane Mott, "Accounting Issues: 576 Companies Have Voluntarily Adopted Option Expensing Under the Fair Value Method," Bear Stearns (April 29, 2004); see Attachment 3.

[49] Congressional Budget Office, "Accounting for Employee Stock Options," Summary, Section 2 of 3, page 2, and Section 3 of 3, pages 5 and 6.

[50] Hearing on H.R. 3574: Stock Option Accounting Reform Act, Before the Subcommittee on Capital Markets, Insurance and Government Sponsored Enterprises of the Committee on Financial Services, Summary of Testimony of Robert C. Merton (March 3, 2004).

[51] Michael B. Clement, "Accounting: The Case for Expensing Stock Options," Goldman Sachs Global Equity Research (April 7, 2004), page 1.

statements.[52] Few accrual-based accounting measurements can claim absolute reliability, but most parties agree that financial statement recognition of estimated amounts that are approximately right is preferable to the alternative—recognizing no amounts.[53]

Mandatory Expensing of Employee Stock Options Will Eliminate Broad-Based Stock Option Plans

If broad-based employee stock option plans are a good business decision, meaning that the benefits derived from those plans exceed their costs, mandatory expensing of fixed plan employee stock options should not lead to the elimination of broad-based stock option plans. Many other forms of compensation, including pension plans and Employee Stock Purchase Plans, have been and continue to be "broad-based" at many enterprises, notwithstanding that those and other forms of compensation, other than fixed plan employee stock options, are reported as an expense.

As indicated above, Wal-Mart Stores, Inc., Netflix Inc., and Home Depot, Inc., have historically offered broad-based stock option plans to many nonexecutive employees and have indicated that voluntarily adopting fair value expensing for all employee stock options will not result in any curtailment of those programs. The CEO of Netflix Inc. recently commented:

> Thoughtful Silicon Valley CEO after CEO lines up to say that closing the stock option loophole will curtail the innovation economy as we know it. But Amazon, Microsoft and my company, Netflix, all voluntarily converted last year to expensing, have continued to give broad-based equity incentives, and innovation continues unabated. Stock options may be the symbol of the Silicon Valley culture, but it is not the essence. We innovate because it thrills us, not because of some accounting treatment."[54]

[52] As an example, Intel Corporation's ("Intel") Form 10-K for fiscal year ended December 27, 2003, includes a disclosure of "Critical Accounting Estimates" in Management's Discussion and Analysis of Financial Condition and Results of Operations. That disclosure describes "difficult and subjective judgments" in five specific areas that Intel acknowledges "have a significant impact on the results we report in our financial statements." Those five areas include goodwill, non-marketable equity securities, inventory, long-lived assets, and income taxes. Intel Form 10-K, pages 32-34.

[53] Steven Milunovich and Richard Farmer, "Tech Stock Options—The Invisible Cash Flow Drain," Merrill Lynch Comment, page 5.

[54] Reed Hastings, "Expense It!" *The Wall Street Journal.*

Mandatory Expensing of Employee Stock Options Will Have Negative Economic Consequences

Some opponents of the proposal argue that the recognition of compensation cost based on fair value may have undesirable economic consequences, including harmful implications for US technology leadership and job creation.[55] As indicated above, they often suggest that the required recognition of compensation cost from equity-based payment arrangements is likely to cause some enterprises to reduce, eliminate, or otherwise revise those arrangements. Some also contend that recognition of compensation cost for employee stock options will raise the cost of capital for enterprises that make extensive use of those options. All of those assertions seem to be based on the presumptions that (1) most, if not all, current equity-based arrangements are inherently desirable regardless of their cost and (2) Opinion 25's accounting requirements have only desirable economic consequences. The Board considers neither presumption to be either supportable or relevant in establishing accounting standards for equity-based payment arrangements.

The Board's operating precepts require it to consider issues in an evenhanded manner, without attempting to encourage or to discourage specific actions. That does not imply that improved financial reporting should have no economic consequences. To the contrary, a change in accounting standards that result in financial statements that are more relevant and representationally faithful, and thus more useful for decision making, presumably would have economic consequences. For example, required recognition of compensation cost based on the provisions of the proposal would result in comparable accounting for all forms of employee compensation. The Board believes that any decision to reassess and modify existing equity-based payment arrangements would be based on information that better represents the costs and benefits of various forms of compensation.

Some investors and others have noted the dramatic increase in the number of stock options awarded to employees during recent years. The Board understands that the vast majority of stock options awarded to employees are fixed plan employee stock options for which enterprises that continued to use the accounting requirements of Opinion 25 recognized no compensation expense. The accounting under Opinion 25 treats most fixed plan employee stock options as though they

---

[55] Some commentators have found it ironic that defending US jobs is used as an argument against the FASB proposal, when many high technology and venture capital enterprises are at the same time trying to convince Congress and other State legislators not to impose restrictions on outsourcing as they actively promote the movement of jobs overseas. Steven Milunovich and Richard Farmer, "Tech Stock Options—The Invisible Cash Flow Drain," Merrill Lynch Comment, page 6. Some recent articles discussing support of outsourcing by representatives of the high technology or venture capital industries include Don Clark, "Another Lure of Outsourcing: Job Expertise," *The Wall Street Journal* (April 12, 2004); Ann Grimes, "Venture Firms Seek Start-Ups That Outsource," *The Wall Street Journal* (April 2, 2004); and Karl Schoenberger, "Fears Over Offshoring Inflated, Says AeA, " *Mercury News* (March 24, 2004).

were a "free good," which implies that the services received in exchange for those options are obtained without incurring a cost. But employee services received in exchange for stock options are not free. Stock options are valuable equity instruments for which valuable consideration is received—consideration that should be recognized regardless of whether it is in the form of cash, goods, or services from employees or other suppliers. Accounting for fixed plan employee stock options as though they imposed no cost on the enterprise that issues them may encourage their substitution for other forms of compensation, such as stock options or other instruments with performance or market conditions that may be preferable in a particular situation. Requiring recognition of compensation cost based on fair value increases the neutrality of financial reporting and removes an accounting incentive for an entity to choose a form of incentive compensation—fixed plan employee stock options—that may not be the most advantageous in its circumstances.

Many would agree that an enterprise's expenditures for a broad range of items, such as pensions, education and training, environmental remediation, or occupational, health, and safety programs, are expenditures that should be encouraged. Those items, however, like all forms of employee compensation, are a cost of the enterprise and properly reported as expenses in financial reports.

Of note, the above observations have generally been supported by many economic experts who have reviewed the issue, including Federal Reserve Chairman Alan Greenspan,[56] former Federal Reserve Chairman (and current chairman of the Trustees of the International Accounting Standards Committee Foundation) Paul A. Volcker,[57] Nobel Prize winning economists Robert C. Merton[58] and Joseph E. Stiglitz,[59] the Financial Economist Roundtable,[60] the Republican Staff of the Joint Economic Committee of the US Congress,[61] the Conference Board Commission on Public Trust and Private Enterprise,[62] and the Congressional Budget Office.[63]

---

[56] Dear colleague letter from The Honorable Pete Stark, Joint Economic Committee, Congress of the United States, "Greenspan Says Congress Impeding FASB Stock Options Rules Would be a 'Bad Mistake;'" Federal Reserve System Chairman Alan Greenspan, Remarks at the 2002 Financial Markets Conference of the Federal Reserve Bank of Atlanta, Sea Island, Georgia (May 3, 2002), pages 5 and 6.

[57] Hearing before the Subcommittee on Capital Markets, Insurance and Government Sponsored Enterprises of the Committee on Financial Services, Testimony of Paul A. Volcker (June 3, 2002), pages 3 and 4.

[58] Hearing on H.R. 3574: Stock Option Accounting Reform Act, Before the Subcommittee on Capital Markets, Insurance and Government Sponsored Enterprises of the Committee on Financial Services, Summary of Testimony of Robert C. Merton.

[59] Joseph E. Stiglitz, "The Roaring Nineties" (October 2003), pages 115-139.

[60] Statement of Financial Economist Roundtable on the Controversy over Executive Compensation (November 24, 2003).

[61] Joint Economic Committee, Republican Senate Staff, Economic Policy Research, "Understanding the Stock Option Debate," Report 107-04 (July 9, 2002), page 18.

[62] The Conference Board, "The Commission on Public Trust and Private Enterprise, Findings and Recommendations, Part 1: Executive Compensation," page 6.

[63] The Congressional Budget Office, "Accounting for Employee Stock Options," Section 3, pages 4 and 5.

Some Observations about H.R. 3574

As many experts have indicated, the provisions of H.R. 3574 are seriously flawed and violate fundamental concepts of financial accounting and reporting.[64] The FASB is particularly concerned about the provisions in H.R. 3574 that would prohibit the SEC from recognizing as "'generally accepted' any accounting principle established . . . relating to the expensing of stock options," unless the standard includes certain specific requirements and until an economic impact study of unlimited duration has been completed.[65] The Board strongly opposes such an effort to block improvements to the financial accounting and reporting for equity-based compensation for several reasons, including the following.

First, HR 3574 would override the Board's independent, objective, open, and ongoing due process to make unbiased decisions on the substance and timing of improvements to the accounting for equity-based compensation. As indicated above, such intervention would be in direct conflict with the expressed needs and demands of many investors and other users of financial reports. Such intervention also would appear to be inconsistent with the language and intent of the Act and the related Policy Statement, both of which were intended to enhance the independence of the FASB.

Second, HR 3574 would have an adverse impact on the FASB's efforts to achieve timely convergence of high-quality international accounting standards in this important area and again appears to be inconsistent with the language and intent of the Act and the related Policy Statement, both of which indicate support for the FASB's convergence efforts. As indicated above, enterprises in 90 countries around the world will begin reporting all equity-based compensation as an expense, in a manner generally consistent with our proposal, beginning on January 1, 2005.

Finally, and perhaps most importantly, HR 3574 would establish a dangerous precedent in that it would send a clear and unmistakable signal that Congress is willing to intervene in the independent, objective, and open accounting standard-setting process based on factors other than the pursuit of sound and fair financial reporting. That signal would likely prompt others to seek political intervention in future technical activities of the FASB.

---

[64] Letter from Edward Nusbaum, CEO, Grant Thornton LLP, To the Honorable Richard H. Baker, United States House of Representatives (March 17, 2004), page 4; Summary of the Testimony of Robert C. Merton, Before the Subcommittee on Capital Markets, Insurance and Government Sponsored Enterprises of the Committee on Financial Services, H.R. 3574: Stock Option Accounting Reform Act. See Attachment 2 for additional comments from experts and others on H.R. 3574 and other proposed legislation.

[65] H.R. 3574, Section 3(a)(3).

For all of the above reasons, HR 3574 would likely result in a giant step backwards in the recent and ongoing efforts by Congress, the SEC, the FASB, and many other parties, to restore public confidence and trust in the integrity of financial reporting.

Conclusion

In conclusion, let me assure you that you, and the users, auditors, and preparers of financial reports, including small business financial reports, can have confidence that the Board will continue to actively reach out and solicit input in response to our proposal. That input will be carefully considered in an open, thorough, and objective manner. Our ultimate goal is to develop an accounting standard that will faithfully report the underlying economic effects of equity-based compensation transactions and, thus, significantly improve the transparency and integrity of financial reporting in the US.

Thank you again, Chairman Baker. We would welcome the opportunity to respond to any questions.

UNITED STATES
SECURITIES AND EXCHANGE COMMISSION
WASHINGTON, D.C. 20549

THE CHAIRMAN

May 3, 2004

The Honorable Paul E. Kanjorski
2353 Rayburn House Office Building
U.S. House of Representatives
Washington, DC 20515

Dear Congressman Kanjorski:

On March 31st, the Financial Accounting Standards Board issued a proposal that, if adopted, would require companies to record as compensation expense the fair value of all stock options granted to employees. As is often the case when the FASB proposes a change in accounting practice, this proposal has generated significant debate. Over the years, the Securities and Exchange Commission (SEC) has encouraged such debates because they lead to better standards, and I am hopeful that will be the case for this issue as well.

The Federal securities laws give the SEC broad authority over the accounting principles to be followed in the preparation of public company financial statements.[1] Practically since its inception, however, the SEC, while preserving its full statutory authority, has looked to the accounting profession for leadership in establishing and improving accounting principles. Over the years, various accounting standard setting bodies have been formed to carry out this function. Most of these bodies, however, included part-time members, who remained partners in accounting firms and under the possible influence of clients and other interested parties.

In the late 1960s, the accounting profession, recognizing that the credibility of its standards was at risk, and with encouragement from the SEC, formed a committee, chaired by former SEC Commissioner Francis Wheat, to study and recommend a better process. The final report, published in March 1972, recommended the formation of the FASB as an independent body that would be removed from the influence of active members of the accounting profession and their clients. This recommendation was widely endorsed by industry, financial analysts, accounting educators, and practicing accountants.

Following the formation of the FASB more than 30 years ago, the SEC issued a policy statement affirming that the FASB would provide an institutional framework that would permit responsible actions flowing from research and consideration of all points of view. The Commission also noted the collective experiences of the members of the FASB and the commitment by the accounting profession to provide substantial resources to that Board.

Less than two years ago, in the Sarbanes-Oxley Act of 2002, Congress reaffirmed and strengthened the Commission's mandate to oversee private sector standard setting bodies such as the FASB, and to assure the independence of such bodies. The Act specifically provided a legal framework for the Commission to determine whether a standard setting body meets critical

---

1 *See* Sections 7, 19(a) and items (25), (26), and (27) of Schedule A of the Securities Act of 1933, sections 12, 13(b)(1) and 17(e)(2) of the Securities Exchange Act of 1934, sections 5(b), 14, and 20 of the Public Utility Holding Company Act of 1935, and sections 8, 30(e), 31, and 38(a) of the Investment Company Act of 1940.

conditions essential to ensuring the integrity of its processes.[2] Further, the Act authorized the imposition of a mandatory annual accounting support fee on public companies – thereby removing the dependence of the standard setting body on voluntary funding from industry and the accounting profession and assuring it of a steady source of revenue.[3]

On April 25, 2003, the Commission formally recognized the FASB as a standard setting body meeting the criteria established by the Sarbanes-Oxley Act. The Commission has twice subsequently determined that the FASB's support fee meets the Act's requirements, most recently on February 20 of this year.

The FASB's process for standard setting allows for extensive, thorough, deliberative consideration and open procedures in order to establish standards so that companies can provide relevant and reliable information to the public. Accounting standards that fail to accurately portray events can skew company results, reinforce investor skepticism, and set back efforts by Congress, the Commission, accounting professionals and others who have been engaged in restoring public confidence in the integrity of financial reporting in the United States. The FASB's process includes extensive consultation, public meetings and hearings, written input on proposed standards, and public re-deliberation where appropriate, and includes consideration of the impact on smaller businesses. The process is designed to provide ample and appropriate opportunity for the public to air their views and concerns, while providing the FASB with the opportunity to thoughtfully consider all aspects of those concerns before reaching a final decision. The SEC oversees the work of the FASB to assure that their process operates in a fair and open way and that the results serve the interests of investors.

For the policy reasons described above, recently underscored by the Sarbanes-Oxley Act, I strongly support an independent and open standard-setting process for establishing accounting principles for U.S. public companies. Accordingly, I believe that the process established by the FASB to consider the pending stock option proposal should be allowed to run its course.

Sincerely,

William H. Donaldson
Chairman

cc: The Honorable Michael G. Oxley
The Honorable Barney Frank
The Honorable Richard H. Baker
The Honorable Richard C. Shelby
The Honorable Paul S. Sarbanes
The Honorable Michael B. Enzi
The Honorable Christopher J. Dodd

---

2 Section 108(a) of the Sarbanes-Oxley Act of 2002 (codified at Section 19(b)(1) of the Securities Act of 1933).
3 Section 109(e) of the Sarbanes-Oxley Act of 2002.

Subcommittee on Capital Markets, Insurance and Government Sponsored Enterprises
Hearing regarding H.R. 3574
Additional Questions
Submitted by
Congressman Brad Sherman
For Robert H. Herz
Chairman
Financial Accounting Standards Board ("FASB")

1. **What effect would the zero volatility assumption described in H.R. 3574 have on the value of stock options for the top 5 employees of companies?**

   It is generally accepted that a large part of a stock option's fair value is the result of the volatility of the underlying stock price, and there is no real-world traded stock whose volatility is zero. Thus, the effect of the zero volatility assumption described in H.R. 3574 would be to significantly undervalue the stock option compensation expense for the top 5 employees of companies. For example, a November 26, 2003, *BusinessWeek* Commentary by Louis Lavelle indicated that under the zero volatility assumption described in H.R. 3574 the stock options Cisco Systems awarded in fiscal 2003 to their top 5 employees would be worth about a third of their Black-Scholes value.

2. **Please estimate the percentage of stock option value held by people earning a salary of over $100,000 a year.**

   A General Social Survey for 2002, conducted by the National Opinion Research Center at the University of Chicago, indicated that 4 percent of workers earning less than $15,000 received stock options, compared with 41 percent of workers earning more than $75,000 a year. A 2002 Gallup Poll of Media Use and Consumer Behavior for the San Francisco Market indicated that those Silicon Valley households with stock options had a median income of $122,000. Finally, a Pilot Survey on Stock Options Incidence in Private Industry in 1999, conducted by the Bureau of Labor Statistics, indicated that 0.7 percent of private-sector non-executive employees earning less than $35,000 received stock options, compared with 12.9 percent for non-executive employees earning $75,000 and above.

3. For the top 10 issuers of employee stock options, what is the maximum and minimum expense when calculating the expense using the unadjusted Black-Scholes model and the binomial method?

A maximum and minimum expense using the unadjusted Black-Scholes model and the binomial model for the top 10 issuers of employee stock options cannot be calculated because the company-specific facts and circumstances necessary to make an estimation are not publicly available. That is not to imply, however, that the measurement approach contained in Financial Accounting Standards Board's ("FASB" or "Board") Exposure Draft, Proposed Statement of Financial Accounting Standards, *Share-Based Payment* ("Proposal"), may result in compensation expense amounts that are so unreliable as to impair the comparability of financial statements. In the public deliberations leading to the development of the Proposal, the Board explicitly addressed that issue. After extensive work, the Board concluded that estimating the fair value of employee stock options based on currently available valuation techniques would generally result in sufficiently reliable compensation expense amounts that would improve the comparability of financial statements. In reaching that conclusion the Board noted that the Black-Scholes-Merton formula and the binomial model are based on the same well-established economic theory. Provided the inputs are identical, the fair values calculated under either the formula or the related model will generally be the same. Under the Proposal, nonpublic enterprises would be permitted to determine compensation expense based on the difference between the current fair value of their shares and the exercise price of outstanding employee stock options, i.e., based on the "intrinsic value of those options." Public enterprises also would be permitted to use this simpler alternative approach in circumstances in which, after a diligent effort, they conclude that it is not possible to determine with sufficient reliability the fair value of the employee stock options they have granted. The Board also noted that the use by most enterprises of the APB Opinion No. 25, *Accounting for Stock Issued to Employees* ("Opinion 25"), intrinsic value method has impaired and would continue to impair not only the comparability, but the relevance and reliability of financial statements by omitting a potentially significant component of the total cost of employee services. The Board's conclusion is supported by the July 2003 United States Securities and Exchange Commission's *Study Pursuant to Section 108(d) of the Sarbanes-Oxley Act of 2002 on the Adoption by the United States Financial Reporting System of a Principles-Based Accounting System* ("SEC Study"). The SEC Study was critical of Opinion 25 and concluded that accounting standards could result in greater comparability if they were more "objectives-oriented" allowing accounting professionals to operationalize accounting treatments in a manner that best fulfills the objective of the standard and thereby best captures the underlying economic reality. The Board's conclusion is also supported by the fact that thousands of public enterprises have been estimating the fair value of employee stock options, generally consistent with the approach contained in the Proposal, and have been reporting those amounts in their audited financial statements for eight years. Some of those enterprises use the binomial model in making those estimations.

Moreover, more than 575 enterprises, 116 of which represent 41 percent of the S&P 500 index based on market capitalization, have estimated and reported all of their employee stock options as an expense in their audited and certified financial statements generally consistent with the Proposal's approach. Again, some of those enterprises use the binomial model in making their estimations. Effective at the beginning of this year, many Canadian enterprises were required to expense all employee stock options based on a measurement approach generally consistent with that contained in the Proposal. Beginning in 2005, International Financial Reporting Standards will require thousands of other foreign enterprises in over 90 countries around the world to do the same. Not surprisingly, many valuation experts and many other parties, including Federal Reserve Chairman Alan Greenspan and the Congressional Budget Office, generally agree that employee stock options can be reliably valued under the Proposal's approach. It is widely acknowledged that far more complicated financial instruments, including long-dated and complex derivatives, and convertible bonds containing long-dated options, are valued in the marketplace daily and that value is routinely reported by enterprises in their audited and certified financial reports. Uncertainties inherent in estimates of the fair value of employee stock options are generally no more significant than the uncertainties inherent in measurements of, for example, loan loss reserves, valuation allowances for deferred tax assets, asset impairment calculations, and pensions and other postretirement benefit obligations. Moreover, the implementation guidance contained in the Proposal is far more extensive than the guidance provided in the accounting literature for the measurement of those other items. Of note, most accounting estimates that are currently reported in audited and certified financial statements are not mechanical calculations but require that enterprises use appropriate measurement techniques, relevant data, and management judgment in making those estimates. Few accrual-based accounting measurements can claim absolute reliability, but most parties agree that financial statement recognition of estimated amounts that are approximately right is preferable to the alternative—recognizing no amounts. Finally, the Proposal's Notice for Recipients includes six issues seeking additional input on the measurement issues raised by the Proposal, including whether the Proposal provides sufficient guidance to ensure that the fair value measurement is applied with reasonable consistency. The input received on those issues and all other issues will be carefully considered by the Board, consistent with the FASB's Rules of Procedure, at public meetings prior to the issuance of any final standard to improve the accounting for equity-based compensation.

O